WHAT'S HAPPENED TO THE HUMANITIES?

WHAT'S HAPPENED TO THE HUMANITIES?

Edited by
Alvin Kernan

PRINCETON UNIVERSITY PRESS   PRINCETON, NEW JERSEY

© 1997 by Princeton University Press
Published by Princeton University Press, 41 William Street,
Princeton, New Jersey 08540
In the United Kingdom: Princeton University Press, Chichester, West Sussex

Library of Congress Cataloging-in-Publication Data
What's Happened to the Humanities?/edited by Alvin Kernan.
p.   cm.
Includes bibliographical references and index.
ISBN 0-691-01155-9 (cloth: alk. paper)
1. Humanities—Study and teaching (Higher)—United States.
2. Humanities—Philosophy. 3. Learning and scholarship—United States—History.
I. Kernan, Alvin B.
AZ183.U5G46 1997
001.3′071′173—dc20   96-28325

Publication of this book has been aided by a grant from
The Andrew W. Mellon Foundation

This book has been composed in Adobe Bauer Bodoni

Printed in the United States of America by
Princeton Academic Press

10 9 8 7 6 5 4 3 2 1

Contents _____

Foreword   vii
William G. Bowen and Harold T. Shapiro

Introduction: Change in the Humanities and Higher Education   3
Alvin Kernan

NUMBERS

1. Democratization and Decline? The Consequences of
Demographic Change in the Humanities   17
Lynn Hunt

2. Funding Trends in the Academic Humanities, 1970–1995:
Reflections on the Stability of the System   32
John H. D'Arms

CLASSROOMS

3. Ignorant Armies and Nighttime Clashes: Changes in the
Humanities Classroom, 1970–1995   63
Francis Oakley

4. Evolution and Revolution: Change in the Literary
Humanities, 1968–1995   84
Margery Sabin

BOOKS, LIBRARIES, READING

5. Humanities and the Library in the Digital Age   107
Carla Hesse

6. The Practice of Reading   122
Denis Donoghue

THEORY

7. "Beyond Method"   143
Gertrude Himmelfarb

8. Changing Epochs   162
Frank Kermode

9. The Pursuit of Metaphor   179
Christopher Ricks

INSTITUTIONS

10. The Demise of Disciplinary Authority   201
     Louis Menand

11. Scholarship as Social Action   220
     David Bromwich

*Appendix: Tables and Figures on B.A.s and Ph.D.s in the
Humanities, 1966–1993*   245

About the Contributors   259

Index   261

Foreword _____

WILLIAM G. BOWEN AND HAROLD T. SHAPIRO

HUMANISTIC scholarship—especially the close reading and interpretation of texts—has always been an important part of our cultural inheritance, particularly since the eighteenth-century flowering of biblical philology and hermeneutics. The twentieth century has witnessed not only a redefinition of the humanities and a new disciplinary organization of teaching and research in this and other areas, but also the successive development of a number of new approaches to the interpretation of texts. In the most recent decades, some would say that certain components of the humanities have changed more than any other area of study at the universities. One clear result is that serious humanistic scholarship now includes a much wider variety of approaches than it did a generation ago. At the same time, a good deal of controversy has developed—especially in the last few decades—as partisans of alternative approaches have contended with each other for influence over the direction of humanistic scholarship and related educational programs. Although the center of a good deal of the debate has been the field of literary criticism, many areas of the humanities have been affected—and indeed transformed—by the discussions that have surrounded such concepts as structuralism, poststructuralism, deconstruction, feminism, and gender, ethnic, and cultural studies. These controversies have certainly helped to enhance our understanding of particular texts and brought a fuller understanding of the nature of our cultural contexts; yet there are those who feel that some of the more radical of the new approaches threaten—if pursued to extremes—to devalue and trivialize the cultural artifacts themselves and to undermine the cultural values from which they arose.

It is not our intention in writing this foreword to enter these controversies. Neither of us is expert in these fields, and others have provided very well articulated expressions of the spectrum of positions on these questions. Rather, the purpose of this foreword is first to thank Professor Alvin Kernan and his colleagues for providing this group of essays, some of which were presented at the Princeton Conference on Higher Education and all of which are the result of work supported by The Andrew W. Mellon Foundation in the hope of providing some new insights into the changes that have had an impact on the study of many of the humanistic disciplines. The essays themselves are very usefully described and placed in context in Professor Kernan's introduction to this volume. Although the essays collected here cover a wide variety of topics, they should not be viewed as an attempt to cover all the important issues and/or areas. Second, it is important to note that, although this group of essays addresses primarily the context of English literature and history, the issues they discuss are reflected to some extent across the whole domain of humanistic scholarship. Finally, the essays as a group reflect a combination of descriptive analysis (i.e., attempts to understand just what is going on) and evaluation (i.e., particular opinions regarding recent developments). In this latter respect, we, as economists, take no particular point of view regarding the ultimate impact of these changes on the various fields of humanistic studies. The essays have been ably chosen by Professor Kernan, and we let them speak for themselves.

WHAT'S HAPPENED TO THE HUMANITIES?

Introduction

Change in the Humanities and Higher Education

ALVIN KERNAN

INSTITUTIONALLY, in the standard academic table of organization, the university catalogue—the knowledge tree of contemporary western culture—the humanities are the subjects regularly listed under that heading: literature, philosophy, art history, music, religion, languages, and sometimes history. This branch of knowledge is separated from the branch of the social sciences and from the branch of the biological and physical sciences. These three branches together form the arts and sciences, or the liberal arts, as they are sometimes known, which are as a group separated in turn from the professional disciplines—such as medicine, education, business, and law—which, at least at one time, concentrated on practice rather than theory.

Historically, the humanities are the old subjects, which in many forms and under a variety of names—the nine muses; the liberal arts; quadrivium and trivium; rhetoric, dialectic, and logic; humane letters—were the major part of Western education for over two millennia. In the modern college and university they have mutated into a number of specialized subjects, such as art history, religious studies, classics, national literatures, and musicology. Perhaps because they are the old subjects, they are also the least abstract, the most immediate—not the most prestigious, but the most intimate—to humanity's sense of itself in the world. They shape the stories we tell, our ways of thinking, what our collective past has been, how we communicate and persuade with language, and, perhaps most powerfully of all, the music that stirs our depths: these are, *mutatis mutandis*, the basic humanistic ways of knowing, the most instrumental to life as it is ordinarily lived.

Socially, in the latter twentieth century, the humanities, along with some of the "softer" social sciences like anthropology and sociology, have been the battlefields of an extended *Kulturkampf*. These subjects have proven extremely sensitive to pressures for social change in the society at large, to the wave of populist democracy, to technological changes in communication, to relativistic epistemologies, to demands for increased tolerance, and to various social causes, such as black studies, feminism, and gay rights. Every liberal cause—from freedom of speech and the Vietnam War to anticolonialism and the nonreferentiality of language—has fought bitter and clamorous battles in these subjects. The revolutionary spirit extended into the intellectual realm, and truth itself as well as fact, the foundations of Western rational inquiry, were confronted by deconstructive philosophies that replaced knowledge with interpretation and dethroned objectivity in the name of subjectivity. Where the old humanities were once ethnocentric in their concentration on western Europe, they have become increasingly multicultural, pluralistic, and politicized.

This turmoil in the humanities has been part of, and offers an insight into, a much larger change in American higher education as a whole that has been taking place since World War II. "A substantial change of scale is a change of enterprise," remarks Christopher Ricks, and a few numbers establish the nature and direction of the change of "enterprise" in higher education. In the years between 1960 and 1990, according to figures from the National Center for Educational Statistics, the number of institutions of higher education increased from 2,000 to 3,595. The greatest increase was in the publics, which grew from 700 to 1,576, while the privates, which had earlier dominated higher education, went from 1,300 to 2,019. Full-time enrollments increased from 3.5 to 15.3 million, with the share accounted for by the public institutions increasing from 60 to 80 percent of the total. The area of the greatest growth was in the new community colleges, which enrolled only 400,000 students in 1960 but had 6.5 million by 1990. The proportion of women increased from 37 to 51 percent of the total of undergraduate enrollments in this time period, and that of minorities from 12 to 28 percent. To support this growth, federal aid to students went from $5.1 to $11.2 billion. To provide teachers for the increased number of students, the number of doctoral degrees granted grew from about 10,000 to over 38,000 a year, and overall faculty numbers increased from approximately 281,000 to over 987,000. Research payments were increased accordingly by the federal government, which between 1960 and 1990 increased R&D funds from $2 billion constant 1960 dollars to $12 billion.

These numerical changes are of course the substructure of much more visible surface disturbances. Socrates said that "the modes of music are never disturbed without unsettling of the most fundamental political and social conditions," but who would have thought that the sounds of Elvis and the Beatles, electrically amplified until they drowned out every other sound, would announce new political and social conditions on campus? The sweet smell of marijuana floated through the dormitories, and the sound of gunfire crackled in the groves of academe. *Et in Arcadia ego*! Free-speech movements coarsened the vocabulary of higher education, and student protests, strikes, and sit-ins were only the most visible of many continuing challenges to *in loco parentis* authority. Democratic egalitarianism found its intellectual counterparts in pluralism, a multicultural curriculum, and the relativistic concept of truth—one person's ideas are as good as another's—which has been the intellectual "loss leader" on campus for many years now. In time, new manners and new epistemologies were followed by new politics. Affirmative action brought increasing numbers of minorities into the classrooms, a feminist movement established itself at the center of academic concerns, and all intellectual activities were declared to be means of seeking power. Margery Sabin sums up the pattern of change in the following way: "radical social protest in the late 1960s; deconstruction in the 1970s; ethnic, feminist, and Marxist cultural studies in the 1980s; postmodern sexuality in the 1990s; and rampant careerism from beginning to end."

Educational institutions, like all other social institutions—the family, the state, the church—obviously do change radically from time to time. In *The Uses of the University* (1967), Clark Kerr noted the appearance as early as the 1950s and 1960s of a new kind of institution of higher education, which he called the "multiversity, a city of infinite variety," a term he coined to call attention to a progressive weakening of any unifying force at the educational center—either geographical, curricular, or philosophical—of the old research universities, which he defined as a "unified community of masters and students with a single 'soul' or purpose." In the thirty years since Kerr told us that a "multiversity" was replacing the old research universities, the democratic social revolution in education has continued to the point that by now it might be better to call the new institution a "demoversity," if you will allow the word, tending toward the empowerment of the many rather than the unified one, questioning traditional centralized authority and all forms of elitism.

These tectonic shifts in higher education have not, I think it is fair to say, been kind to the liberal arts in general, and to the humanities in particular. Again we can turn to numbers, those assembled in the appendix, where Figure 1 shows the decreasing role that the liberal arts have occupied in American education over the last century. What has happened to the humanities in more recent years, when better figures have been available, is demonstrated in Tables 1 and 2. They show conclusively that while the absolute numbers of bachelor's and doctoral degrees in the humanities have increased slightly in the last thirty years, the humanities have lost ground at both levels as a percentage of the total number of degrees conferred in a time of maximum growth. Where bachelor's degrees in the humanities were 20.7 percent of the total awarded in 1966, in 1993 they were only 12.7 percent; and where doctoral degrees in the humanities were 13.8 percent of the total awarded in 1966, in 1993 they made up only

9.1 percent. It is true that both bachelor's and doctoral degrees have recovered somewhat from a deeper slump in the 1980s, and it has been argued that the numbers for the mid-1960s—the point at which reliable figures are first available—are perhaps historically high. Furthermore, the liberal arts in general, not just the humanities, have lost ground during this period. But the inescapable point would still seem to be that as the demoversity has taken shape, the humanities, in plain words, have become a less and less significant part of higher education. This is not, as Figures 7–11 detail, so much the case in the elite institutions as in the community colleges and more service-oriented educational institutions, where vocationalism has swept the board. Yet this does not change the fact that the humanities are playing a less important part within the totality of higher education in America. During the same period the social sciences little more than held their own in percentages of bachelor's and doctoral degrees, but the natural sciences were hit as hard as the humanities.

The following essays explore in depth some of the changes in the humanities that have accompanied the paradigm shift in higher education from university to demoversity. They offer sharply drawn pictures of what has actually happened: Has the phenomenology of reading changed? Who pays for humanistic studies? What is taught in the humanities classrooms? Has professionalism broken down? What has happened to enrollments in the humanities? Have demographic changes led to institutional changes? Does the transition from a print culture to an electronic culture have consequences for the text-centered humanities? Has positivism been replaced by relativism as the governing epistemological concept in the humanities? With what results have the humanities made themselves into the conscience of the society?

The essays focus on the kinds of change—in demographics, in patronage, in reading—for which it is possible, if not to be entirely objective, at least to be sufficiently factual to be able to discuss the issues meaningfully. They tell us what has actually happened, rather than arguing about what should have happened or what might have happened. Moral and intellectual judgments are not absent, of course—how could they be?—but there has been a major effort here to describe what has actually happened in the humanities rather than to praise or blame it. Francis Oakley catches the spirit of the volume when he remarks, in his study of changes in the humanities classroom, "it is tempting to assume that in the absence of some formidably massive and intricate exercise in empirical investigation we are doomed in this matter of changes in humanities instruction to being cast adrift on an ocean of anecdotage masquerading as generalization or of ideology purporting to be fact. But that is a temptation, I believe, to which we should refuse to yield."

We properly begin with some rudimentary numbers, the basic demographic and economic facts. Lynn Hunt takes the raw materials of demographics and follows them through to their effects on teachers, whose day-to-day working lives are moving, she believes, like leaves following the unseen winds of demographic change. A continuing increase in the number of students going to college, the degree to which humanistic studies are becoming women's subjects, the ongoing pressure of minorities for representation in the colleges, the inevitability of multiculturalism, and a financial squeeze that is unlikely to ease in a time of slower economic growth—these and other forces are changing not only the folkways but also the intellectual views of universities. More and more part-time and temporary faculty are being hired to save money and tenure commitments, leading to an increasing proletarianization of the teaching faculty. Two-worker faculty families remake fundamental social relationships; a disproportionate increase in the number of administrators and nonfaculty professionals shifts the educational center; and the failure of senior faculty to retire breeds generational strife. Multiculturalism and postmodernism, and the changing intellectual life of the university in general, Hunt argues, are not anomalies but responses to the demographic pressures.

Who are the humanities' patrons, and what kind of support are they offering these days? This is the critical money question that John D'Arms poses and explores in a convincing way. He analyzes expenditures by a number of highly visible traditional sources of support—the National Endowment for the Humanities (NEH), the National Humanities Center, the American Council of Learned Societies, a number of major foundations, and university humanities centers—as well as the patterns of public philanthropy—to find that responsibility for the humanities is being increasingly shifted to the colleges and universities and that they cannot, or will not, make up the losses from other sources. The general trend of support is sharply and worrisomely down—catastrophically so in the critical case of the NEH—and it is clear, D'Arms concludes from the funding patterns, that people, including Congress, think of the humanities as increasingly marginal contributors to the sum of knowledge and the well-being of society.

Francis Oakley undertakes the difficult task of trying to get some solid purchase on the much-debated question of the extent of changes in humanities classrooms, mainly the kinds of courses offered and their contents. He reads catalogues from different times, looks at the statistics showing the number of humanities majors, compares the study of the humanities in different types of colleges and universities, analyzes a number of studies of course content, and supports his evidence with a state-of-the-art bibliography on these and other matters that have generated so much heat. His own upbeat conclusion is that there have indeed been large changes: for example, the increase in the number of course offerings, the growing composition/literature course ratio in English departments, and a veritable explosion in courses dealing with women's and ethnic issues. But these changes—particularly in the elite institutions where the humanities have held their own better than elsewhere—have been, he argues, largely incremental. He finds that basic courses like "American History" and "Modern Literature" are still being taught, though not necessarily in the same way.

Margery Sabin explores this same issue in a somewhat different way by looking in depth at several points at which the confrontation of the old order of literary studies with postmodern ways of thinking and writing appears with particular sharpness: change in the literary section of the catalogue at Amherst College over thirty years; Frederick Crews's Marxist attack on "capitalist scholarship" at the 1969 meeting of the Modern Language Association and the fumbling attempts of the president of the organization, Henry Nash Smith, to respond by defending complexity; a meeting of the English Institute in which Edward Said and other worthies used a "scorched earth strategy" to discredit, in Said's words, a "conservative philosophy of gentlemanly refinement, or sensibility." Professor Sabin sums up by saying that "from 1968 until recently, ambitious, aggressive energies in the humanities fed on the perception of a monolithic traditional structure, which served as a kind of backboard for the play of challenge and protest. That structure, never as firm or uniform as portrayed, has now crumbled from neglect as much as from battering." But she refuses to accept this division as final and ends on a note of compromise by offering two detailed studies of teaching programs, one in literature at Williams College and one in writing at the University of Pittsburgh, in which old and new values have been successfully recombined.

Technology has also played a part in educational change. Several of our authors point out that the humanities are text-centered and are therefore affected more than the laboratory- and computer-centered sciences by the ongoing shift from Gutenberg to electronic modes of communication. John D'Arms and Denis Donoghue point out, in passing, that interest in the visual arts seems to be increasing even as interest in literature is decreasing, but Carla Hesse spells out in detail the consequences for the humanities of the growing troubles of the library and the printed book. Caught "between the two blades of an economic scissors," increased production of printed materials and reduced budgets, libraries are more and more seeking salvation in various types of digitalization, but the "electronic library is rapidly recasting our understanding of the key institutions of modern literary culture—the book, the author, the reader, the editor, the publisher, and the library—in terms of time, motion, and modes of action, rather than space, objects, and actors." The humanities were at home in—were indeed an integral part of—the Gutenberg world, but they may well find the electronic world fatally hostile to their most central values, Hesse concludes, unless humanists make the library "a key site of struggle over how we reconstitute public culture in the wake of digitalization."

At the heart of this transition in humanistic communication, and of education in general, is the practice of reading. The humanities might almost be said traditionally to have been elaborate exercises in various kinds of reading and writing, and quite obviously they are vitally affected by the kind of contemporary reading problems defined by the frequently heard term "literacy crisis," by the constantly falling verbal scores on SAT tests, and by the problem that E. D. Hirsch, Jr., has styled declining "cultural literacy": a decrease in the extent or quality of information derived from reading. Denis Donoghue probes beneath these functional reading difficulties to locate and describe a changing phenomenology in the different interpretations of several poetic passages in Shakespeare's *Macbeth*, a play with a particularly rich verbal texture. Donoghue is not concerned with poor schools and students who sit seven hours a day in front of the television, but rather with those postmodernist literary critics who—far from being illiterates—are as it were the expert and official readers of the present time, the contemporary models of what a reader should be. Where older critic-readers such as F. R. Leavis and William Empson read "intensively," and with a sense of the ambiguity of language, newer critics like Terry Eagleton and Madelon Gohlke read "extensively" and with an odd sense of language as transparent. Where the older critics read in literary texts like *Macbeth* "to exercise or incite one's imagination, specifically one's ability to imagine being different," the postmodernists cut through the "symbolic action" of the language to locate a basic political meaning—"read until you find the villain"—such as the oppression of women (including the witches and Lady Macbeth) by a bloody-minded, power-mad masculine society. Words from a recent Amherst catalogue, noted by Sabin, catch precisely the program of this new kind of reading: "The course will approach reading as an act of consumption and appropriation." Donoghue, I believe, objects to this way of reading, which he considers reductive; but what really concerns him most is that the new, thin way of reading threatens to vaporize the sense of the fullness of the world that the older, intensive way of reading fostered.

"For the scholar," says Gertrude Himmelfarb, "the method is the message," and her essay describes changes that have taken place in the way that historians and other humanists approach, question, and organize their evidence, and in what they consider their proper conclusions. In our time, she argues, we have seen a fundamental shift from a "modernist" to a "postmodernist" methodology in which the past is considered radically and immutably ambiguous, in which not even an approximation of truth is possible, in which the bias of the investigator is consequently inescapable and objectivity an illusion. Derrida showed the way to views of research and writing as independent of any prior reality, whereas Foucault argued that "knowledge" is only a tool of power. By no means all humanists have as yet entirely bought into these views, says Himmelfarb, but she demonstrates that they have by now spread widely enough to have discredited many of the older, more (though by no means altogether) positivistic methodological practices, from footnotes to narrative form.

The methodological change Himmelfarb describes is explored by Sir Frank Kermode under the terms of an epistemological shift. *Episteme* has become a potent theoretical term, referring to ways of thinking about things so fundamental that they determine consciousness and control understanding of historical and social events. To the "abolitionists"—Kermode's term for the postmodern theorists and activists—the approaching millennium has brought an apocalyptic end to the old "modernist" episteme: "aesthetic ideology, tradition, *grands récits*, canonical works." In its place, they contend, is a new postmodern episteme: skeptical if not downright nihilistic, subjective, political, and scornful of such concepts as "totality," "reason," and "truth."

The old episteme is said by postmodernists to have been absolutely and entirely displaced. Kermode is not so sure. "Does epistemic change come in different sizes or is it always catastrophic and total?" He agrees that the changes in the humanities have been both deep and extensive. But he reviews, with great learning and subtlety, past changes that suggest that epistemic *coupure* is never so complete as is claimed. The Renaissance, for example, never really was done with the medieval past, and indeed it may be impossible at all times and in all places for the *"anti-passéiste"* to achieve his Maoist revolutionary purpose. And so it may be once again, he quietly ventures, that a "saving remnant," a "clerisy," will continue to preserve a kind of older literary sensibility that may still be perceived to have some value.

In this matter of epistemic change, readers will, I think, find of particular interest Christopher Ricks's description of the efforts of theory to replace "principles" in literary studies. Metaphor is the stone on which Ricks sharpens his question of "Why, or when, is it proper to desist from further elaborating of the argument, from further philosophizing?" Since literature might almost be called a type of extended metaphoric language (certainly metaphor has been literature's primary trope), any effort by Keats's "cold philosophy" to list it in "the dull catalogue of common things" is of the greatest import. Likewise, any effort to defend its "charms" is a defense of the citadel of literature itself. Working in an ironic and witty way, Ricks exposes what he calls "the futility of boundless pursuit" as he opens up the failure of theory to define, in aspect after aspect, the nature of metaphor. In the end, he finds such "intractabilities as might honorably give us not only pause but also remission" and concludes that the failure of philosophy in this critical project should not lead to scrapping the idea of metaphor, as some theorists have proposed, but to a recognition that there are areas in which it is better not "to consider too curiously." Literature, I believe he is saying—he is delightfully difficult to pin down—by the very nature of its language, has an inbuilt resistance to theory that will in the end protect it from being demystified.

The humanities, of course, have a social and institutional presence, as well as a financial and an intellectual one, and it is in this context that Louis Menand and David Bromwich explore the changes of recent years. Menand locates a deep contradiction in the present condition of the humanities. He tells the story of the developing professionalization of the study of the humanities over a century and the way in which these professional values were institutionalized. However, by demystifying the profession, recent theoretical developments have undermined its professional claims to authority and control of education. At the same time, the increasing pressures of a diminishing job market have put a premium on professional status and raised its value for those seeking permanent, high-status tenure appointments. Thus we have the ever-difficult-to-explain situation in which, as the market for new Ph.D.s in the humanities goes down, the number of applicants to graduate schools continues to go up. Those who do not make it in the job lottery are increasingly radicalized by low-paying part-time work and become more and more anti-establishment, anti-professional. Yet the only hope for a job and status is the profession. Menand identifies with great precision and real feeling these contradictions in the academic humanities at the present time that continue to disrupt the social life and intellectual values in these subjects.

David Bromwich, in his essay "Scholarship as Social Action," turns his attention to the widespread impression, to which he subscribes, "that since the 1960s the place of advocacy in teaching and research has become so prominent as almost to constitute in itself a separate description of what scholarship in the humanities is." Not so very long ago scholars did not see their scholarship as the instrument of their political beliefs and social values (though their work might well follow their interests in these matters) but as, in Max Weber's words, a way to "teach . . . students to recognize 'inconvenient' facts—facts that are inconvenient for their party positions." With extraordinary subtlety, Bromwich winds himself into the various ways in which the older ethos of responsibility to facts has changed since the Vietnam War into a view of research and teaching as politically minded activities. He drills test holes into a variety of fascinating intellectual events to show the complex, indirect ways by which we have learned to construct "user-friendly pasts" and to give priority to "lost causes" rather than successful ones in the definition of history. The flummoxed Enola Gay exhibit at the Smithsonian provides the occasion for a "thick description" of the ways in which the American history-making imagination has been corrupted, and the recent attempt at formulating national standards for the teaching of history offers a rich scene of not only "professional timidity, acquiescence, and a muddled eclecticism," but a historical view that no longer sees persons but only "social causes and effects." "Guilt spawns theory," says one of Bromwich's sources, and that trenchant sentence catches exactly the inquiring tone of his exploration of the curious ways in which the intellectual world changes its social functions.

This volume of essays is one of the studies of higher education being sponsored by The Andrew W. Mellon Foundation and published by Princeton University Press. Many people and many institutions have contributed to the publication of this study of the humanities, and I want to make at least a gesture toward thanking them for their help. William G. Bowen, the president of The Andrew W. Mellon Foundation, originally suggested the study, and the Mellon trustees financed its preparation. Bill Bowen's sharp eye for issues, his unvarying good will, and his constant support have been critical to the progress of the work.

The issues discussed in the volume were identified at two conferences on the present state of the humanities. The first took place in the fall of 1994 at the National Humanities Center (NHC) in Research Triangle Park, North Carolina, where a group of distinguished scholars—Thomas Crow, Denis Donoghue, Lynn Hunt, Lawrence Lipking, Louis Menand, Alexander Nehamas, Annabel Patterson, Richard Rorty, and Alan Ryan—read papers and discussed the humanities in a lively and well-informed give-and-take discussion. Stephen Marcus was particularly helpful in shaping the issues and identifying the right people to work on them. Robert Connor, the director of the NHC, and his staff, especially his associate Kent Mullikin, both ran the conference and participated in it in most helpful ways. To Robert Connor, a distinguished classicist, we are particularly indebted—as are the humanities in this country in general—for his insight and leadership in these difficult times.

The second conference was held at Boston University under the auspices of the University Professors' Program and its director, that fine historian and specialist in Latin American issues, Professor Claudio Veliz. Professor Veliz arranged for a group of distinguished humanists to deliver lectures on the subject of where the humanities are and where they are going. Peter

Berger, David Bromwich, John Ellis, Gertrude Himmelfarb, Irving Kristol, Christopher Ricks, Roger Scruton, Alan Wolfe, and others helped to make this a memorable occasion for getting some sense of the humanities' past and future. John Silber, a philosopher and the president of Boston University, and Jon Westling, the provost and president-designate, were kind enough to enter fully and learnedly into the discussions. To all I am very grateful for their wisdom and their good-natured help, and I owe to Claudio Veliz the greatest debt for the care and intelligence with which he put everything together.

My debt to the distinguished authors represented in this volume is obvious, and I will say only that it has been a privilege to work with such intelligent people. I owe debts, too, to the staff here at the Princeton office of The Mellon Foundation: to Dorothy Westgate, who typed the materials again and again with her usual speed and perspicacity; to Fred Vars, who produced the graphs for me; and specially to Joan Gilbert, who used her remarkable talent for figures to supervise the compilation of the statistics that form the basis for the tables and figures in the appendix.

I should not fail to mention Walter Lippincott, the director of Princeton University Press, and our editor, Peter Dougherty, who attended the conference at NHC and has shepherded the project along from the beginning. To all, my heartiest thanks, and the hope that we will contribute something useful to an understanding of the humanities and to higher education in a time of great change.

NUMBERS

One

Democratization and Decline?

THE CONSEQUENCES OF DEMOGRAPHIC CHANGE IN THE HUMANITIES

LYNN HUNT

TEACHING and research in the humanities are shaped by various factors, not all of which are immediately evident either to the public or to humanities scholars themselves. This essay examines the role of some of those silently acting but nonetheless effective agents in remaking the world of higher education. The focus will be on the intersection of two major structural trends: the ever-progressing democratization of higher education and the less certain but nonetheless potentially momentous decline in the status of the humanities. How are these trends connected to each other? More generally, what are the likely consequences of demographic changes in and for the humanities sector of higher education? I do not argue that economic and demographic changes will determine all the social and intellectual outcomes, but it does seem likely that they will shape those developments in significant ways.

My basic lines of argument can be briefly summarized: (1) Scholars in the humanities must meet the demographic and cultural challenge of an ever more multiethnic and feminine student population in an era of declining resources and perhaps declining prestige, especially for their field. (2) All faculty, but perhaps especially those in the humanities, face the potentially divisive social side effects of age cohorts that have different sex and minority ratios and different professional experiences and expectations—effects that could be exacerbated by the rise of the two-earner partnership and uncertainties about the retirement of the senior faculty. (3) Intellectual trends in the humanities will inevitably be affected by declining prestige, dwindling resources, and internal social divisions. I do not mean to paint a bleak portrait of our future, for in many ways higher education has never been more successful anywhere in the world than it is now in the United States. But a reminder of an old definition of the difference between optimism and pessimism might come in handy: the optimist proclaims that we live in the best of all possible worlds, while the pessimist fears this is true.

Democratization

American higher education has been undergoing an ever-accelerating process of democratization since the 1870s. In 1870 52,000 students enrolled in American universities and colleges; twenty years later their number had more than doubled to 157,000, and by 1910 the total had reached 355,000.[1] The number of students leapt to over 2 million after World War II and rapidly increased to 15 million by 1994. According to projections published in the September 1, 1995, almanac issue of the *Chronicle of Higher Education*, college enrollment will remain static until 1998, when it will recommence its inexorable climb, reaching 16 million by 2005.[2] In recent decades this growth has been due largely to an increase in the proportion of high school graduates going on to college. In 1983 32.5 percent of high school graduates went on to college; in 1992 the figure reached 41.9 percent.[3] However, in 1993 the percentage declined slightly to 41.4 percent.[4] If the percentage of high school graduates going on to college continues to stagnate or decline, the process of democratization might also stagnate or decline, thus reversing or at least halting a century-long development.

Democratization of higher education is probably more advanced in the United States than anywhere else in the world; in the 1980s, only Canada and Sweden even came close to sending as many young people on to higher education, and Australia, France, the USSR, and West Germany sent only about half as many of their nineteen- to twenty-four-year-olds to university (in the United Kingdon the proportion was even lower).[5] In North America the percentage of the *total* population studying at the "third level" (which includes all institutions of higher education) has climbed from 4 percent in 1970 to 5.3 percent in 1991 (a 32 percent increase in just twenty years). In Europe the comparable figures are 1.4 percent in 1970 and 2.1 percent in 1991 (a 50 percent increase); in Africa, 0.1 percent in 1970 and 0.4 percent in 1991 (a 300 percent increase, albeit from a much lower level). In many other countries (indeed in most of the world, but especially in Europe), government policy has shifted in the direction of admitting more students to university-level study, which may mean that these countries will face social and intellectual tensions similar to those that Americans have confronted on campuses over the last decades.

If the worldwide trend toward expanding higher education does continue, it will generate pressures on the physical plants and faculties of universities and colleges, since the number of institutions is not increasing by much if at all, schools are expanding their plants only very slowly, and the size of faculties may not continue to expand as it has in the past. In the United States, the total number of institutions offering higher education nearly doubled between 1870 and 1920, doubled again between 1920 and 1960, increased by 57 percent between 1960 and 1980, and even increased by 12 percent between 1980 and 1990, but the rate of growth in our institutions has now tapered off to about 1 percent a year.[6] Worldwide, the faculty/student ratio at the third level has remained virtually stagnant, declining slightly from a ratio of 13.22 students per faculty member in 1970 to 13.46 in 1980 and 13.67 in 1991.[7]

Although higher education has become more available to almost every kind of social group in the United States, women have made the most spectacular gains. In the 1980s alone, for example, the number of bachelor's degrees awarded to men increased by 7 percent while the number of those awarded to women rose 27 percent. Women now make up 55 percent of the student population, and the number of women among the faculty is increasing too, albeit at a slower pace. In 1987, 27 percent of full-time college professors were women.[8] By 1992, this had risen to 33.5 percent.[9] The humanities have one of the highest proportions of women faculty: 33 percent in 1987 (the most recent year for which such comparisons are available), compared to 2 percent women faculty in engineering, 17 percent women faculty in natural sciences, and 22 percent in the social sciences. Only health and home economics had a higher percentage of women faculty in 1987.[10]

The entrance of women into the academy has been particularly apparent in the humanities at the doctoral level; the proportion of doctoral degrees conferred on women in all disciplines increased from one in ten in 1966 to over one in three by 1993, while the proportion of humanities doctorates conferred on women grew from about one in five to virtually one in two in the same time period (Figure 12, appendix). Women have long taken B.A. degrees in the humanities, and at this level there has been less change. While overall the proportion of B.A. degrees conferred on women rose from about one-third in 1966 to nearly one-half in 1993, the proportion of women gaining B.A.s in the humanities remained remarkably steady, ranging between 50 and 60 percent in the research universities and 55 and 65 percent in the liberal arts colleges (see Figures 13 and 14, appendix). At the B.A. level, then, women have maintained their traditional interest in the humanities, but the real increase has come in nonhumanities fields.

Accompanying (but not exactly paralleling) the increase in women students has been the less dramatic but still significant increase in the numbers and percentages of minority students. In 1993 minority students made up 22.6 percent of college and university students; in 1992 13.2 percent of the faculty were minorities.[11] (In the humanities 11 percent of the faculty were minorities in 1987. This figure put them in the middle of all fields, which ranged from 13 percent minorities in engineer-

ing [almost entirely Asians] to 6 percent in agriculture and home economics.[12]) Changes in immigration patterns may well raise the number of
minority students coming to colleges and universities. Between 1931 and
1960, Europeans made up 58 percent of immigrants to the United States,
Canadians 21 percent, Latin Americans 15 percent, and Asians only
5 percent. Between 1980 and 1984, in contrast, Europeans made up only
12 percent of the immigrants and Canadians just 2 percent, while Latin
Americans comprised 35 percent and Asians 48 percent.[13] But the consequences of this change for the humanities are not yet clear, for unlike
white women, minority students do not gravitate toward the humanities
for their majors or doctorates.

Minority students take fewer B.A.s and fewer doctorates in the humanities than whites (see Figures 15 and 16, appendix). It is worth noting that
only education and the social sciences produced proportionately more
women Ph.D.s than the humanities in 1993, whereas all other fields—including the natural sciences—produced more minority Ph.D.s in 1993
than the humanities.[14] Thus, though demographic changes might put
feminism and multiculturalism inevitably on the intellectual agenda, their
impact on the humanities should be viewed as less than self-evident.
Perhaps a paradox is at work here: the humanities have responded most
vehemently in intellectual terms to the changes within the student body,
but they have not shared equally in all those changes; humanities faculty
teach their subjects somewhat differently because of changes in the student body, but they have not actually attracted those different students to
serious study of the humanities. It is possible that minority students have
been especially alert to the potential decline in status of the humanities or
that they have felt that the humanities are inherently more elitist and
white in subject matter because the humanities are more closely tied to
Western culture than the social or natural sciences.

A Decline in Status?

The increasing "feminization" of the humanities (and to some extent of
higher education more generally) raises serious questions about long-term
consequences, for the feminization of work almost always has led to a
decline in skill status in other occupations in the past. One measure of the
relative status of the humanities can be found in comparative pay scales.
In a national faculty salary survey of 1993–1994, researchers found that
the average salary (all ranks included) for foreign languages and literature
was $41,038, for English $41,346, for philosophy and religion $43,489, and
for history $45,337. During the period 1966–1993, history and philoso-
phy and religion had much lower proportions of women receiving doctor-

ates than foreign languages or English (Figure 12, appendix). Similarly, nonhumanities fields were generally characterized by higher average salaries than the humanities: biology $44,390, mathematics $45,000, physics $52,660, economics $52,755, and engineering $62,280.[15] There is a correlation between relative pay and the proportion of women in a field; faculty in those academic fields that have attracted a relatively high proportion of women are paid less on average than those in fields that have not attracted women in the same numbers.

The potential for a decline in status has become more likely with the increased use of part-time positions for teaching. Already in 1989, before the effects of economic recession and stagnation became apparent, one quarter of four-year-college faculties were part-time and fully one-half of those teaching at two-year colleges were part-time.[16] Women comprise 42 percent of the part-time faculty, and 43.2 percent of women faculty members work on a part-time basis as compared to 30 percent of the male faculty.[17] As more and more positions go part-time or temporary and more and more teaching is done by lecturers and adjuncts, the social structure of the university faculty is likely to become proletarianized at the bottom. There are intellectual consequences as well. A recent study of *full-time* but non-tenure-track faculty has shown that compared to untenured faculty on a tenure track they had less interest and engagement in research, less of a sense that they could influence matters in their department, and more of a sense that they had made the wrong career choice and might soon leave academia.[18]

The size of the faculty has been increasing, by 30 percent between 1976 and 1989, when the number of students increased 25 percent, but the teaching environment has been subtly transformed even for full-time, tenure-track faculty. The number of teaching and research assistants has increased hardly at all, by only 2 percent between 1976 and 1989. The number of administrators and nonteaching professionals employed by the university has increased most of all, by 43 percent for administrators and by 123 percent for "nonfaculty professionals" (many of whom we would probably consider administrators). The university staff as a whole is getting bigger, but the relative presence of faculty, secretaries, and janitors is actually declining.[19] By 1991, the percentage of faculty within the total staff of institutions of higher education had declined from 34 percent in 1976 to 32.5 percent, the percentage of nonprofessional (janitorial, secretarial) staff had declined from 42.4 percent to 37.3 percent, and the percentage of instruction and research assistants had declined from 8.6 percent to 7.8 percent, while the presence of nonfaculty professional staff had increased from 9.6 percent to 16.8 percent.[20] As the university becomes increasingly bureaucratized to meet financial pressures, the humanities—preeminently a teaching sector—are unlikely to prosper.

If the humanities are perceived as especially "soft" because they have become "feminized" (admitting more women to their ranks as students, B.A.s, doctoral candidates, and faculty), and especially contentious because they "man" the forward trenches of the "culture wars," they may suffer disproportionately from decreases in funding, declines in faculty size, or increases in adjunct and part-time teaching. Such a trend would exaggerate a decline in status. This decline may already have been registered in comparative numbers of doctoral degrees, which in the humanities have declined from a high of 14.8 percent of all doctoral degrees in 1973 to a low of 8.4 percent in 1988–1989 (rising marginally to 9.2 percent in 1992), compared to a more steady state in the social sciences (rising from a low of 14.6 percent in 1966 to a high of 18.8 percent in 1977). The natural sciences had long dominated (32.3 percent of doctorates in 1966), but they have also declined somewhat (to 23.7 percent in 1993; see Table 2, appendix), though no doubt for different reasons (many of the students in the natural sciences, especially at the doctoral level, are now foreign-born, reflecting declining interest in the natural sciences among native-born students). At the B.A. level, both the humanities and the natural sciences seem to be suffering from a long-term malaise; as the number of B.A. degrees overall has more than doubled (from 1966 to 1993), the proportion in the humanities has steadily dropped from just over 20 percent in the late 1960s to a low of about 10 percent in the mid-1980s, increasing only to 12 percent in the early 1990s. Similarly, the proportion in natural sciences has dropped steadily from 11 percent in the late 1960s to under 7 percent in the early 1990s. At the B.A. level, as at the doctoral level, the social sciences have achieved more of a steady state, claiming 15 to 17 percent of the B.A.s in the late 1960s, then rising slightly, then declining slightly, only to end again at 15 percent in the early 1990s (Table 1, appendix).

The now seemingly permanent stagnation or slow growth of Western economies and the consequent cuts in national and state-level funding for higher education will exacerbate the effects of these trends, encouraging university administrations to downsize faculties, keep the lid on faculty salaries, hire more part-timers with lesser or no benefits, and devote more and more university time and personnel to the raising of funds. This atmosphere of constraint has unpredictable but momentous effects on scholarly life, that is, on the social and intellectual structures that shape the humanities.

One potential effect, already evident in some universities, is the demand that faculty teach more students, either in bigger classes or in more classes per faculty member. In general this means teaching more with fewer resources. This requirement will eventually influence the kind of teaching that is performed: less face-to-face interaction with students, more multiple-choice tests, bigger and fewer discussion sections, fewer papers, and so on. Some of the public universities seem to be pointing in just this direction.

Social Pressures

Economic constraints, feminization, and the turn toward part-time employment are creating a kind of class or caste system within the universities, with proletarianized part-time or non-tenure-track lecturers and adjuncts at the bottom and junior faculty with uncertain or temporary positions on the next highest rung; followed by regular ladder faculty with tenure who have no prospects of outside offers or much inside advancement; topped off by a relatively small group of "stars" who have secure positions, high salaries, a steady stream of graduate students, and the prospect of continual advancement. This new hierarchy is already reflected in severe salary compression in the assistant, associate, and even full professor ranks; economic stagnation will only make these effects more prevalent and more divisive. This trend seems to affect all the disciplines alike: the average salary of a new assistant professor in English is only about $9,000 less than the salary of an average associate professor and the range is similar in other fields (biology $8,000; mathematics $9,000; economics less than $7,000).[21]

The entrance of new groups into the faculty has distinctly changed the social dynamics within the university in just the last twenty to thirty years. In the 1960s Jews finally gained full admission to faculty positions, followed by women in the 1970s and ethnic minorities in the 1980s. Reactions to these changes cannot be measured precisely, but it seems that resistance and obstruction have been correlated largely with recentness of entry to the profession: Jews are on the whole accepted (with many exceptions), women are somewhat accepted, and minorities still meet greater resistance. In any case, the atmosphere of a club of gentleman scholars has largely disappeared, or at least begun to dissipate.

The pace of change should not be exaggerated, however. Between 1972 and 1989 the proportion of women faculty in all institutions of higher education rose only from 21.4 percent to 28.3 percent. The proportion of nonwhite faculty grew from just 5 percent to 9.1 percent (figures for women and minorities vary from study to study depending on the institutional base included). But these averages mask significant differences between types of schools: private universities averaged only 20.3 percent women on their faculties in 1989 as opposed to 21.3 percent in public universities, 27.1 percent in public four-year colleges, 30.8 in private four-year colleges, and 39.2 percent in public two-year colleges. (Once again, the lower the status, the higher the proportion of women; the converse is also true.) The variation in minorities, however, was less pronounced: from 6.7 percent in private four-year colleges to 10.6 percent in public two-year colleges in 1989.[22]

Change has been more marked in recent hires. In 1989 38.6 percent of the new hires were women (compared to 24.4 percent of the current faculty) and 13.8 percent of the new hires were minorities (compared to 9.8 percent of the current faculty). The figures for 1972 were much lower for women: 24.1 percent of the new hires in that year (20.5 percent of the current faculty in 1972 were women, so the increase in percentage of women faculty was not great). In 1972 only 8.3 percent of the new hires were minorities (5.6 percent of the current faculty were minorities in the same year).[23]

The remaking of the university has not come without a struggle. The statistics show that changes in the faculty have not followed automatically from changes in the student body or in the pool of doctoral candidates. The statistics cannot explain this discrepancy, but other kinds of evidence have been uncovered (for those who have not experienced it firsthand). Peter Novick has demonstrated how history professors resisted the democratization of their profession. One secretary of the American Historical Association wrote in the early twentieth century, "One has it [the aesthetic sense] by inheritance or by long training. . . . It is more apt to be found in persons who are born of and trained in families of long standing in the upper classes of society than in persons who have sprung from the class that is accustomed to the plainer ways and thinking of the world. The leading historians of the past, for the most part, belonged to this class." This original prejudice against scholars from the lower classes translated in the twentieth century into anti-Semitism and discrimination against women and minorities. In a recommendation for J. H. Hexter, a Jewish student and now a prominent historian of England, Crane Brinton wrote, "I'm afraid he is unemployable, but I'd like to make one last effort in his behalf." One recommender described another Jewish scholar and eventual Harvard historian, Oscar Handlin, as having "none of the offensive traits which some people associate with his race." Daniel J. Boorstin was depicted as "a Jew, though not the kind to which one takes exception." One can only imagine what was said about women and minorities. Daniel J. Boorstin himself told the American Historical Association Committee on Graduate Education in 1959 that he had not "had a single really keen woman student" and as a result was "not in favor of encouraging women students any more than they have been encouraged in the past."[24]

If there is a continuing correlation between the pool of applicants and the faculty chosen (and there is such a correlation, however imperfect in the past), the proportion of women faculty in the humanities will continue to grow: in 1993 47.5 percent of the new Ph.D.s in the arts and humanities were female (compared to 33 percent of the humanities faculty in 1987). The same does not hold, unfortunately, for minorities; in 1993 only 10.9 percent of the new Ph.D.s came from minority groups (whereas minorities comprised 11 percent of the humanities faculty in 1987).[25] The disparity between women and minorities should be cause for alarm; at every level, the humanities attract women candidates in greater numbers than minorities. Although this is true to some extent in every field of study, the discrepancy is greatest in the humanities; it is among the most success-ful in attracting women faculty and among the least successful in attract-ing minority faculty. In 1987, for example, the ratio of women to minority faculty in the humanities was 3:1 whereas in both the social sciences and the natural sciences it was 2:1 (in large part, admittedly, because there were fewer women in those fields).[26]

The diversification of the faculty has created an unprecedented social situation in which the rules of interaction are less than clear. The confu-sion about social codes has been aggravated by social differences between age cohorts within higher education, the vagaries of the job market, the rise in two-earner partnerships, and the continuing wave of early retire-ments. The potential for social conflict within the academy has been on the rise, while the factors that might mitigate it have been in decline.

Those who currently teach within the university know that different age groups have had very different experiences in higher education. These differences can be attributed in part to the fluctuations in the job market for faculty positions. A huge cohort, the cohort of the expansion of positions in the 1960s (largely made up of white men), is now approaching retirement, just when mandatory retirement has been eliminated. A few universities have developed early retirement schemes; others have pro-duced incentives to encourage retirement between the ages of sixty-five and seventy. Early evidence seems to suggest that faculty are now gener-ally less likely to retire before age seventy. [27] If tension is created by the reluctance of the older cohorts to retire, it will affect the humanities in particular for the humanities are the oldest sector in the university: in 1987 47 percent of the humanities faculty were fifty years old or older as compared to 37 percent in both the natural sciences and the social sciences.[28] Conversely, where early retirement schemes are put into effect, the humanities will suffer the most noticeable losses in personnel. They will also suffer disproportionately from downsizing since they are on the verge of losing the most positions in the near term.

My own cohort (with the first significant influx of women), those who entered the job market in the 1970s during a time of constriction but who eventually gained a quite large number of positions, might be left prematurely holding the reins of power and facing recurring internecine struggles over budget cuts and curricular realignments. This intermediate group is smaller in the humanities than in the natural or social sciences; in 1987 34 percent of the humanities faculty were in their forties as compared to 39 percent in the natural sciences and 41 percent in the social sciences (perhaps because these fields expanded later). This cohort, however, has great advantages over those who follow, for it at least had a common experience in college and graduate school: the experience of vibrant social movements in the 1960s and a consequent sense of mission. Moreover, careers in this cohort had been established by the time constant budget crisis set in for most universities in the 1990s.

The 1980s cohort is perhaps the least advantaged of all because it is the product of a very constricted job market and very different social and political times, especially for higher education. This group is arguably isolated because it is smaller in number; in the humanities only 18 percent of the faculty was under forty in 1987 as compared to 24 percent in the natural sciences and 22 percent in the social sciences. They run the risk of being alienated by the structural changes occurring within the university (which threaten to lower the profile of the humanities), a risk that is enhanced by changes in the social life of the university and by the now relentless pressure to try to escape from the compressed ranks of assistant and associate professors. Moreover, this cohort eventually may be swamped in number by the 1990s cohort if (and this is very much an "if") a large wave of retirements results in new positions.

Changes in the economy and in customs have encouraged the rise of two-earner partnerships, which have had an impact on the university along with other sectors of society. Wives now work, many of them within the university. No one sex is assigned the invariable role of social facilitator in the couple. Since everyone works all day, no one has the energy to organize the dinner parties of old with eight, ten, or twelve colleagues sharing a festive meal laboriously prepared by a dutiful (and unemployed outside the home) wife. As a result, socializing and social life in general have almost disappeared in favor of official functions and much more informal interaction (but generally, I would argue, simply less interaction). Junior faculty feel left out, even though there is no "in" that is clearly identifiable. The result is that there is not much of a mechanism for smoothing over the tensions already cited. Just at the moment when economic pressures create the potential for internal strife, social bonding within the university has weakened. Esprit de corps rests only tenuously on common interests, especially in disciplines that are increasingly fragmented by specialization (as most are).

Uncertainty about retirement might exacerbate these developments. Early retirement schemes remove the stratum of the university population that has traditionally played the role of arbiter, mediator, and facilitator. Ironically, the apparent resistance to retirement in schools without early retirement schemes could increase social tensions for the opposite reason; if senior faculty are perceived as staying beyond the point of productivity and thereby blocking progress by younger scholars, their very presence would generate tensions between the age groups. In either case, the older faculty will be unable to exercise the role of sage elders, mitigating conflict in the interest of the community. In either case, the social environment is in danger of deterioration.

Interesting evidence of age differences can be found in a 1989 survey of faculty attitudes. Younger faculty were less likely to believe that their institutions had made affirmative action a priority or aimed to create a diverse multicultural environment and less likely to agree that faculty in their own institutions were sensitive to issues of minorities or that many courses included minority or feminist perspectives. Those fifty-five and over were more likely to believe that their institutions put a premium on affirmative action and a multicultural environment and that the faculty were sensitive to minority issues and offered many courses with minority and feminist perspectives. Women were as likely as men to believe that their institutions promoted affirmative action for minorities but less likely to believe that they did the same for women; otherwise the difference between age cohorts was much greater than the difference between men and women. Similarly, the difference in age cohorts overshadowed the differences between ethnic groups. Whites were *less likely* to believe that their institutions wanted to promote affirmative action than were their African American and Hispanic colleagues (only Asian Americans were a bit less likely to believe this than whites). Whites were also less likely than any minority group to believe that their institutions hoped to develop appreciation for a multicultural society or create a diverse multicultural environment.[29] The difference between age groups within the faculty has great significance for the long-term future of the humanities and the university as a whole.

I do not mean to paint a nostalgic picture of the past, when a gentleman's club often functioned through various forms of prejudice and unspoken exploitation. But I do mean to suggest that present-day faculty and administrators should think about the social conditions of their employment as much as the economic ones. This is especially true in the humanities, which by their disciplinary nature have been connected in some fashion with notions of a life worth living.

Intellectual Consequences

I have placed considerable emphasis on the economic and social conditions within the university because I believe that they may fundamentally
transform the intellectual options facing us. The rise of new fields of
knowledge on the backs of multiculturalism and postmodernism (ethnic,
gay and lesbian, women's, and postcolonial studies among others), increasing interdisciplinarity, and the attractions of cultural studies—to
name some of the important trends in my part of the humanities—all take
on a different meaning when looked at in the light of faculty downsizing,
feminization of the work force, the rise of part-time employment, perennial budget crisis, and the disappearance of mechanisms for resolving
social conflict within the academy. New fields appear now not in an
atmosphere of buoyant expansion as in the 1960s, but in a fiercely
contested zero-sum game in which new positions must displace older ones.

Although new forms of knowledge are not a symptom of decline but
rather of the robust growth of higher education for so many decades, they
may well coexist now with certain forms of decline in status, prestige, and
power for the humanities as a sector. As higher education has expanded,
the humanities have not grown apace (and neither have the natural
sciences); new fields have attracted many of the new students and therefore an important share of the funding. The humanities have become the
site of political and academic contention just when they have become more
vulnerable within the university, i.e., as their relatively older faculties
retire without replacements, have become markedly more feminized than
other faculties, and attract relatively fewer undergraduates and doctoral
students compared to faculties in other fields. (Needless to say, I am not
arguing that the humanities should purge women from their ranks in order
to improve their status!)

The current situation may give rise to any number of paradoxes. Cultural studies, for instance—resisted in many quarters as faddish, overly
theory driven, and/or Marxist-feminist—may end up providing deans
with a convenient method for amalgamating humanities departments
under one roof and reducing their faculty size. Similarly, interdisciplinarity may only make the case that humanities faculty are all interchangeable
and hence that many are expendable. Interdisciplinarity has tended to
weaken the argument for chronological coverage (the need to have someone who specializes in a particular approach sometimes supersedes the
need for someone who covers a particular century or movement) and
might thereby facilitate downsizing. In short, the decline of old intellectual
models has its potential costs as well as benefits. Intellectual change
cannot be made to depend on a cost-benefit analysis, but the negotiation

of economic and social tensions might be enhanced by a broader understanding of the trends that are shaping our decisions.

The only intellectual trends that seem to follow inexorably from the changing demography of higher education are feminism and multiculturalism, if these are taken as broad affiliations rather than fixed ideological positions. The rise in number of women and minority students, the increase in number of women and minority faculty (but especially women faculty), and the expansion of education to previously excluded social classes must exert some pressure on the structure of knowledge, especially in the humanities and social sciences, whose subject matter is sensitive in one way or another to social configurations. The increasing emphasis on the social construction of knowledge and identity probably stems from these same changes, for previously excluded groups are especially sensitive to the ways in which social structures and social meanings have shaped their lives (if only because such influences worked to exclude people like them from higher education in the past). Even if affirmative action admission and hiring policies were to be effectively dismantled tomorrow, the process of change in values would most likely continue apace because it is rooted in the democratization of the university (both the student body and the faculty), which has proceeded, however fitfully and contestedly, since at least 1870, that is, since the days when the modern university first took shape.

Moreover, feminism and multiculturalism in the curriculum depend not only on changes in the consumers and producers of knowledge but also on changes in world politics; in humanities courses this means that as Europe has receded from world dominance in favor first of the superpower rivalry of the United States and the former Soviet Union and now of a more even free-for-all in which the Pacific Rim carries increasing weight, so too the emphasis will shift in at least some measure from a seemingly automatic Eurocentrism to a more diverse world perspective. It is not just the identity of the students in the class that forces change, but also the realities of geopolitics today. We may and no doubt will still teach the common values that shaped Western civilization because we still share them with Europeans, but we will also have to make an effort to understand how the new world we live in has come to be.

Understanding that world also includes understanding the forces that shape the American university as a place for acquiring and transmitting knowledge and values. This essay has been an exercise in a particular kind of self-reflexivity. Rather than look at the intellectual trends themselves, I have shifted focus to consider structural changes in the size and composition of the student body and the size and composition of the faculty in the humanities. We do not always clearly see these structural changes, though we live every day with their consequences as some colleagues retire, new ones are hired, positions are lost, and sometimes others of a different sort are gained. It might be helpful to keep those broader, silent forces in mind as we prepare for education in the next century.

Notes

1. These estimates are provided in National Center for Education Statistics, *Digest of Education Statistics 1994* (Washington, D.C., 1994), 175. For a general discussion of trends, see Christopher J. Lucas, *American Higher Education: A History* (New York, 1994), 140.

2. *The Chronicle of Higher Education Almanac* 42, no. 1 (September 1, 1995): 16. Some of the summary statistics are available as well on line from *Academe This Week* and in more complete form as a subscriber service from *Academe Today*, both of them produced by the *Chronicle of Higher Education*.

3. *The Chronicle of Higher Education Almanac* 41, no. 1 (September 1, 1994): 16.

4. *The Chronicle of Higher Education Almanac* (1995): 16.

5. This statement is based on the figures provided in Clark Kerr, Marian L. Gade, and Maureen Kawaoka, *Higher Education Cannot Escape History: Issues for the Twenty-First Century* (Albany, N.Y., 1994), 89. The figures are: United States 50 percent (37 percent full-time), Australia 22 percent, Canada 42 percent (31 percent full-time), France 23 percent, Sweden 33 percent, United Kingdom 14 percent, USSR 22 percent, and West Germany 23 percent. Figures are given for nineteen- to twenty-four-year-olds, not eighteen- to twenty-four-year-olds.

6. My calculations are based on the data given in *Digest of Education Statistics 1994*, 175.

7. I have calculated the percentages of students out of the total population and the faculty/student ratios from the data given in *Digest of Education Statistics 1994*, p. 415. Country-by-country data can be found in *UNESCO Statistical Yearbook 1995* (Lanham, Md., 1995).

8. *Chronicle of Higher Education Almanac* (1994): 33.

9. *Chronicle of Higher Education Almanac* (1995): 22.

10. *Digest of Education Statistics 1994*, 232.

11. *Chronicle of Higher Education Almanac* (1995): 14, 22.

12. *Digest of Education Statistics 1994*, 232.

13. Roger Daniels, *Coming to America: A History of Immigration and Ethnicity in American Life* (New York, 1990), 335.

14. *Chronicle of Higher Education Almanac* (1995): 18.

15. College and University Personnel Association, *1993–94 National Faculty Salary Survey* (Washington, D.C., 1994), especially 3–14.

16. National Center for Educational Statistics, *Digest of Education Statistics 1993* (Washington, D.C., 1993), 166.

17. "Report on the Status of Non-Tenure-Track Faculty," *Academe* 27 (July-August 1993): 39–46.

18. Roger G. Baldwin, Jay L. Chronister, Ana Esther Rivera, and Theresa G. Bailey, "Destination Unknown: An Exploratory Study of Full-Time Faculty off the Tenure Track," *Research in Higher Education* 34 (1993): 747–61.

19. *Digest of Education Statistics 1993*, 225.

20. *Digest of Education Statistics 1994*, 227.

21. *1993–94 National Faculty Salary Survey.*

22. Jeffrey F. Milem and Helen S. Astin, "The Changing Composition of the Faculty: What Does It Really Mean for Diversity?" *Change* 25 (March-April 1993): 22 (Table 1).

23. Ibid., 23 (Table 2). The authors do not explain the slight discrepancy between their figures for all institutions in Table 1 (cf. their footnote 13) and Table 2.

24. Peter Novick, *That Noble Dream: The "Objectivity Question" and the American Historical Profession* (New York, 1988), 171, 172–73, and 367. Novick says nothing about the irony of the situation suggested by the last quote.

25. *Chronicle of Higher Education Almanac* (1995): 18.

26. *Digest of Education Statistics 1994*, 232.

27. David Card and Orley Ashenfelter, "Faculty Retirement in the Post-Mandatory Era: Early Findings from the Princeton Retirement Survey." Unpublished paper presented at the Princeton Conference on Higher Education, March, 1996.

28. All data on age groups come from *Digest of Education Statistics 1994*, 232.

29. Milem and Astin, "The Changing Composition of the Faculty," p. 25 (Table 4). Age groups were divided into under thirty-five, thirty-five to forty-four, forty-five to fifty-four, fifty-five to sixty-four, and sixty-five and over. The trends tended to be uniform: for example, those under thirty-five were less likely than those aged thirty-five to forty-four to believe that their institutions put a priority on affirmative action for minorities, those aged thirty-five to forty-four were less likely to believe this than those aged forty-five to fifty-four, and so on. The differences are not always great, but the trend is apparent in each case.

Two

Funding Trends in the Academic Humanities, 1970–1995

REFLECTIONS ON THE STABILITY OF THE SYSTEM

JOHN H. D'ARMS

WHO have been the patrons—the Maecenates and the Medici, the Pierpont Morgans and the Paul Mellons—of the humanities in this country's leading universities and colleges during the past twenty-five years? What trends in patterns of financial support can be detected over time, and what vectors and forces can be identified as the principal drivers of change? A list of patrons with any pretension to completeness would include at least two agencies of the federal government; private philanthropic foundations large and small; a wide range of independent fellowship providers, including both residential centers and national research libraries; corporate sponsors; and private individuals. Overshadowing all of these, of course, are the universities and colleges themselves, and the various supporters that combine to form their distinctive networks of patronage: parents and students paying tuition and fees; graduates and other individuals, past and present, bearing gifts destined for the annual fund or for endowment; state legislatures, federal and corporate sponsors, private and family foundations. A full discussion of trends would demand year-by-year analyses of numerous budgets and generate discourse bristling with numbers and percentages; it would also require careful scrutiny of the attitudes, as well as the behavior, of leading individual donors, and of the psychological factors that prompt them to choose to validate their wealth in specific ways.

Since there exist no systematic data, collected over time, that might provide a partial guide to sources, levels, and patterns of funding, even an outline of an attack on so large a topic requires the discipline of a highly selective approach. My solution has been to single out a small but influential subset of humanistic patrons—the National Endowment for the Humanities (NEH), the largest philanthropic foundations, a few independent fellowship providers (the American Council of Learned Societies [ACLS], the National Humanities Center [NHC], and the John S. Guggenheim Foundation), a group of major donors to a single university—and, drawing upon available budgetary information for specific years, to attempt to show how the fluctuations in contributions from this subset of patrons illustrate more general trends. For the sources of financial patronage of the humanities lie both within and outside the academy; even if the universities themselves have always been and must remain the senior partners, the strong complementary role of external patrons creates a dynamic interplay among funding sources that is critical for the continued stability of the system.

Shifts in disciplinary boundaries yield many legitimate ways of mapping the intellectual territory that falls under the rubric of the humanities. Interests of clarity thus require a working definition of the humanities as conceptualized for the purposes of this essay. By the terms *scholarly humanities* and *academic humanities*, used interchangeably throughout this chapter, I mean all fields of study that are normally grouped together within colleges of arts and sciences, that are identified as departments and programs in humanities, and in which the Ph.D. is the highest earned degree.[1] I further include two fields sometimes classified as social sciences: all periods of history and, within anthropology, the subfields of ethnology and archaeology. Room needs also to be found for emerging interdisciplinary fields and groupings that have to date only intermittently begun to offer the Ph.D.—cultural, ethnic, and gender studies; literature and law— and the campus-based humanities centers that may house these and other disciplinary clusterings. Important aspects of the scholarly infrastructure—general and specialized libraries, museums, other collections, university presses—have not been wholly ignored. My definition, in short, has endeavored to include all aspects of the academic humanities as would be readily recognizable by faculty members and administrators in the approximately three hundred institutions classified by the Carnegie Foundation as Research Universities I and II, and Baccalaureate Colleges I.[2] This is a small universe, comprising less than 10% of all U.S. institutions of higher education, but a universe possessing educational and societal influence unquestionably disproportionate to its size, and the universe likely to be of most interest to the readers for whom the present volume is intended.

The National Endowment for the Humanities

In 1980, the authors of *The Humanities in American Life* noted that the divisions of Fellowships and Research Grants at the NEH, whose programs were then the principal channels through which the Endowment strengthened the scholarly foundation for humanistic study, were then awarding only 22 percent of all Endowment funds, in contrast to the 60 percent awarded for such purposes during the first years of the NEH's existence.[3]

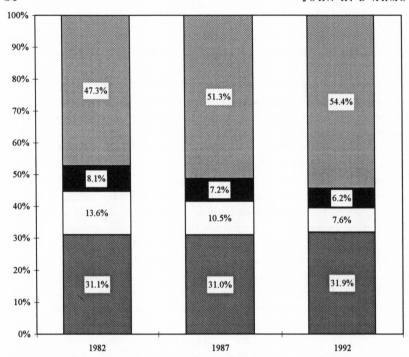

FIGURE 2.1. Recipients of NEH grants. *Key:* ▨, universities and their affiliated scholars; □, four-year colleges and their affiliated scholars; ■, individuals and scholars who received regrants; ▧, all other recipients (including libraries, historical societies, elementary and secondary education, and state and public programs.)

But those percentages took no account of challenge grants, or of grants from all NEH divisions that benefited colleges, universities, and the members of their faculties. The results of a new attempt to estimate actual NEH allocations to all aspects of the academic humanities, and to track recent trends in funding for these by comparing figures for the years 1982, 1987, and 1992, are displayed in Figure 2.1 and Table 2.1.[4]

In nominal dollars, total NEH budgetary obligations (less administrative expenses) increased steadily between 1982 and 1994 and declined only slightly when measured in constant dollars.[5] Particular fluctuations within sectors are set forth in Table 2.1 and Figure 2.1, but three findings with major implications for funding trends require emphasis here. First, the academic sector as a whole has been losing ground steadily to state and public programs: the latter's budget share grew from approximately 40 to 50 percent between 1982 and 1992 (Figure 2.1).[6] Second, both the universities and the colleges have experienced marked declines in support from the office of challenge grants (53.4 and 80.5 percent, respectively), despite steady annual increases in allocations to this program. Since challenge grants are the single program of the Endowment that focuses on the long-term health of institutions by requiring them to generate matching dollars, primarily to build endowments, fewer awards of challenge grants are a cause for concern, insofar as they signal insufficient attention to long-term institutional needs, and therefore also to future financial stability.[7] Third, we should draw attention to the astonishing increase, in the university sector, in funding for preservation and access.[8] Although the congressional commitment to protect deteriorating collections of books and other paper-based materials in university (and other) libraries is clearly to be applauded, these new allocations create a misleading impression of NEH support for universities over the decade: in the absence of such funding, the university share of NEH funding, in constant 1992 dollars, would have declined by nearly 25 percent.

We estimate that when complete data for 1994 become available, they are certain to confirm continuation of the trends outlined here—above all, that of a greatly expanded role for state and public programs. Of course, the trends just summarized all pale into insignificance given present threats to the Endowment's very existence. Should the present Congress finally vote to approve the FY 1996 funding agreed to by the House and Senate conference committee, the NEH can anticipate, by the most optimistic estimate, a budgetary decline of close to 40 percent from 1995 levels and a total budget, measured in constant dollars, reduced to what it was in 1972—nearly a quarter of a century ago.

Fellowships and Foundations

The uncertain future of the NEH lifts into still higher relief the place of foundations in the scholarly support system, especially those foundations with assets of $100 million or more that historically have supported humanistic scholarship on a sustained basis. Here I propose to illustrate recent trends by concentrating on a single but significant aspect of foundation funding: competitive peer-reviewed research fellowships, awarded to individual faculty investigators. Over the past thirty years these have come to be one important measure of the perceived health of the academic humanistic enterprise, so much so that they are described in a recent study as "the lifeblood of scholarly research in the Humanities."[9] The fellowships awarded by the ACLS, the NHC, and the John S. Guggenheim Foundation are among the best known, most actively sought, and most prestigious (in a larger sample, the Institute for Advanced Study and the Center for Advanced Study in the Behavioral Sciences should certainly be included). Although these three institutions present distinct organizational

TABLE 2.1
NEH Disbursements, 1982–1992, by Category of Recipient

	Corrected for regranting, 1992 dollars			Percent change 1982–1987	Percent change 1987–1992	Percent change 1982–1992
	1982	1987	1992			
A. Recipients of NEH Grants						
Universities and their affiliated scholars	52,791,460	47,662,381	50,718,688	−9.7	6.4	−3.9
Four-year colleges and their affiliated scholars	23,059,764	16,133,449	12,016,457	−30.0	−25.5	−47.9
Individuals and scholars who received regrants	13,790,675	11,104,581	9,860,135	−19.5	−11.2	−28.5
Two-year colleges	1,273,287	1,113,539	638,039	−12.5	−42.7	−49.9
Elementary and secondary education	613,964	434,951	1,435,781	−29.2	230.1	133.9
Radio, television, or film	5,084,070	11,584,852	9,081,344	127.9	−21.6	78.6
Nonuniversity library, museum, or historical societies	16,705,383	22,847,215	29,825,791	36.8	30.5	78.5
Professional societies	4,390,587	1,721,065	2,645,918	−60.8	53.7	−39.7
State and other programs	52,262,682	41,045,627	42,880,887	−21.5	4.5	−18.0
Total	169,971,872	153,647,660	159,103,040	−9.6	3.6	−6.4
B. Recipient Was a University or Affiliated Scholar						
Education programs	7,494,547	10,943,135	9,083,561	46.0	−17.0	21.2
Fellowships and seminars	13,643,088	10,604,604	9,471,504	−22.3	−10.7	−30.6

Public programs	2,774,711	5,368,069	2,552,484	93.5	-52.5	-8.0
Research programs	19,419,667	15,347,583	14,382,721	-21.0	-6.3	-25.9
Preservation	349,344	1,694,487	11,003,890	385.0	549.4	3049.9
Planning and assessment studies	36,431			-100.0		-100.0
Challenge grants	9,073,672	3,704,502	4,224,528	-59.2	14.0	-53.4
Total	52,791,460	47,662,380	50,718,688	-9.7	6.4	-3.9

C. Recipient Was a Four-Year College or Affiliated Scholar

Education programs	3,947,305	5,689,070	4,096,577	44.1	-28.0	3.8
Fellowships and seminars	4,028,948	3,937,711	3,531,740	-2.3	-10.3	-12.3
Public programs	571,904	901,593	51,552	57.6	-94.3	-91.0
Research programs	1,118,865	1,086,908	1,631,670	-2.9	59.1	45.8
Preservation			125,859			
Planning and assessment studies	139,116			-100.0		-100.0
Challenge grants	13,253,626	4,518,164	2,579,059	-65.9	42.9	-80.5
Total	23,059,764	16,133,446	12,016,457	-30.0	-25.5	-47.9

profiles—a federation of scholarly organizations, a residential center, and a private foundation—three factors argue for grouping them together as a class: their respective commitments to supporting all fields of humanistic scholarship, their highly respected selection committees, and their collective importance nationally as fellowship providers (in 1982, 250 scholars received fellowships from these three sources alone, nearly as many as the total awarded by the NEH).[10]

Up through the mid-1980s, the fellowship program of the ACLS benefited from major endowment grants from the Ford, Rockefeller, and Andrew W. Mellon foundations.[11] When the NHC opened the doors of its new building in 1978, the Ford, Rockefeller, and Mellon foundations and the Carnegie Corporation had all assumed most of the preliminary cost of planning and locating the center in North Carolina, and Rockefeller made two major early grants for fellowship awards.[12] At the Guggenheim Foundation, 122 fellowships were awarded to scholars in the humanities in 1972. A decade later these numbers had dropped to below 100, but average awards had risen to prevent a severe loss in purchasing power.[13]

The most striking impression to emerge from the systems of support prevailing at the ACLS and the NHC into the early 1980s is the disproportionately large funding role being played by a very small number of sources: the NEH and a few of the largest independent foundations. The NEH, through annual grants for fellowships and challenge grants, has remained a steady and substantial supporter in subsequent years. But of the three major foundations that had anchored the core fellowship programs, only Mellon has maintained its record of substantial grantmaking into the 1990s;[14] at both the Ford and Rockefeller foundations new sets of priorities prevail.[15] Nor have other large foundations stepped forward to take their places: the Carnegie Corporation, the Pew Charitable Trusts, and the John D. and Catherine T. MacArthur foundations have all been approached, and declined to support unrestricted fellowship competitions administered by independent organizations.[16]

That the priorities of large foundations were shifting to other areas was clear as early as 1986, when the president of the Mellon Foundation analyzed all grants contributed by the thirty largest foundations to the various categories of the humanities as the NEH then classified them; he estimated that total grantmaking amounted nationally to approximately $50 million, well below half of what the NEH alone was spending on the same activities.[17] A fresh calculation in 1992, based on the grantmaking patterns of more than eight hundred of the largest foundations, reached essentially the same conclusion; the author somberly observed that "the humanities have remained a tiny percentage—less than one percent—of all foundation giving."[18]

How best to illustrate the impact of the virtual disappearance of large foundations as patrons of the ACLS and the NHC? The capacity of those two institutions, and of the Guggenheim Foundation, to attract new resources for endowments, and so to sustain fellowship awards at earlier levels, can be gauged by comparing reported fellowship data at fixed yearly intervals between 1982 and 1994. At the ACLS, total expenditures for the central fellowship program in actual and constant (1994) dollars were $2.015 million ($3.130 million) in 1982. They have since fallen steadily, to $1.820 million ($2.379 million) in 1987, to $1.020 million ($1.080 million) in 1992, to $1.050 million in 1994. In 1982, the Council had a broad portfolio of programs in place, offering a wide variety of scholarly assistance: sixty-nine senior fellowships, with average awards of $14,042 (worth $21,812 in 1994 dollars), thirty-seven fellowships for recent recipients of the Ph.D. (average awards: $8,205 [$12,745]), twelve fellowships for a special program in Modern Society and Values (average awards: $8,500 [$13,203]), and ninety-four smaller grants-in-aid of less than $5,000. By 1994, the ACLS was reduced to offering senior fellowship awards exclusively: sixty-nine, with average awards worth only $15,192.[19]

Similar data reported by the NHC reveal a generally upward trajectory from 1982 through 1992, followed by a decline. In actual dollars, the Center's total expenditures for fellows' stipends rose steadily through 1992 before dropping in 1994. Although average stipends increased throughout the period (appreciably for the first ten years, though only marginally thereafter),[20] numbers of funded fellows have been declining steadily over the period, from thirty-nine in 1982 to thirty-one in 1994. The Center's trustees preferred the policy of maintaining stipend levels at competitive rates to that of offering smaller awards to more scholars. Even so, measured in constant (1994) dollars, the purchasing power of fellows' stipends has eroded seriously since 1987, and the value of average stipends too has lost some ground.[21] The Center is a residential institution, which provides studies, a variety of academic support services, dining facilities, and fellowship funding and travel expenses to almost all members of each year's cohort of fellows; it is also a youthful institution, which began both its operations and its serious quest for permanent endowment only in 1978. As a consequence, the Center's trustees must struggle annually to generate income (from endowment, gifts, and grants) sufficient to maintain stipends at competitive levels without sacrificing the high quality of support services that makes the Center especially attractive to scholars.

As we saw previously, the Guggenheim Foundation awarded 273 fellowships in 1982, 94 of these in the humanities; the average award was $18,311 ($28,493 in 1994 dollars).[22] Over the next five years, funding conditions improved somewhat: in 1987, although the numbers of all fellowships and of the humanities' share remained unchanged, average awards had increased to $23,209 ($30,339 in constant dollars). Two years later, however, a dramatic reversal of this trend began, and by 1990 total numbers of fellowships had dropped to 143, humanities fellowships to 53, a 44 percent decline from 1987 levels. These conditions have persisted. In 1992 and 1994, although the ratio of humanities to total Guggenheim fellowships remained better than 1:3, only fifty humanists were able to be funded in 1992 and fifty-three in 1994. The purchasing power of these many fewer fellowships has also declined relative to 1987 levels. Since 1994, the Foundation has felt constrained to seek support publicly from other foundations and former fellows.[23]

Funding and the Visual Arts

Cumulatively then, the total number of fellowships in the humanities awarded by the ACLS, the NHC, and the Guggenheim Foundation has fallen from just over 250 in the early 1980s to just over 150 in 1994—that is, by nearly 40 percent—and purchasing power has also seriously eroded.[24] Before proceeding to evaluate the broader significance of this decline in funding, we should take note of two other types of change, which can be best illustrated by developments at the Guggenheim Foundation and at the NHC, respectively, over these years; both changes have implications for the balance of forces in the support system for the scholarly humanities.

First, at the Guggenheim Foundation the distribution of awards by broad disciplinary field has changed significantly between 1986 and 1993. Figure 2.2 shows that whereas the percentage of humanities to total fellowships has remained constant over the period, the number of fellowships in the arts has increased by 10 percent, slightly exceeding the percentage of fellowships in the humanities in 1993. Moreover, when we compare subcategories within the arts, most noteworthy is the dominant position of the visual arts—painting, photography, sculpture, video, and film. Indeed, since 1966, visual artists have received more fellowships than members of any other arts subcategory,[25] and, in the four years beginning in 1992, more fellowships than the artists in all other subcategories combined. A corresponding shift of interest, toward the visual components of culture, can be detected within the broad category of humanities fellowships, to judge from the Foundation's annual reports on the scholarly topics with which academic humanists are engaged: more art and architectural history; more topics in cultural studies with explicitly visual dimensions; more awards to scholars jointly appointed in English and film, or in English, modern culture, and media; more professors whose appointment titles combine English with American studies, comparative literature, or humanities, and who are pursuing projects like "Photography and Cultural Authority in Ante-bellum America," or "Cin-

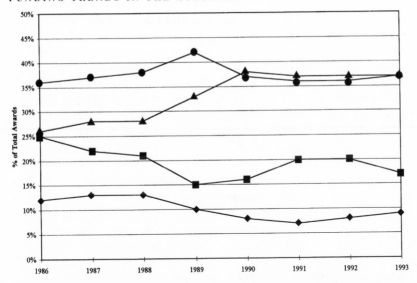

FIGURE 2.2. John S. Guggenheim Memorial Foundation awards distribution by field, 1986–1993. *Key:* –■–, science; –◆–, social science; –●–, humanities; –▲–, arts. (Source: John S. Guggenheim Foundation Report of the President, 1992.)

ema, Deconstruction, and Autobiography," or "Memorial Images in 18th Century English Art and Literature."[26]

These impressions are inevitably somewhat subjective, since reported titles of projects can be no more than approximate guides to their actual contents. Furthermore, the impressions derive from titles of funded projects only, not from actual applications, and of course selection committees are guided by judgments of scholarly quality, not by numerical distributions of applications by disciplinary field, in making their decisions. The Guggenheim evidence offers only a single sample: it could be tested against reports from other major providers of fellowships—the ACLS, the NHC, and the NEH—for signs that scholarly interests there are also shifting toward what is visual in culture and away from what is exclusively text-based.

Yet there can be little serious question but that the Guggenheim evidence faithfully reflects broader national trends. One observer has recently characterized "the steady increase in the nature and volume of arts activity" as "the most dramatic (cultural) statistic in the years following World War Two."[27] Another cites the many factors that led to the emergence of the visual arts, beginning in 1950, "as the dominant set of aesthetic forms in our society": New York's becoming the major international creative crucible for painting, sculpture, and other visual arts; the

establishment of photography, film, and video as pervasive presences in
national life; the maturing of art history as a major field of humanistic
study in the United States, and with it a much larger portion of university
graduates who appreciate the visual arts; and, accompanying all of this,
the powerful new preeminence of art museums as a cultural force.[28]

As further evidence for the extension of these visual trends into the
territory of humanistic scholarship, we may note one of the findings of a
recent study, sponsored by the Association of American University Presses:
the rate of publication of scholarly monographs in art, art history, and
architecture increased by more than 100 percent during the decade 1978–
1988, despite the high costs incurred in producing heavily illustrated
books of this kind.[29] The programmatic objectives of a scholarly symposium held at the Institute for Advanced Study in 1993 are also symptomatic. Anthropologists, historians, musicologists, and authorities on
literature and film gathered, along with art historians, to "explore the
phenomenal growth since World War II of interest in the visual arts . . .
among professionals in other fields of the humanities and social sciences."
Finally, new research in cultural studies—exploring the tensions between
images and texts, between "opticality" and "logocentrism," between "the
interrogation of the eye" and "antiocularcentric discourse"[30]—indicates
how markedly some parts of the scholarly landscape have changed since
the days when a major foundation could define the humanities as primarily text-based and could link the advancement of humanistic knowledge
closely to the safeguarding of collections of books, manuscripts, and other
documents in important centers of learning.[31]

As regards funding patterns, the most obvious lesson to be learned from
these trends is just how overwhelmingly the arts have come to dominate
the competition for the portion of the nation's philanthropic resources
available for culture. In 1992, foundations alone spent an estimated
$1.36 billion to support the arts, an increase of 12 percent over the
previous three years and more than double the amount donated ten years
earlier.[32] In contrast, current estimates place foundation grantmaking for
all academic humanities, by the broadest possible definition, at only
$50 million.[33] The arts attract support in ways that most sectors of the
academic humanities find increasingly difficult; it follows, by extension,
that we should expect to find prospects for financial stability much more
favorable at research centers situated within, or closely associated with,
major arts institutions.

The success of the Center for the Advanced Study of the Visual Arts
(CASVA), the scholarly arm of the National Gallery of Art, provides an
excellent case in point. Although CASVA is the almost exact contemporary
of the NHC—where, as we have seen, financial challenges are ongoing—
CASVA's endowment has grown from $5 million in 1982 to $27.3 million

in 1994, as a result of a major challenge grant from the Mellon Foundation and substantial subsequent individual gifts for endowed chairs. Numbers of resident fellows increased from twelve to eighteen over the same period; the Center now annually funds fourteen nonresident predoctoral fellowships; the annual operating budget, consisting of a balanced mixture of endowment income, annual grants, and federal funds for staff support, grew from $250,000 in 1980 to nearly $2 million in 1995.[34] To be sure, centers such as CASVA, or the Getty Center for the Study of the Arts and Humanities, present a picture of fiscal robustness that is clearly atypical, even for institutions at which commitment to the visual arts is the animating feature. Still, they offer a most instructive contrast both with independent residential centers such as the NHC (with its much more inclusive range of humanities disciplines) and with another group of cultural institutions of the first importance for academic humanists: the nation's leading independent research libraries: the Huntington, Pierpont Morgan, Newberry, and Folger Shakespeare libraries and the American Antiquarian Society. While the two new centers for the visual arts have flourished, these oldest research libraries in the United States, with their unparalleled collections of rare books and manuscripts, have changed from income-spenders to fund-seekers; since 1971 recurring deficits have become the norm at all of them.[35]

The Shift to the Academy

The second change of broad significance for funding patterns can be documented from a valuable set of records kept by the NHC that enables us to compare the total annual disbursements at the Center for fellows' stipends with the totals contributed by other sources for the same purpose. The data fall naturally into three distinct time periods. In the first phase, through 1986–1987, the Center was the leading stipendiary provider: in that year the NHC made payments of approximately $1 million as compared with $800,000 from other sources. During the second phase, external sources alternated with the Center as principal funder until 1990–1991, when the relative shares provided were virtually identical: in other words, during that period the Center was unable to sustain its earlier pace of stipendiary funding.[36] The year 1990–1991 ushers in the third phase and constitutes the watershed: in each of the following four years, the Center has taken second place in stipendiary funding to other providers, whose contributions have outstripped those of the NHC by amounts varying from $45,000 to $370,000.[37]

Thus, as stipendiary provider, the status of the NHC has shifted over the past decade from that of senior to junior partner. And from the experience of the NHC, where available data allow us to track these changes over time, we may safely assume that a similar shift in status has been occurring also at the ACLS and Guggenheim. Since average ACLS awards are now substantially lower than those at the NHC, whereas those from Guggenheim are only marginally higher, no tenured faculty member could reasonably expect to support himself or herself for an academic year on such modest stipends. Who, then, are these other providers that are being called upon to bridge the annually widening gap between fellowship stipends and scholars' academic salaries?

We should not expect a straightforward answer to that question, since scholars now commonly find themselves constrained to patch together a portfolio of support from any and all available sources in order to fund periods of leave at levels that at least approximate their annual academic salaries. On the other hand, there can be little doubt that the chief source, increasingly, has come to be the universities and colleges themselves. Reports from senior administrators at numerous campuses, particularly those of research universities, have a common theme: beginning in the late 1950s with the forward thrust of the research universities, expanded research opportunities and incentives became the norm—for all faculty, but especially for natural scientists, whose practices provided the model for university-based research. Humanists, riding the coattails of their colleagues in experimental and social sciences, were also beneficiaries as institutions formulated more generous leave policies for both junior and senior faculty. Today, even though funding prospects in most fields are far less bright, those earlier commitments to supporting research remain largely intact. Universities have remained willing to carry the costs of staff benefits during periods of leave and to "top up" fellowships, particularly those conferred by what are perceived to be the most prestigious external sources—the NEH, Guggenheim, the NHC, and the ACLS.[38] As has been rightly seen, such institutional behavior reflects the still-prevailing university value system, in which "personal and institutional legitimacy is obtained predominantly through research achievements."[39]

Funding balances, then, have shifted. The role of the independent fellowship providers has contracted, and that of the colleges and universities has expanded to take their place: such investments align closely with institutional values that privilege research. It is also important to note that these relatively modest cost shifts have occurred while academic institutions have been making a new and far more substantial set of commitments to the humanities enterprise: to the interdisciplinary humanities centers and institutes that, since their modest beginnings in the late 1970s, have now become a familiar feature of the campus landscape. By 1992, fifty-three U.S. universities were sponsoring formal organizations of this kind, variously titled and with differing programmatic objectives.[40] Thirty-eight centers surveyed in 1991 were already then reportedly awarding more fellowships than those conferred by the major national providers.[41]

To be sure, it is difficult to know how to interpret this finding, since conditions attached to accepting fellowships at the campus-based centers are far more restrictive than those of such providers as Guggenheim or the NEH: centers' fellowships are generally more modest in stipendiary terms, are usually of shorter duration, and often demand high intellectual "entrance fees," such as some teaching responsibility and active participation in advancing a center's annual theme. Responses to a new survey of twenty-nine of the larger humanities centers, conducted in 1995 for the purposes of the present study, indicate that this group was awarding, on average, eight internal faculty fellowships and three external fellowships by 1992 (again, the reported dollar amounts are much smaller, and periods of funded leave much briefer, than those of the major independent providers).[42]

Since fellowships and some programs at these centers have been partially funded through occasional grants from a few major foundations (notably Rockefeller, MacArthur, and Mellon), and through challenge grants from the NEH, a truer test of the scale of host universities' commitments is the size of annual operating budgets. Precise breakdowns of such costs are unavailable. But for all twenty-nine centers, annual average administrative expenses had reportedly risen from $95,000 in 1982–1983 to $110,000 in 1992–1993; more revealingly, while the seven centers that opened between 1988 and 1992 were averaging $66,000 for administration, the fifteen centers in existence in 1982–1983 were spending an average of $129,000 ten years later. We should note that these administrative expenses are almost certainly underreported, since they presumably omit the fixed costs to the university of space, heat, and light. In any case, given such major new commitments at home, how realistic is it to expect universities to increase still further their contributions to off-campus residential centers such as the NHC—whether indirectly, by assuming still more of the costs of assisting faculty to accept fellowships there, or through more direct forms of support? The results of a recent experiment by the trustees of the NHC, when contrasted with earlier experience at the ACLS, is perhaps a sign of the times. In 1969, in conjunction with its sixtieth-anniversary funding campaign, the ACLS successfully appealed to the colleges and universities whose faculty had been the chief beneficiaries of ACLS fellowships to initiate annual contributions as Associates of the Council; there are now some 170 institutional Associates paying annual membership fees. When the NHC explored the feasibility of a similar initiative in 1993, responses were not encouraging; universities now appear far more reluctant to add to their previously existing numbers of institutional memberships.

We may now attempt to summarize our findings thus far. We have seen, first, that at the NEH—by far the largest source of external support for the academic humanities—state and public programs, not research and fellowships, have dominated the grantmaking over the past decade; grants to universities, colleges, and their affiliated scholars have accounted for well below half of NEH funding; only substantial growth in the program of preservation and access has enabled the academic sector's share to remain at earlier levels. Moreover, the trends of the recent past appear positively benign in comparison with prospects for the future. As of November 1995, the NEH anticipated an overall reduction of nearly 40 percent in its FY 1996 budget, from $172 million to $110 million. State programs are expected to remain immune from these cuts, since congressional appreciation for the work of the state councils is viewed by many as the strongest bulwark protecting the Endowment from extinction. By the most optimistic current estimate, funds earmarked for fellowships and research—the programs of major interest to colleges, universities, and their affiliated scholars—will drop by 50 percent from FY 1995 levels.

Second, when viewed through the prism of the financial vicissitudes suffered by selected independent fellowship programs, the retreat of major philanthropic foundations with a strong historical record of support for the scholarly humanities—especially the Ford and Rockefeller foundations and the Carnegie Corporation—emerges as a clear trend. Other large foundations identified as potential replacements have opted to pursue other priorities instead. With the conspicuous exception of the Mellon Foundation—which is currently providing an estimated 50 to 60 percent of the $50 million flowing annually to the humanities from large foundations—cultural grantmaking by these major philanthropic organizations is overwhelmingly targeted toward the arts.

Third, our inspection of the funding trends among the three leading national providers of fellowships for the humanities outside the NEH (the ACLS, NHC, and Guggenheim Foundation) documents a 40 percent decline in the total number of fellowships offered between 1982 and 1994, as well as a decline in purchasing power. For the two of these providers whose fellowship programs are heavily dependent upon annual regrants from the NEH—each year, NEH funding constitutes between 35 and 50 percent of the fellowship budget of the ACLS, and between 35 and 40 percent of that of the NHC—the pressures to strengthen existing endowments and to identify alternative sources of fellowship funding now become particularly acute. For the Guggenheim Foundation, now strenuously engaged in a major campaign to add an additional $10–20 million to its $150 million endowment,[43] several years will need to pass before numbers of fellowships can be restored to pre-1988 levels, and it seems wholly unrealistic to expect that the Foundation will ever again experience conditions as favorable as those in the early 1970s, when it was awarding between 330 and 360 fellowships annually.

Nearly fifty years ago, the Ford Foundation's Gaither Report concluded that "the history of philanthropic support for the humanities may bear the subtitle 'the short and simple Annals of the Poor.' "[44] Although one hesitates to draw so stark a conclusion from the evidence presented thus far, that evidence does at least attest to a major shift in the balance of funding forces in the scholarly humanities. To a degree previously unrecognized— or at least not to my knowledge made quite so explicit—the costs of the enterprise are being transferred away from the foundations and from the federal sector and back to the colleges and universities themselves—the very institutions that, of course, are already providing the major funding for the scholarly activities of faculty. Can one reasonably expect these institutions to sustain now, and expand in future years, what is already clearly a dominant role? Are such sustained commitments feasible, especially in the current economic climate, in which the leaders of even the best-endowed and carefully managed colleges and universities are struggling with shrinking resources, striving to contain rising costs and to restrain growth, even engaging in selective downsizing?

Answers to questions like these, if properly developed, would extend this essay well beyond reasonable length, and even then would be highly speculative. Prudence suggests a more limited approach, an attempt to identify the most promising potential sources from which colleges and universities might seek the new funding required to sustain the scholarly humanities at approximately present levels. Most institutions, even those with modest endowments, will struggle to resist subsidizing faculty research and scholarship by increasing tuition and fees, since some share of the costs of scholarship—higher salaries and benefits, fewer teaching responsibilities (especially for faculty whom universities compete to attract or retain), more research leaves for more faculty at junior, midcareer, and senior levels—is already being passed along to students and their families, to a degree that varies considerably among institutions, and that is therefore difficult to calibrate. Inevitably, if we are to assess the capacity of colleges and universities to remain the principal patrons of the scholarly humanities, we need to consider the role of patronage of another type: private giving by alumni, parents of students, and other individuals.

The Private Patrons of Universities and Colleges

Of the reported total of $10.7 billion in gifts to all of higher education in 1992, alumni and other individuals accounted for more than half, far outpacing all other sources.[45] Since the early 1980s, the organized quest for private dollars through major capital campaigns has become a standard feature of institutional life; ever shorter time spans elapse between the conclusion of one campaign and the beginning of the next; at the largest research universities, public as well as private, campaign goals of a billion dollars or more, inconceivable fifteen years ago, are now not uncommon. And yet, college and university "fund-raisers find it increasingly difficult to obtain endowment for chairs and programs in the humanities."[46] That opinion, which has long been circulating quietly in the philanthropic circles closest to academe, has come to be voiced aloud with greater frequency since the widely publicized episode early in 1995, when an alumnus of Yale rescinded a $20 million donation designated for the teaching of courses in Western Civilization. What basis have such opinions in fact? How far can they be said to reflect reality?

Whatever the perceived difficulties, countervailing examples can be adduced to show that efforts to attract individual patrons to the academic humanities can meet with real success. Nineteen of the twenty-nine campus-based humanities centers surveyed in 1995—including five of the seven centers that began operations as late as 1987—have reportedly secured private gifts for endowment. Nine of these nineteen are seeking to enlarge present endowments; seven of those nine believe their endowment objectives to be realistic. Stanford's Humanities Center reports receipt within the past few months of a private additional gift of $1 million to its endowment, bringing the total to $5.5 million; the center at Northwestern has raised $4 million over the past three years; the endowment at the University of Oregon's center stands at $250,000 and is growing. When one extends inquiry beyond the relatively small world of these centers to the academic departments and multidisciplinary programs that constitute the larger humanistic universe, the pages of alumni newsletters and other university publications carry the news, almost weekly, of major private gifts for newly created chairs—$4.7 million for Jewish studies at Princeton, for example; $2 million for expository writing at Harvard; a first installment of $375,000 donated for a new interdisciplinary center at Washington and Lee.

Such examples might be multiplied to show that private patrons, large and small, of the academic humanities are hardly an endangered species. On the other hand, senior academic officers and their development staff, are far more forthcoming about their successes than about their failures, disappointments, or frustrations. We may legitimately wonder too how many of the newly endowed chairs, building projects, and programmatic initiatives eventually allocated to the humanities had their origins as undesignated gifts, which were quietly steered to their ultimate destinations by university administrators, committed to seeing that the humanities also be perceived to benefit in at least some way from universitywide campaigns. Among humanities institutes and centers, ten of the twenty-nine surveyed, or just over one third, remain wholly unendowed, despite reports of energetic solicitation of persons deemed "strong donor prospects," and administrators at several centers endorse the perception of one of their colleagues, who wrote "the humanities are not a priority."

But the same donors who may be unwilling to support a center often show greater interest in funding a particular humanities department or other initiative. Such facts as are publicly available are patently too few to reconcile these conflicting impressions and opinions, still less to illuminate current or recent shifts in the attitudes and behavior of alumni and other private donors. An alternative approach—a somewhat closer inspection of private humanities patronage, present and past, at a single university—may prove instructive. Although a case study is no substitute for a more comprehensive report, one institution's experience might nonetheless point the way toward a broader understanding of funding trends.

At the University of Michigan, all apparent signs suggest that the rate of private giving to the humanities has accelerated during the present $1 billion capital campaign. By the fall of 1995, two-thirds of the way toward completion, a University progress report indicated that private donors had endowed three new chairs in the humanities, designated for rabbinic literature, philosophy, and the Institute for the Humanities. With the addition of this last-named chair, Michigan's Humanities Institute, assisted by a challenge grant from the NEH, had generated nearly $12 million in outright private gifts and pledges toward its overall goal of $20 million—among the largest endowments reported by all the campus-based humanities centers surveyed, and an unusual accomplishment for a young institute, created only in 1987. In a separate initiative, to endow annual faculty awards for distinguished scholarship and graduate teaching in the humanities, the graduate school needed only six months to raise the requisite $600,000, all of this from private individuals.

But these examples of private patronage must be placed in broader context. First, the humanities have received just three of a total of fifty-eight newly endowed university chairs. Humanities faculty will occupy fewer than 25 percent of the chairs (thirteen) designated for arts and sciences. All of arts and sciences have a smaller share than either medicine (fifteen) or business (fourteen), although the numbers of tenured instructional faculty in arts and sciences are a third again as many as those in medicine, and almost nine times as many as those in business. Indeed, tenured faculty in the division of humanities alone outnumber all of those in business by well over 2:1. Five of the new chairs are designated for the law school, where there are forty-two tenured faculty: humanists outnumber lawyers by more than 4:1. Finally, in order to gain a clearer sense of the degree to which chairs represent real growth, we would need to know how many were intended to be incremental positions, and how many, instead, to endow existing positions, currently supported on general funds. However this may be, let us imagine that Michigan's newly appointed professors have been convened in a university classroom containing sixty chairs arranged in rows of ten: the three professors of humanities will not be conspicuous in this assembly.

Next, at the Institute for the Humanities, private donors have indeed responded in exemplary fashion to the director's vision for the humanities and to his energetic advocacy for their needs. It belittles neither their generosity nor his achievement to observe that University provosts and deans have also had a decisive influence on these patterns of private giving: the initial endowment grant of $2 million and the newly created chair arrived as undesignated gifts, which were channeled to the director by University administrators determined to move the Institute along the path to fiscal self-sufficiency. And again, although the gift for the new chair in philosophy actually materialized during the course of the present campaign, the family made their original bequest in stages between 1940 and 1948; realization of this deferred benefaction had to await the final settlement of the estate, a process which has taken nearly fifty years.

Indeed, if we situate this last major gift to the humanities where it historically belongs, in the context of the years just before and after World War II, an entirely new prospect opens up, one which invites entry into a period of academic culture and associated private philanthropy sharply alien from those of the present day. It is striking to consider just how many of the major projects, collections, and initiatives in the humanities at Michigan were launched and institutionalized before the 1960s.[47] Forty large and handsomely illustrated volumes in the Michigan Humanistic Series appeared between 1904 and 1950, paving the way for what eventually became the University of Michigan Press. Henry S. Frieze, man of culture and learned philologist, aimed to heighten his students' aesthetic sensibilities as well as to sharpen their intellects, believing both objectives to contribute to the development of moral character. He founded the University Art Museum in 1857, traveling to Europe at his own expense and buying the classical artifacts to fill it. The Museum's new home was completed in 1910 with a gift of $140,000 from University graduates and christened Alumni Memorial Hall. Thomas Spencer Jerome, alumnus from Saginaw and long-time resident of the island of Capri, endowed in 1919 a major lectureship on aspects of the ancient world that has continued uninterrupted to the present day. The *Medieval English Dictionary*, an immense collaborative editorial project that, with the assistance of major grants from the Mellon Foundation and the NEH, is only now drawing to a conclusion, began in 1930. F. W. Kelsey, the entrepreneurial classicist, attracted private funding that financed the acquisition of the University's famous collection of Greek papyri (1918) and archaeological expeditions to the Mediterranean (1919). The Detroit attorney and philanthropist Horace Rackham was a chief contributor to these projects, as he was to the Museum of Archaeology that would eventually bear Kelsey's name (1929). Horace and Mary Rackham's own major benefactions were the graduate school (1938) and a multi-million-dollar endowment to accompany it. William L. Clements, University alumnus and regent and Bay City industrialist, was also a collector of books, maps, and documents from the American colonial period and beyond. He viewed the new library that was designed to replicate Rome's Villa Madama and that was to bear his name (1923) as "a temple of American history"—but also in his sights were earlier models, the John Carter Brown Library at Brown University (1904) and the Huntington Library in San Marino (1919). An enterprising professor of history began to collect Michigania and documents related to the history of the University in 1935: the Michigan Historical Collections finally found a permanent home and a new name in the 1970s, thanks to a gift from the widow of U.S. congressman and University regent Alvin M. Bentley.

Common to all or most of the philanthropic patrons and academic entrepreneurs leading this early humanistic parade at Michigan are, first, a confidence in the power of learning—above all, text-based learning—as a path to both intellectual and moral cultivation, and, second, a readiness to invest in such enterprises as one of the approved ways to validate acquired or inherited wealth. Additionally, one is struck by the special acquisitive flavor that animates some of this early philanthropy. A number of these patrons and scholarly entrepreneurs were collectors first and foremost, less interested in making cash donations or bequests than in finding permanent homes for the beloved books and artifacts in their personal collections.

But beginning with the post–World War II period and accelerating swiftly thereafter, academic growth shifts away from the text-based humanities—first to the perceived objective certainties of natural sciences and positivist social science (the Institute for Social Research); later away from the arts and sciences as a whole and into less "academic," more "professional" arenas. The medical school and its new hospital dominated developments here, but so also did engineering and business, both of which were significantly strengthened and enlarged during the late 1970s and early 1980s. These early years of the 1980s also saw the inauguration of the first major universitywide development campaign. This centrally organized quest for private and corporate donations was viewed as essential, owing to the negative impact of national recession on state allocations to the University, and owing also to the escalating costs and declining federal support for big science—especially for scientific facilities and instrumentation. Finally, though it is a secondary development, the emergence of the performing and other arts as clearer and more distinct identities is another feature of the postwar years: witness the new Saarinen building at the School of Music (1964), independent schools of art and architecture in the early 1970s, the invigoration of established programs in theater and dance, and the creation of new ones in film and video studies.

Hardly surprisingly, these trends are closely linked to new and different types of philanthropic patronage. First, one detects fewer individual patrons with strong personal attachments to the traditional values of high culture, and many more who are committed instead to pragmatic and interventionist approaches to the solution of such pressing social problems as health or primary and secondary education. Second, the acquisitive pleasures of collectors are now concentrated far more exclusively on art; whereas the University Museum of Art has benefited notably from this trend, the great museums in the major metropolitan centers, understandably, are even stronger magnets for donors. Third, more institutional patrons moved closer to center stage: the mission-oriented agencies of the federal government (the National Institutes of Health, the National Science Foundation, and the departments of Defense and Energy); philanthropic foundations with strictly defined social agendas, strongly disposed to favor applied research in their grantmaking; and industrial or corporate sponsors (automobile, chemical, pharmaceutical, and high-technology companies). The strengthening of the arts, already mentioned, was further solidified in 1971 with the dedication of the privately funded Power Center for the Performing Arts. In sum, at the University of Michigan, it is not so much that academic humanities began to lose their momentum, or the backing of their patrons, by the 1960s; rather, the humanities, once located near the center of the University's mission, have moved toward the periphery, pushed closer to the margins by the arrival of more powerful new fields, forces, and funding.

The Future of Patronage

So panoramic a historical sweep, of course, oversimplifies what is in detail a more complicated picture. And even if the Michigan case study is broadly accurate in outline, considerable adjustment would be required before it could be fitted to other universities and colleges, with their differing institutional histories, traditions, and rhythms of philanthropic growth. Still, national statistics, beginning in the early 1970s, document the steadily declining numbers of undergraduate and doctoral degrees conferred in arts and sciences generally, and in the humanities in particular;[48] and other evidence suggests that the experience at Michigan is broadly consistent with national trends. If that is so, what prospects can one see for the academic humanities continuing to play a vital, if inevitably somewhat more restricted, role in advancing the university's overall mission in the future? In particular, how confident can we be that the humanities will attract the patrons who can help to assure this?

Some forces clearly lie quite beyond the power of humanists to influence or control. The slowing of national economic growth began in the 1970s, just after U.S. higher education had experienced the single largest period of expansion in its history.[49] If, as many thoughtful observers believe, the entire higher education enterprise has become too large to be sustained at present levels, there will continue to be adverse financial consequences for the humanities, not least because decline in national prosperity inevitably drives students away from concentrating in the "softer" fields of the liberal arts and toward those academic and professional areas that hold out brighter economic prospects. Moreover, throughout the period of the Cold War, while humanists were still training their interpretive sights on the masterpieces and monuments of Western civilization, national ideals and the humanistic canon converged, only to split apart during U.S. intervention in Vietnam and later, with the collapse of the Berlin Wall, the anxieties of an ill-defined "new world order," and the emergence of a global marketplace. Finally, enormous personal fortunes have been amassed in this country over the past twenty-five years. The percentage of this wealth that will eventually flow into philanthropic channels is a question of major importance for the future of all U.S. nonprofit institutions. Higher education's share of this percentage will be affected by many factors, including the degree of societal confidence in leading colleges and universities as the major engines for upward economic and social mobility. In this regard, the current trends in foundation grantmaking to colleges and universities need to be carefully scrutinized. A series of custom searches undertaken at my request by the Foundation Center for the purpose of this study yield results that are not encouraging. Whereas total giving by the one hundred foundations with the largest assets has increased notably over the years in question—from $1.8 billion to $2.7 billion to $3.2 billion in constant (1993) dollars—the college and university share of this grantmaking, which rose slightly from 32.6 to 33.2 percent between 1982 and 1989, dipped sharply in 1993, when it constituted only 26 percent of the total.[50]

But in some ways, it may be respectfully suggested, we in the humanities might be doing more to help our own cause. In what now seems the far more coherent and optimistic intellectual world of the early 1960s, voices of academic humanists resonated with confidence, as they engaged in exploring with students—of literature and history, of classics and philosophy—fundamental questions concerning human life and its meaning.

Investigative conditions in today's postmodernist academic world have markedly changed. Exploration of questions with the most profound human consequences—about the causal relationships between neurobiological processes and conscious experience, for example, or about the predictive power and empirical consequences of rational choice theory—is being pursued outside humanistic territory: by biologists, neuroscientists, and cognitive psychologists, or by economists, psychologists, and political scientists. Fresh disciplinary combinations of investigators in these areas are offering accounts of their subject matter that are changing the world as we once understood it.

Within the humanities too, fundamental and unsettling questions of great consequence continue to be explored. Few of us would wish to deny the demographic and political realities that have given rise to some of the best multicultural scholarship, or would seriously question the value of rigorous and sympathetic study of the history and aesthetic expressions of previously subordinated groups and ignored traditions—including non-Western traditions. Similarly, the intellectual contributions of post-modernist theoretical approaches have significantly affected the way in which many of us go about our work, especially the fundamental idea that reality, instead of being wholly objective and independent of its interpreters, is to some degree shaped, or "constructed," by particular readers, viewers, communities, and cultures. On the other hand, in their reformulations of such fundamental human concerns, have not our scholarly communities been distancing themselves from the broader society that supports us? We are perceived as more successful at unsettling and undermining traditional values and societal roles than at connecting our findings with "lasting works (images, buildings, music, writings in poetry and prose) considered significant or revealed or great or beautiful,"[51] so as better to illuminate the human dilemma.

Other contributors to this volume address both the complex origins and course of, and the hopeful signs of eventual emergence from, the epistemological doubt and disciplinary fragmentation that have replaced the earlier confidence and coherence of the humanities. Suffice it only to say here that, viewed from the perspective of those persons best equipped to carry forward the private patronage of the humanities—parents paying their children's college tuition and fees, and loyal alumni who have the capacity to make large gifts—some of the present humanistic debates are likely to appear offputting, highly esoteric, or both. Prospective donors, quite understandably, need to be convinced of the value of major investments. Can wealthy alumni of the class of 1965—who still believe, based on their own college experience, that the study of the humanities contributes to leading enriched, more meaningful lives—be persuaded to see connections between their understanding of the humanities and scholarly agenda in which—from their perspective—truth is held to be largely contingent, reality mostly constructed, meaning and value no more than relative and culturally conditioned?

I am left uneasy and yet cautiously optimistic. We can hope to quicken the interests of our private patrons if more of us in the academic humanities will, in Seamus Heaney's words, "make the Orphic effort to haul life back up the slope against all the odds."[52]

Acknowledgments

I am most grateful to the several friends and colleagues who have assisted in the preparation of this essay, and especially to former University of Michigan graduate students Colleen Heflin and Mark Long, from the School of Public Policy, and Dr. Caroline Winterer, from the Department of History.

Notes

1. Classics; languages and literatures ancient, modern, and comparative; American culture; art history; linguistics; the theory, composition, and history of music; philosophy; and religion.

2. Ernest L. Boyer, foreword to *A Classification of Institutions of Higher Education: 1994 Edition* (Princeton, N.J.: Carnegie Foundation for the Advancement of Teaching, 1994).

3. *The Humanities in American Life*, Report of the Commission on the Humanities (Berkeley and Los Angeles: University of California Press, 1980), 168–69.

4. I know of no previous attempt to determine the actual university and college share of annual NEH budgets. In consultation with Jeff Thomas and Larry Myers at NEH, and drawing upon NEH's formal program and divisional classifications as our point of departure, Colleen Heflin, Mark Long, and I have sought to identify all activity that could reasonably be defined as support for the humanities and their practitioners in a university, college, or similar setting: not only research and study fellowships, or major collaborative scholarly projects, or awards to centers for advanced study, but also grants to the colleges and universities themselves, designed for curricular initiatives and reform, for public programs, and for challenge grants and other initiatives to undergird the scholarly infrastructure (the preparation of scholarly editions, translations, academic library catalogues, and other reference materials; grants to the libraries of these institutions for the preservation of books and other paper-based materials). We have then distributed the total dollars allocated for these initiatives among three new categories of grant recipients: (1) universities and their affiliated scholars, (2) four-year colleges and their affiliated scholars, and (3) individual scholars—usually with university or

college affiliations—whose fellowships or grants reached them through a two-step process: dollars first awarded to an independent scholarly organization (such as the ACLS or the NHC) then "regranted" to individual scholars through selection committees appointed by those organizations. (No attempt has been made to apportion shares of funding, in this third category, among universities, colleges, and independent scholars; we estimate that independent scholars comprise no more than 10% of the total.) Although this methodology yields results that may overstate the degree to which colleges, universities, and their individual faculty members—as distinct from other sectors—have actually been benefiting from grantmaking throughout the various divisions of the Endowment, those benefits have clearly been seriously underestimated by the methods used in the past; we have tried to supply a corrective by supplying figures that are intended to constitute an outer bound.

5. Budgetary "obligations" (NEH terminology) by year in nominal and constant (1994) dollars: 1982: $111,632,000 ($173,403,000); 1987: $125,078,000 ($163,504,000); 1992: $137,534,000 ($145,572,000); 1994: $157,748,000.

6. Within the academic sector of recipients (universities, colleges, and individuals who benefited from regrants), while the portion of total NEH dollars awarded to universities and their affiliated scholars held steady at around 32 percent, the buying power of these awards declined by almost 4 percent over the decade, measured in 1992 dollars. The share awarded to the four-year colleges, meanwhile, has declined by nearly one half, from 13.6 to 7.6 percent (a decline of almost 48 percent in constant dollars), and regrants have dropped from 8.1 to 6.2 percent (a loss of 28.5 percent in constant dollars; see Table 2.1 and Figure 2.1).

7. Since the NEH changed its rules and began to permit second applications for challenge grants by 1983, these sharp downward trends cannot be explained by reference to constraints imposed by the agency.

8. In 1982, $350,000 in funds for preservation was awarded to institutions of higher education. After congressional intervention in 1988, the budget for preservation grants grew steadily, and $11 million was awarded to higher education institutions in 1992.

9. Douglas Greenberg, *Fellowships in the Humanities, 1983–1991*, ACLS Occasional Paper no. 18 (New York: American Council of Learned Societies, 1992), 1.

10. On these numbers, see Kenneth L. Goody, *The Funding of the Arts and Artists, Humanities and Humanists in the United States* (New York: Rockefeller Foundation, 1983), 50–51.

11. Ford contributed more than $2 million to the sixtieth-anniversary campaign of the ACLS in 1980, and another $1 million five years later. Rockefeller, also a steadfast supporter of the Council in earlier years, contributed $1 million during the ACLS's endowment campaign in 1985–1986; Mellon made the same commitment. The source of these and all other figures is the president's office of the ACLS. I am grateful to Hugh O'Neill and to Barbara Henning for their most helpful assistance.

12. For the role of the Rockefeller Foundation, I have profited, here and elsewhere, from Joel Colton and Malcolm Richardson, *The Humanities and "the*

Well-Being of Mankind": A Half-Century of the Humanities at the Rockefeller Foundation (1982, unpublished).

13. Average Guggenheim awards in 1972 were $10,167, representing just over $34,000 in constant (1994) dollars. The figure for 1982 (ninety-four humanities fellowships) was $18,311 ($28,443) and that for 1983 (ninety-nine fellowships) $18,921 ($28,211). Annual reports of the John S. Guggenheim Foundation.

14. The ACLS received a matching grant of $1.25 million for endowment in 1991; the NHC a grant of $4 million in 1991 ($1.75 million as a matching grant for endowment).

15. At the Ford Foundation, the organizational shift away from Humanities and Arts to Education and Culture, reflects priorities now targeted toward "expanding opportunities for the disadvantaged, . . . fostering . . . diversity in the arts and education, . . . and teaching and scholarship in the social sciences, particularly in area studies, African American studies and women's and gender studies" (Ford Foundation Annual Report, 1994, 55). The total program budget for Education and Culture in 1994 was $46 million, reduced from $53.9 million in 1993. The Rockefeller Foundation's program in Arts and Humanities encourages "artists and scholars and their institutions to reach out across the divides . . . of class, culture, ethnicity, generation, geography and tradition"; through its own annual competitions since 1983, the Foundation has committed approximately $22.5 million to a fellowship program that supports such cross-cultural dialogue (Rockefeller Foundation Annual Report, 1994, 34). The total program budget declined from $14.5 million in 1993 to $12.5 million in 1994.

16. Greenberg, *Fellowships in the Humanities*, 17n26.

17. William G. Bowen, Testimony to the Interior and Related Agencies Subcommittee of the House Committee on Appropriations, in support of the FY 1989 Appropriation for the National Endowment for the Humanities, Washington, D.C., March 17, 1988, 7–8, with Chart 2 and Table 1 (drawing on 1986 data).

18. Richard Ekman, Secretary, A. W. Mellon Foundation, Statement at a Public Meeting of the President's Committee on the Arts and the Humanities, Washington, D.C., January 25, 1995, 2.

19. Data courtesy of the president's office, ACLS.

20. Fellowship stipend totals and average awards: 1982: $606,129 ($15,531); 1987: $725,669 ($20,157); 1992: $809,250 ($24,000); 1994: $749,000 ($24,565). These and subsequent figures have been supplied by the administrative offices of the NHC. I am most grateful to Kent Mullikin and Sandra Copeland for their kind aid.

21. NHC total stipends and average stipends measured in constant 1994 dollars: 1982: $941,529 ($24,125); 1987: $948,608 ($26,350); 1992: $856,564 ($25,403); 1994: $749,000 ($24,565).

22. The sources of these and other Guggenheim data are the annual reports of the John S. Guggenheim Foundation.

23. For 1992: 148 total awards, 50 humanities fellowships; average awards were $26,318 ($27,856 in constant 1994 dollars). The figures for 1994 were 147, 53, and $27,667, respectively. For current fundraising efforts by the Foundation, see note 43.

24. Actual figures for 1982 were 252 and for 1994, 153—a decline of 39.3 percent.

25. These include the performing arts, fiction, poetry, and musical composition. Fiction and poetry, of course, are "text-based" arts.

26. This cursory summary derives from a detailed review, for all years from 1959 to 1995, of all project titles of fellowships in the humanities, classified into the following four subcategories: text-based humanistic study (history, literature, scholarly editions, philology, ancient and modern languages, linguistics, biography); history of art and architecture; humanistic study based upon both texts and visual sources; and philosophy.

27. Stanley N. Katz, "Can the Arts Enter the Philanthropic Mainstream?" in *Arts Funding: A Report on Foundation and Corporate Grantmaking Trends*, ed. N. Weber and L. Renz (New York: Foundation Center, 1993), 23.

28. Neil Rudenstine, in *The Economics of Art Museums*, ed. Martin Feldstein (Chicago: University of Chicago Press, 1991), 81–82.

29. Herbert S. Bailey, Jr., *The Rate of Publication of Scholarly Monographs in the Humanities and Social Sciences, 1978–1988* (New York: Association of American University Presses, 1990), 18–21.

30. See, e.g., W. J. T. Mitchell, *Iconology: Image, Text, Ideology* (Chicago: University of Chicago Press, 1986); Barbara M. Stafford, *Body Criticism: Imaging the Unseen in Enlightenment Art and Medicine* (Cambridge, Mass.: MIT Press, 1991); Martin Jay, *Downcast Eyes: The Denigration of Vision in 20th Century French Thought* (Berkeley and Los Angeles: University of California Press, 1993).

31. The Report of the Rockefeller Foundation in 1931 defined the humanities as including "the liberal and historical arts, literature, philology (ancient and modern languages), and archaeology" (cited by Colton and Richardson, *The Humanities and "the Well-Being of Mankind,"* 21).

32. Loren Renz et al., *Arts Funding Revisited: An Update on Foundation Trends in the 1990's* (New York: Foundation Center, 1995), 3 , with Table 2. The figures for 1992 may be somewhat inflated owing to unusually large donations by the Lila Wallace–Reader's Digest Fund.

33. Ekman, Statement at a Public Meeting of the President's Committee on the Arts and the Humanities, 2–3. See also Nina K. Cobb, *Looking Ahead: Private Sector Giving to the Arts and the Humanities* (Washington, D.C.: President's Committee on the Arts and Humanities, 1996), where, however, the primacy of arts funding should have been more forcefully stated.

34. This information was kindly supplied by the dean of CASVA, Henry A. Millon, and Helen Tangires, staff assistant, in October 1995.

35. See the excellent new study by Jed I. Bergman, *Managing Change in the Non-Profit Sector: Lessons from the Evolution of Five Independent Research Libraries* (San Francisco: Jossey-Bass, 1996). For the impact of the electronic revolution on text-centered humanities, see the essay by Carla Hesse in this volume.

36. The shares of the NHC and of other providers (shown in parentheses), in 1994 dollars: 1987–1988: $948,608 ($969,974); 1988–1989: $957,279 ($743,473); 1989–1990: $943,095 ($1,075,060); 1990–1991: $802,491 ($789,356).

37. Annual figures, in constant 1994 dollars: 1991–1992: $70,000; 1992–1993: 370,000; 1993–1994: $45,000; 1994–1995: $92,000.

38. Greenberg, *Fellowships in the Humanities*, 19.

39. See Jonathan R. Cole, "Balancing Acts: Dilemmas of Choice Facing Research Universities," *Daedalus* 122 (Fall 1993): 23.

40. The 1991–1992 membership directory of the Consortium of Humanities Centers and Institutes lists fifty-three U.S. members; since only a fraction of these centers are declared members of the Consortium, actual numbers are much higher.

41. Greenberg, *Fellowships in the Humanities*, 18.

42. Survey conducted by the author, with the assistance of Colleen Heflin and Mark Long, from the University of Michigan, 1995.

43. K. W. Arenson, "Guggenheim Foundation, Long a Donor, Is Now Having to Seek Donations," *New York Times*, October 31, 1995, A12.

44. William G. Bowen, testimony in support of the FY 1989 appropriation for the National Endowment for the Humanities, 1–2.

45. *Giving USA: The Annual Report on Philanthropy for the Year 1992* (New York: AAFRC Trust for Philanthropy, 1993), 126.

46. A. Delbanco, *The New Yorker*, March 27, 1995, 8.

47. In what follows, in addition to published sources, I have relied heavily on an excellent unpublished study by my research assistant, Caroline Winterer, on patrons of the humanities at the University of Michigan, 1850–1995.

48. See the appendix to this volume, Tables 1 and 2. Agglomerated data such as these may oversimplify, by disguising actual rates of change in specific types of institutions and in certain fields. For important discussion, see Sarah E. Turner and William G. Bowen, "The Flight from the Arts and Sciences: Trends in Degrees Conferred," *Science* 250 (October 26, 1990): 517–521; and, more recently, Joan Gilbert, "The Liberal Arts College: Is It Really an Endangered Species?" *Change* (September-October 1995): 37–43.

49. For the decline of national economic growth, linked closely to the slowing of productivity, see most recently Jeff Madrick, *The End of Affluence* (New York: Random House, 1995), and the article by the same author in *The New York Review of Books*, September 21, 1995, 13–17; for a recent summary, with statistics, of the expansion in U.S. higher education, see Francis Oakley, *Community of Learning: The American College and the Liberal Arts Tradition* (New York: Oxford University Press, 1992), 75–98.

Between 1965 and 1970, 150,000 new faculty entered the professoriate, lifting the overall numbers to 600,000; the number of new positions created and filled during these years was larger than the total number of faculty positions that had existed in 1940 (147,000). And of course, the case for decline in humanities funding presented in the preceding pages is closely tied to the numbers of humanities faculty. It is important to know whether numbers of humanities faculty in the institutions discussed have grown or declined over the period 1970–1995. Unfortunately, there exist no reliable data. The National Center for Education Statistics estimates that in 1987 there were approximately 75,000 full-time faculty in the humanities in all U.S. postsecondary institutions (four-year colleges, universities, and community colleges, this last category being assumed to constitute at least 25 percent of the total). The Center further estimates that this number had declined very slightly, to 74,000, by 1992. (These figures have been provided by

Dr. Peter Syverson, vice president, Council of Graduate Schools, to whom I am very grateful.) Within the selective institutions discussed in this essay, however, I am convinced that numbers of humanities faculty have remained stable and possibly have even increased. This impression is based upon more than unofficial reports from many major campuses. The recently published study by the National Research Council on research doctorate programs in 274 universities found that, between 1982 and 1993, average numbers of faculty had increased in all humanities, anthropology, and history programs that had participated in both the 1982 and 1993 studies—even though numbers of Ph.D.s in these fields had declined over the same period. See M. L. Goldberger, B. A. Maher, and P. E. Flattau, eds., *Research Doctorate Programs in the United States: Continuity and Change* (Washington, D.C.: National Academy Press, 1995), 44, Table 3-10, and Appendix R (699–701, 705, 709–10, 713–15, 718–19, 725).

50. The actual college and university shares, in constant (1993) dollars, were $605.2 million (1983), $907.2 million (1989), and $826.6 million (1993). The percentage of these funds flowing to Arts and Culture (the rubric under which the humanities are included in the Foundation Center's classification system) declined from 5.8 percent in 1983 to 4.1 percent in 1989, then rose slightly to 4.2 percent in 1993. (Loren Renz, the Foundation Center, New York, September 28, 1995.)

51. Roger Shattuck, *Perplexing Dreams: Is There a Core Tradition in the Humanities?* ACLS Occasional Paper no. 2 (New York: American Council of Learned Societies, 1987), 4.

52. Seamus Heaney, *The Redress of Poetry* (New York: Farrar, Straus & Giroux, 1995), 158.

CLASSROOMS

Three

Ignorant Armies and Nighttime Clashes

CHANGES IN THE HUMANITIES CLASSROOM, 1970–1995

FRANCIS OAKLEY

IF THE title of this essay suggests the presence of a measure of confusion in the debates of the past decade and more about the state of the humanities, it is intended to do so. It is intended also to signal the fact that a residual undertow of agnosticism still tugs away uneasily even at this rather modest attempt merely to identify the principal changes over the past twenty-five years in *what* is actually being taught in the undergraduate humanities classroom and in *how* it is being taught. For that is my topic. And yet, to the degree to which that attempt stops short of passing judgment on the desirability of such changes, one would have thought that the task involved would be a comparatively easy one.

During those years, after all, the dawning recognition that the invention of the computer had ushered in some sort of "second Industrial Revolution" encouraged millennial expectations of an "unprecedented technological revolution" destined to transform the way in which students learned, certainly in the natural and social sciences, perhaps also in the disciplines lying at the very heart of the humanities.[1] The available evidence, however, indicates very clearly that no such definitive transformation has yet occurred. It is true that contemporary students are much more visually oriented and visually sophisticated than were their predecessors a quarter of a century ago. Film and video now have, accordingly, a somewhat larger presence in the classroom, as also in efforts at course-related enrichment outside the classroom, and one gets the impression that students are spending more time sitting in the flickering dark than was formerly the case. But the television-driven pedagogic "revolution" that some were predicting in the 1960s has simply not occurred.[2] Nor, except possibly in programs of distance learning and in the use of e-mail to foster discussions out of class, have forms of computer-aided instruction moved close to center stage. Even if we take American faculty as a whole (natural and social scientists as well as humanities people), those pioneering the exploitation of computer-aided instruction constitute less than 5 percent of the total,[3] and the percentage for those in the humanities is undoubtedly much

smaller than that. Similarly, until the year 1994–1995, those making use
of any sort of computer-aided instruction fell only into the 4 to 16 percent
range, and the figure for courses in the humanities will again undoubtedly
be smaller than that.[4] Though in the decades to come all of this is probably
destined to change (and the year 1994–1995 saw a dramatic acceleration
in usage),[5] the assessment that Lawrence Douglas made in 1983 to the
effect that computer-assisted education in history was a "revolution yet to
come" remains just as valid twelve years later—valid, moreover, not only
for history, but for the humanities in general.[6]

The picture, however, becomes a good deal less clear, and one's ability
to speak with confidence accordingly diminished, when one broadens the
scope of the inquiry to encompass other changes of a very different type
impinging on instruction in the humanities. Over the past quarter of a
century, it should be recalled, during a period marked by a historic and
truly massive increase in the numbers of students flooding into the undergraduate programs of our colleges and universities, our ears have been
assailed by a persistent drumbeat of educational commentary of the
"eclipse of the liberal arts," "crisis of the humanities," "erosion of the
humanities," "flight from the humanities" genre, evoking and lamenting,
among other things, the precipitous contemporary decline in the numbers
of American students willing to commit themselves to the study of the
humanities disciplines. Meanwhile, those very disciplines (and especially
English, comparative literature, history, and art history) have been experiencing the upheaval of the spirit discussed elsewhere in this volume and
reflecting not only the sharp linguistic turn in so much of our thinking but
also our era's intense preoccupation with the categories of gender, race,
ethnicity, social class, and sexual orientation, as well as the impact of the
growing (and related) body of commentary that is "postcolonial" in its
inspiration. If the programs of the annual scholarly meetings, the agendas
of the mounting number of humanities conferences, and the contemporaneous surge in theoretical and methodological discussion together constitute any sort of accurate guide, this great perturbation has in no small
measure transformed the characteristic ways in which academics in the
humanities go about their intellectual business, no less than the dominant
focus of their disciplinary preoccupations.

Not surprisingly, such seismic shifts have come to be viewed in quite
conflicting ways. But whatever one's particular judgment about the current health of the humanities, it has become customary, hewing to "the
old-fashioned idea that scholarship drives the curriculum,"[7] simply to
assume that intellectual perturbations of the nature and scope experienced
over the past quarter of a century cannot but have had a transformative
impact on what goes on in the classroom itself. That has certainly been the
guiding assumption of those educational critics who, for the past decade

and more, have been prone to wondering if "the flight from the humanities" might not, after all, have had something to do with what students were actually encountering in their humanities classes. "It may well be the case," or so Roger Kimball suggested in 1990, "that the much-publicized decline in humanities enrollments recently is due at least in part to students' refusal to devote their college education to a program of study that has nothing to offer them but ideological posturing, pop culture, and hermeneutic word games."[8] Nonetheless, it is my purpose now to suggest that the existence of any direct or straightforward linkage between the debates raging in the realms of scholarship and criticism, on the one hand, and what is going on in the humanities classroom, on the other, is not to be taken, Kimball-fashion, simply for granted. It has, rather, to be established by a patient scrutiny of the available facts—an eminently traditionalist undertaking, I would have thought—and those facts, it turns out, are neither easy to come by nor easy to interpret.

Of course, as I say that, I realize that I am open to the charge of attempting to make something of an analytic banquet out of what is, in fact, a rather small snack. So, in order to obviate, deflect, or at least blunt any such accusation, let me begin by posting three caveats for the benefit of anyone tempted to jump impatiently to quick conclusions on this deceptively simple matter.

First, and most fundamentally, no attempt to arrive at a judgment concerning the impact on the humanities classroom of the intellectual upheavals of the past quarter century is likely to be anything other than misleading if it does not take into account the extraordinary size, range, and institutional variety of the American system of higher education. In 1994, the Carnegie Foundation for the Advancement of Teaching recognized as institutions of higher education some 3,595 universities, colleges, and specialized institutions, of which the specialized institutions, community colleges, and junior colleges make up no less than 61 percent of the total, while the 250 or so institutions categorized in the top ranks of research universities and liberal arts colleges together add up to no more than 9 percent.[9] And yet my own reading suggests to me that the bulk of the critical commentary on the current state of teaching in the humanities—frequently characterized by sweeping and sensationalist claims and a species of disheveled anecdotalism—has been based on what is supposed to be going on at probably no more than a dozen of the nation's leading research universities and liberal arts colleges. I think, for example, of the almost liturgical degree of repetition with which Stanford's decision in 1988 to modify its Western Culture requirement has been invoked in the critical literature—replete with solemn references to the chant in which the Rev. Jesse Jackson led a group of protesting Stanford students: "Hey, hey, ho, ho, Western Culture's got to go!"[10]

But without getting into a discussion of what really happened at Stanford,[11] I would insist that there is, in fact, no easy deduction from what is going on in the humanities classrooms of one of the nation's three or four leading research universities to what is likely to be going on in classrooms right across the whole broad spectrum of American higher education. That is true at even the simplest level about generalizations concerning how many students were actually in those classrooms. During the 1980s, before a measure of recovery began to set in, it was quite common for those of us in education to bemoan the dramatic decline evident in undergraduate interest in the humanities. And humanities degrees had indeed dropped between 1969 and 1986 from a high of 21.4 percent of all degrees awarded to a low of 10.2 percent (see Table 1, appendix). As a result, Kimball himself had a great deal of fun at the expense of the authors of *Speaking for the Humanities* (the American Council of Learned Societies' 1989 pamphlet responding to the Bennett and Cheney reports on the plight of the humanities) for their piecemeal and rather fumbling attempt to question or qualify the evidence indicating a decline in humanities enrollments.[12] But, Kimball to the contrary, their puzzlement was understandable. It was not, after all, the type of institution with which they were affiliated—the top-ranked research university among whose faculty members what Kimball parodies as "ideological posturing, pop culture, and hermeneutic word games" would appear to be most deeply entrenched— that accounted, statistically speaking, for the decline in question. Instead, among the baccalaureate-granting institutions it was the comprehensive universities and colleges, and such other four-year institutions as the state colleges, that had seen the sharpest, most continuous, and most distressing declines in arts and sciences enrollments since the early 1970s. At Cornell and Swarthmore, for example, there were only the most modest fluctuations between 1954 and 1986 in the percentages of arts and sciences degrees conferred and, at Cornell, no real change at all between 1970 and 1986. At Ball State University, on the other hand, where the arts and sciences share of degrees awarded had risen between 1954 and 1970 from 2.5 to 29.9 percent, by 1986 that share had fallen back, quite catastrophically, to 13.3 percent.[13] In relation, then, to higher education as to other things, averages based on aggregated figures can conceal almost as much as they reveal, and it is crucial, when analyzing these adverse trends, to distinguish among institutional sectors.

Caveat number two. Roughly paralleling the differences among the varying types of institutions offering higher education are multiple differences in the priorities and preoccupations of the faculty who teach at them, not least of all differences in the degree of engagement in matters scholarly. "Publish or perish" may be a hallowed cliché among academics and educational critics alike, but we should not allow it to blind us to the fact that statistical surveys and analyses over the past quarter of a century have repeatedly indicated that a majority of American academics view themselves as teachers rather than as "research people," that they are, in fact, inactive in research and succeed somehow, nonetheless, in avoiding perishing while publishing little or nothing. Less than a fourth publish at all extensively, and, as a result, a surprisingly large proportion of the books and articles produced are the work of a smallish group of compulsive scholarly recidivists.[14]

One could, I suppose, assume the direct transfer of the scholarly or critical preoccupations of the more avant-garde among those doing the publishing into their own undergraduate teaching. That assumption does not, however, strike me as necessarily self-evident. In order to go on to assume some sort of cognate transformation in what is being taught in humanities classrooms at large one would have to assume, further, that the mass of faculty who are inactive or only marginally active in scholarship vibrate, nonetheless, to the same intellectual frequencies as those (to pick a much-cited example) who contributed papers to the special session the Modern Language Association (MLA) devoted in 1989 to "The Muse of Masturbation"—a celebrated session naturally pounced upon with glee by Kimball and other conservative critics.[15]

Caveat number three. Even if I am wrong on that score and if the assumption about the direct transfer of scholarly and critical preoccupations into the modalities of undergradute teaching is, in fact, correct, perhaps we should remind ourselves that, with respect to teaching, aspiration not infrequently fails to translate into achievement, and that we would be ill-advised either proudly to proclaim or fearfully to bemoan the transformation of what goes on in the classroom by the rage for theory or the fascination with multiculturalism evident in so much of contemporary scholarship and criticism in the humanities. Given the gritty realities so often encountered in the pedagogic trenches—the number of faculty in a given humanities department and the range of disparate subjects they are called upon to teach; the various abilities, fluctuating interest, and uneven preparation of the students they encounter; the demanding nature or perhaps recalcitrance of the subject matter they are called upon to mediate—classroom reality turns out all too often to bear little relation to intellectual or curricular ideal.

Here, I would suggest, there is a broader lesson to be learned from the attempt made by Anthony Grafton and Lisa Jardine to reconstruct from instructional and classroom materials—textbooks, teachers' letters and diaries, student notes and compositions—what exactly it was that went on in the classroom of the great fifteenth-century humanist teacher Guarino Guarini da Verona (d. 1460). Intellectual historians have usually assumed, accepting "the ideology of Renaissance humanism" as an accurate "historical account of humanist achievement," that the classical education achieved "the formation of character as well as the training of the mind." But what the evidence discloses is the existence of an enormous gap between noble theoretical ideal and the actual grinding preoccupation with grammatical issues and textual detail, which anyone who has had to struggle to master a dead language will ruefully recall, and which appears to have precluded, in fact, the reading over several years of anything more than what would run to several hundred pages in a modern text, and to have left little or no time for reflective consideration of the content of that text.[16]

I cannot help wondering, then, about what we would find if we turned Grafton and Jardine loose as historians upon a similar body of evidence generated by contemporary college instruction, say, in the classics or in modern languages and literatures. Languages still have to be learned, and given the continuing challenge of attaining linguistic competence that undergraduates confront, perhaps it will not be viewed as ungenerous if I express a twinge of skepticism (and especially so when instruction is not conducted in English) about the degree to which the theoretical and critical preoccupations evident at least at the cutting edge of comparative literature scholarship are really likely to inform what actually goes on in the classroom.

And so on. Given the force of these caveats and the fact that they extend even to issues on which we possess some statistical data, it is tempting to assume that in the absence of some formidably massive and intricate exercise in empirical investigation we are doomed, on this matter of changes in humanities instruction, to being cast adrift on an ocean of anecdotage masquerading as generalization or of ideology purporting to be fact. But that is a temptation, I believe, to which we should refuse to yield. During the course of the past decade we have, in fact, been fortunate enough to have had placed at our disposal, at least on some issues and for some fields, a modest body of survey data and statistical reportage. If we aspire at all to weaning commentary on higher education away from the easy indulgence of apocalyptic doomsaying and to nudging it in a more constructively analytic direction (and I must confess that I do), then these data have to be attended to. And it is to them—along with conclusions drawn from my own more impressionistic sampling of the older and very recent course catalogues of institutions drawn from nearly all of the Carnegie categories—that I propose now to turn.[17]

Reading catalogue copy in bulk can be something of a mind-numbing experience, and, of course, as students periodically complain, what it has to say cannot always be relied on. That is especially true when it does not indicate the frequency with which courses are actually given (a surprisingly common occurrence) or when, at large institutions, the survey courses are staffed by a shifting array of unnamed instructors who may be prone to substituting their own choice of readings for those officially advertised.[18] That conceded, and the fallout from original sin, it has to be assumed, being reasonably constant across time, I know of no hard evidence to suggest that such failings were notably less prevalent a quarter of a century ago than they are today. I believe, then, that a comparison of the course listings and descriptions of courses to be found in the catalogues of the same institutions for the years 1969–1970 and 1994–1995 does give a roughly accurate sense of the direction of at least certain types of change.

Five of these changes stand out with a degree of repetitious clarity. First, there is a striking increase in the number of courses listed and presumably offered on some sort of cyclical basis. Observable not only at colleges and universities and in individual departments that have grown in size across the period, but also in those that have not and at which enrollments in the arts and sciences have remained fairly steady, this phenomenon of course proliferation cannot simply be explained as the natural outcome of the overall increase in the size of the American professoriate.[19] Instead, it may also in part reflect the widespread loosening of specific course requirements during the past twenty-five years and the concomitant shift of enrollments into a variety of elective courses.

Second, there appears to have been fairly widespread change not only in the sheer numbers of courses being offered but also in their nature and the way in which they tend, characteristically, to be described. The change in nature seems to be away from a more or less standardized coverage approach, for instance of a genre or period (e.g., "The Latin Epic" or "Recent American History"), and in the direction of more selective and specialized thematic courses (e.g., "Heaven and Hell: The Afterlife in Art," "East and West," or "Women Filmmakers: Resisting/Deflecting/Subverting the Gaze").[20] And the change in description is in the direction of much greater length introduced by more catchy and evocative titles. Indeed, in comparison, catalogue copy from the late 1960s projects fairly consistently an engagingly laconic, take-it-or-leave-it style that lacks the measure of anxious specificity and (occasionally tiresome) self-advertisement so often evident in our contemporary course descriptions.[21] And that particular change, one is tempted to speculate, may have been stimulated by the intensification of student consumerism and by the competitive rigors of a more generally elective curriculum in a setting where (or so my own experience would suggest) student enrollments are likely to swill around in a highly volatile fashion and where the curricular version of Adam Smith's invisible hand appears persistently to be off duty.

The third change evident is a marked and well-distributed increase in the number of interdepartmental and/or interdisciplinary programs offering either majors or minor concentrations,[22] and that change links with the fourth, the accelerated "globalization" of the curriculum. That change is evident not only in the teaching of foreign languages, history, and religion but also in our departments of art history, English, music and philosophy, and not only in our great research universities and leading liberal arts colleges but also in our comprehensive institutions and community colleges.[23] Language instruction in Chinese and Japanese is now comparatively widespread, and a preoccupation with postcolonial theory and writing is growing, as also are course offerings in the art, history, literature, religion, and (to a lesser degree) music and philosophy of Africa, Asia, and Latin America. In its international dimension, then, the American college curriculum is typically and significantly less provincial than it was in the late 1960s.

Something similar is true of the nationally focused sector of that curriculum, for the fifth obvious change (one also intertwined with the growth of interdisciplinary programs) is what gives the impression, at least, of being a veritable explosion since 1969 in the number of course offerings pertaining to American minority populations and ethnic groups, and above all to women's studies, feminisms of one sort or another, and gender-related issues in general. And although the epicenter of this explosion appears to be situated in the curricula of the research universities and leading liberal arts colleges, its reverberations have in some degree affected the course offerings of the other liberal arts colleges, of institutions in the comprehensive sector, and of the community colleges as well.[24] This particular change, indeed, looms so large that it tends to overshadow the more modest but detectable growth in the number of course offerings devoted to such subjects as film, peace studies, business, medical and environmental ethics, and the literature of religious mysticism. It also tends to mask the more sporadic presence of distinctive new offerings reflecting an institution's unusual strength in a particular area or creative responses to the needs and characteristics of the region in which a particular institution is located.[25] Above all, and quite misleadingly, it tends to distract attention from the fact that most of these changes appear to have been achieved by the addition of courses rather than by their substitution for more traditional offerings. For a prominent feature of course listings across the full range of American institutions of higher education is the degree of tenacious continuity they so amply manifest—sometimes to the point of the stubborn reappearance word for word in the 1994–1995 catalogue of a course description to be found a quarter of a century earlier in its 1969–1970 predecessor![26]

It is possible to test the accuracy of these impressions and to nudge them in the direction of greater specificity by turning to a body of survey data gathered by several groups over the course of the past decade and a half. Like the available statistical evidence in general, these data have been almost entirely ignored by those educational critics who have succeeded most persistently in grabbing the headlines.[27] The figures come from surveys focused on three things: on the impact on the curriculum at large and on general education requirements of multiculturalism, globalization, and gender studies;[28] on the changing shape of course offerings and of the major in three disciplines: music, history, and English;[29] and on changes in educational goals and interpretative approach.[30] Let me take them up in turn.

First, multiculturalism, globalization, and gender studies. Here data gathered in 1990–1991, and representing, as it were, a snapshot of conditions at that time, put in perspective by some longitudinal data revealing changes between 1970 and 1985, indicate that about 6 percent of all colleges and universities offer course work in gay and lesbian studies. Between 30 and 40 percent, in fact, offer course work in gender studies and in minority or ethnic studies, with the same percentage having a multicultural general education requirement (though it should be noted that only 12 percent of the institutions having this last requirement focus it on domestic diversity, as opposed to global diversity, or, more usually, some combination of both). To place those figures in context, let me note that 53 percent of all institutions have a general education requirement in Western civilization.[31] As for trend lines, between 1970 and 1985 the number of institutions with a general education *requirement* calling for the taking of at least one course in women's studies grew from 0 to 1.6 percent, for the taking of a course in "Third World Studies" by 5 percent to approximately 8 percent, and for some sort of global education by 10 percent to nearly 15 percent. More surprisingly, perhaps, because it runs directly counter to claims so often made by the critics, the percentage of those requiring a course not simply in Western civilization but specifically in the history of Western civilization also grew across these years and did so by a little over 5 percent to a total of almost 50 percent.[32] These figures, then, make it perfectly clear (if anyone was really in doubt) that the traditional curriculum is far from having been impervious to multiculturalism. At the same time, however, they serve to confirm the impression that change has come by accretion rather than by substitution for what went before. And, as Arthur Levine, the lead author of one of these studies, puts it, these findings certainly render "untenable the notion that multiculturalism is replacing the historic canon."[33]

Second, the changing shape of course offerings and of the majors in music, history, and English. One of Levine's conclusions was that, so far as the humanities are concerned, the leaders among departments introducing a multicultural element into their curriculum are, by far, English and history. About English, thanks to a whole series of studies mounted by the MLA between 1984 and 1991, we know quite a bit. Before I turn to that evidence, however, let me note that some modest and uneven data relating to music offerings as they stood in the 1980s reveal that, although some attention was being paid to world music even in courses not specifically devoted to it, and despite growing concern about that issue, the over-whelming emphasis, at least in the undergraduate curriculum, continued to be placed on Western art music, with symphonic literature receiving by far the most thoroughgoing treatment even in courses designed for non-majors.[34] Let me note, too, that an American Historical Association survey in 1981–1982 revealed that in terms both of the number of departments offering courses in a given field and of the number of courses offered, the history of both the United States and of Europe dominated the scene. Indeed, more departments offered courses in quantitative history and women's history (about 50 and 44 percent, respectively) than in the history of any region of the developing world, Latin America (63 percent) alone excepted.[35]

But what about English? Here we have the materials from which to construct a somewhat more nuanced picture, courtesy of carefully con-structed surveys representative of both the institutional and the faculty profiles of American higher education and focused on a whole range of things from general education requirements in English to the shape of the English major, to the profile of authors being assigned in a selected group of upper-division courses, to the similar profile of authors assigned in the introductory surveys in British and American literature.[36] Given their quality, these studies deserve a far more detailed analysis than I can give them here—the more so in that the survey of upper-division courses has been denounced as "deceptive" in the pages of *Academic Questions*, the publication of the traditionalist-oriented National Association of Scholars.[37] But then I would judge that that critique, while making some reasonable and perfectly arguable points, is marred as a whole by its unwarranted imputation of bad faith to the MLA, by its implausible insistence that the survey data themselves reveal the growing politicization and radicalization of English instruction, and by its hyperbolic claim to the effect that "nothing stands between the public and these facts except the dismaying duplicity of those who speak for the academic establishment."[38]

Whatever the case, and having weighed both reports and criticism, I myself draw five main conclusions from the whole body of material provided by these successive surveys.

First, so far as general education requirements in English are con-cerned, composition rather than literature rules the roost. Whereas the great majority of colleges and universities require at least one term of English composition, only 20 percent require students to take specific literature courses (usually an introduction to literature or a survey of British, American, or world literature), while some 36 percent have no requirements in literature whatsoever.[39] If one is looking for something to worry about, this last finding strikes me as a good candidate.

Second, so far as change in the departmental array of course offerings is concerned, addition rather than substraction or substitution is, indeed, the order of the day, with composition courses of one sort or another again leading the pack. Even the type of course most frequently dropped (and it turns out to be not Shakespeare, not Chaucer, not Milton, but minority literature) was dropped by only 5 percent of the institutions sampled. In contrast, between 20 and 30 percent added courses in film, women writers, minority literature, and upper-level rhetoric or composition, while no fewer than 37 percent added courses in professional or technical writing.[40]

Third, in the twenty years between 1965 and 1985 "the basic configuration of the English major" appears "to have changed only slightly," with most departments still requiring historical coverage of a traditional type, with courses on such topics as literary theory, popular literature, women and literature, and minority literature being tacked on as electives but rarely required for the major.[41]

It is nonetheless conceivable that such soothing evidences of continuity in the subject areas offered or required may mask radical change in the actual content of those courses. But—conclusion number four—the statistics gathered in connection with survey courses in British and American literature and with upper-division courses in Renaissance literature (excluding courses in Shakespeare), in the nineteenth-century British novel, and in American literature from 1800 to 1865 all combine to cast doubt on that possibility. And they should offer at least a measure of reassurance to anyone alarmed by sweeping claims made to the effect that "trendy lightweights" at our colleges and universities have been ignoring the traditional subjects and eliminating from the curriculum the classics of English literature.[42] In effect, here, as elsewhere, the "Apocalypse Now" genre of commentary on higher education has not served us at all well.

In relation, then, to the upper-division courses, the vast majority of respondents reported themselves as teaching a consistent core of specific works, most of them by authors traditionally viewed as the leading writers of their eras (thus, no surprise, the names of Edmund Spenser, Charles Dickens, and Nathaniel Hawthorne loom very large). About 65 percent have recently added works to their lists of required readings, between 25 and 30 percent of such additions being again works by those traditionally regarded as major authors. Between a third and a half have added works less commonly taught, and though the choices of these works are quite scattered, the names that crop up among them are unlikely to surprise (thus, for example, Harriet Beecher Stowe, Frederick Douglass, Margaret Fuller, Oscar Wilde, Mary Shelley, Thomas Carlyle, and Mary Austell).[43]

But then if the picture, as the investigators have proclaimed, is an unexceptionable one of "substantial continuity" modulated by "some changes," the critics of this particular study hotly retort that it was tilted in such a way as to produce a reassuringly traditionalist result, in that (among other things) "upper division courses . . . are taken by few except English majors, whereas it is in the freshman and survey courses that superior works are most often replaced by the likes of Alice Walker's novels."[44] The significance of that last reference should not escape us. It echoes the throwaway remark in a *Chronicle of Higher Education* article by an English department chairman to the effect that he would be willing to "bet that [Alice Walker's] *The Color Purple* is taught in more English courses today than all of Shakespeare's plays combined." That rather zany comment was made in 1988 and it has since been repeatedly invoked, with lugubrious shaking of journalistic jowl, as a simple statement of fact.[45]

Just how ludicrous that is becomes clear when one takes a look at the MLA's 1995 report on its survey data concerning what is being taught in introductory survey courses in British and American literature. For—fifth and final conclusion—although some change has undoubtedly occurred, it is quite undramatic. The list of authors taught on a regular basis is heavily traditional in nature. In terms of frequency of use, the top half-dozen authors named for the American survey are Hawthorne (66 percent), Melville, Whitman, Dickinson, Twain, and Emerson. For the British survey, Chaucer (89 percent), Shakespeare, Milton, Wordsworth, Pope, and Donne head the list. In the rear guard with frequencies less than 1 percent are such authors as Charlotte Brontë, Mary Shelley, Matthew Arnold, James Baldwin, Langston Hughes, Sylvia Plath, and (yes!) Alice Walker. Even Toni Morrison comes in at no more than 1.8 percent—slightly behind (at 2.1 percent) none other than Cotton Mather.[46]

What, then, are we to make of these broadly consistent and mutually reinforcing (if rather soporific) findings—not exactly good fodder for an op-ed piece in the *Wall Street Journal*, and a good deal less energizing, certainly, than claims to the effect that the American professoriate is somehow bent, in what little teaching it is reluctantly conceded still to be doing, on engineering nothing less than the collapse of Western civilization itself. Admittedly, without knowing more than we do about the educational goals of those doing the teaching or the interpretative approaches they characteristically use in mediating their comparatively traditional subject matter, it is hard to give a satisfactory answer to that question. And here survey data of the third type, again gathered by the MLA and that do concern such matters, are not extensive and pose some difficulties of interpretation.[47] For what they are worth, they suggest that the vast majority of instructors set themselves the quite traditional goals of helping students read closely, understand literary forms and genres, and learn the intellectual, historical, and biographical backgrounds necessary for understanding the literature of a given period. Similarly, by way of interpretative approach, two-thirds and more favor such comparatively traditional approaches as the history of ideas and the New Criticism. In fact, the only approach of comparatively innovative stamp that (at 61 percent) comes remotely close in terms of popularity embraces feminist perspectives of one sort or another.[48]

The critics, however (and not altogether without reason), point out that the way in which the questions were posed may well have rendered the outcome ambiguous. Certainly, the question designed to elicit how many favored poststructuralist goals (it turned out to be no more than 12 percent) was so bluntly framed as arguably to have had the effect of dissuading larger numbers from answering in the affirmative.[49] Furthermore, even if we assume these data to be fully reliable, here too averages based on aggregated figures may well conceal some important trends. Indeed when broken down (and as the critics rightly note), they reveal that faculty who received their Ph.D.s since 1980, as well as those of whatever age who teach at Ph.D.-granting universities and are training the faculty of the future, are much more likely than the rest to report themselves as emphasizing such less traditional goals as that of helping students grasp the influence of race, class, and gender on literature and as favoring such less traditional interpretative approaches as the Marxist or the poststructuralist.[50] On that basis, then, the critics go on to conclude that "the trend toward politicized instruction in literary studies is growing and will continue to grow."[51]

Here, however, and by way of conclusion, I would urge the wisdom of keeping one's powder dry and cultivating a measure of residual agnosticism about the postulation of such future trends. In this, as in the use for modeling purposes of financial projections based on seemingly established trends, it is wise to avoid confusing projections with predictions. Past experience suggests not only that present projections may themselves promote the modification of behavior in such a way as to undercut their own value as predictors, but also that it is all too easy in the thick of things to be mistaken about the precise direction even of current trends. Predictions about the future of higher education made as recently as the 1960s and 1970s certainly have a rather sorry look to them now. (Frederick Ness, for example, was worrying about how the populace would be able to cope with all the additional leisure time that, by the end of the century, they were going to have on their hands.)[52] And contemporaneous predictions about intellectual trends really do not look that much better. Few of us pursuing historical work today, I would guess, would be tempted to sign on to the judgment made by even so distinguished a fellow historian as Geoffrey Barraclough as recently as 1979 (and reflecting the post-1950s vogue of empiricist commitments and quantitative aspirations) to the effect that the historicism and soft-core philosophical idealism influential in the interwar years had collapsed, and that the practice of history was on the verge of stepping across the threshold dividing, as he put it, "pseudo-science from science."[53] Similarly, the obituaries for intellectual history so common among social historians in the 1960s and 1970s have proved to be at least as premature as those once fashionable among some advocates of the New Criticism with respect to historically conditioned approaches to literature.[54] And while critics on the right often continue to lump together poststructuralism, feminism, and race-class-gender analysis in general as a complex of related and mutually supportive forces eroding the traditional humanistic verities, it has become increasingly clear with the passage of time that "deconstruction . . . with its microscopically close readings of the text and its emphasis on total irony" is itself in many ways "a development of the old formalistic modes of literary interpretation such as aestheticism or the new criticism."[55] As such, of course, it stands in sharp contrast with those forms of anthropological, sociological, and, above all, historical contextualism that have now nudged it to one side and that constitute something of an ascendant trend, not only in literary and cultural studies, but also in art history and even, in some measure, in music.[56]

Chastened, however, by the misjudgments of the past, I would argue that there is no reason simply to assume that such forms of contextualism, however fashionable they may be at the moment, will necessarily shape the intellectual or instructional orthodoxy of the future. We should recognize that they, no less than the New Criticism or deconstruction, are likely to harbor their own destabilizing elements. Contexts, after all, are not simply given; they have to be chosen or constructed. More often than not they are themselves textually mediated; as such they can be just as opaque and ambiguous as those other texts they are being invoked to illuminate. Indeed, apprehensions are already being voiced lest "the positivities of context be used to resolve the ambiguities of texts."[57]

And that worrisome fact, I would urge, should itself (and however ironically) be made part of the context in which we ourselves, peering anxiously into the future, struggle to achieve some sense of the directions of change in the ways in which scholars and teachers will be approaching the humanities on into the next century.

Acknowledgments

I express my gratitude to Alexandra Steinberg, Williams Class of 1997, for research assistance with this project, and to the many colleges and universities that were kind enough to provide us with copies of their course catalogues for the years 1969–1970 and 1994–1995.

Notes

1. See Kenneth C. Green, "A Technology Agenda for the 1990s," *Change* 23 (January-February 1991): 6–7. The bold prediction of an "unprecedented technological revolution" in the "processing and uses of information," in education as elsewhere, was made over thirty years ago by the physicist Patrick Suppes, "The Uses of Computers in Education," *Scientific American* 215, no. 3 (1966): 206–23 (at 206). Cf. Robert B. Kozma and Jerome Johnston, "The Technological Revolution Comes to the Classroom," *Change* 23 (January-February 1991): 10–23.

2. Here, Steven W. Gilbert's editorial comment in *Change* 27 (March-April 1995): 6, is pertinent. Among other things he insists that "the media have been carrying stories about the ways computer and video technology will revolutionize education during 'the next few months' for 30 years." He adds, however: "They're still wrong, but they become less so with each decade."

3. Kozma and Johnston, "The Technological Revolution Comes to the Classroom," 10–23. Cf. Kenneth C. Green and Steven W. Gilbert, "Great Expectations: Content, Communications, Productivity and the Role of Information Technology in Higher Education," *Change* 27 (March-April 1995): 8–18 (at 15), where they proffer the judgment that "innovation that goes beyond this group has been stalled."

4. Green and Gilbert, "Great Expectations," 10. They reproduce these figures from Kenneth C. Green, *Campus Computing 1994: The USC National Survey of Desktop Computing in Higher Education* (Los Angeles, 1995).

5. The more so in that, despite optimistic predictions, "we have [in fact] little hard evidence to document the real impact of this technology on instruction and scholarly activity"—thus Green, "A Technology Agenda for the 1990s," 6. For the shift in the past year suggesting "that instructional technology has [now] reached the 'critical mass' that it needs to spread throughout higher education," see Thomas J. DeLoughry, "Reaching a 'Critical Mass,'" *The Chronicle of Higher Education*, January 26, 1996, A17 and A20, and Steven W. Gilbert, "Making the Most of a Slow Revolution," *Change* 28 (March-April 1996): 10–23.

6. Cited in James B. Schick, "Microcomputer Simulations in the Classroom," *History Microcomputer Review* 1, no. 1 (1985): 3–6 (at 3).

7. The words quoted are those of W. R. Connor, "Humanities Research," in W. R. Connor et al., *The Humanities in the University: Strategies for the 1990s*, ACLS Occasional Paper no. 6 (New York, 1988), 21.

8. Charles J. Sykes, *Prof Scam: Professors and the Demise of Higher Education* (New York, 1990), 180–81; Roger Kimball, *Tenured Radicals: How Politics Has Corrupted Higher Education* (New York, 1987), xvii. Cf. the similar assertion in William J. Bennett, *To Reclaim a Legacy: A Report on the Humanities in Higher Education* (Washington, D.C., 1984), 16–17.

9. The Carnegie Foundation for the Advancement of Teaching, *A Classification of Institutions of Higher Education: 1994 Edition* (Princeton, N.J., 1994), x, 3–5, and 25–28.

10. See Lynne Cheney, *Humanities in America* (Washington, D.C., 1988), 13; Kimball, *Tenured Radicals*, 2–3 and 28–33; Dinesh D'Souza, *Illiberal Education: The Politics of Race and Sex on Campus* (New York, 1991), 59–93; Martin Anderson, *Imposters in the Temple* (New York, 1992), 148–49 and 195–96. For an account of the degree to which in our recent debates about higher education a handful of anecdotal claims have first been elevated to the status of "evidence" and then obsessively recycled, see Gerald Graff, *Beyond the Culture Wars: How Teaching the Conflicts Can Revitalize American Education* (New York and London, 1992), 16–25.

11. For which, see now W. B. Carnochan, *The Battleground of the Curriculum: Liberal Education and the American Experience* (Stanford, Calif.. 1993), especially 88–111.

12. Kimball, *Tenured Radicals*, 36, commenting on George Levine et al., *Speaking for the Humanities*, ACLS Occasional Paper no. 7 (New York, 1989), especially 21–24 and 35–37.

13. Although accurate, stable, and comprehensive data do not exist nationwide for course enrollments, we do have good data broken down by fields of study. They are provided by the Higher Education General Information Survey, now called the Integrated Postsecondary Education Data System, and since 1962 published annually in summary form by the U.S. Department of Education in *The Digest of Educational Statistics*. Using these data, and supplementing them "with more detailed breakdowns of degrees conferred by sector of education and field of study for the period since 1976," William G. Bowen and Julie Abbe Sosa produced the analysis on which I am drawing; see their *Prospects for Faculty in the Arts and Sciences: A Study of Factors Affecting Demand and Supply, 1987 to 2012* (Princeton, N.J., 1989), 45–65, and Appendix A, 187–90. See also Sarah E. Turner and W. G. Bowen, "The Flight from the Arts and Sciences," *Science* 250 (October 26, 1990): 517–21. For a summary of the general enrollment picture conveyed by these and other statistical sets and analyses, see Francis Oakley, *Community of Learning: The American College and the Liberal Arts Tradition* (New York and Oxford, 1992), 78–93.

14. The surveys conducted in 1969 and 1989 by the Carnegie Commission on Higher Education and the American Council on Education are especially pertinent. For tabulations from the weighted data generated by the 1969 survey, see Everett Carll Ladd, Jr., and Seymour Martin Lipset, *The Divided Academy: Professors and Politics* (New York, 1975), Appendixes A and C, 315–28 and 341–69. The results of the 1989 survey are tabulated in Ernest J. Boyer, *Scholarship Reconsidered: Priorities for the Professoriate* (Princeton, N.J., 1990), Appen-

dix A, 85–126. In addition to Ladd–Lipset and Boyer, see the analyses of Martin Trow and Oliver Fulton, "Research Activity in American Higher Education," in *Teachers and Students: Aspects of American Higher Education*, ed. Martin Trow (New York, 1975), 39–83; Everett Carll Ladd, Jr., "The Work Experience of American College Professors: Some Data and an Argument," *Current Issues in Higher Education* (1979): 3–12; Howard R. Bowen and Jack H. Schuster, *American Professor: A National Resource Imperiled* (New York and Oxford, 1986).

15. See *PMLA* 104, no. 6 (1989): 1028 (session 22); Kimball, *Tenured Radicals*, 145–46.

16. Anthony Grafton and Lisa Jardine, *From Humanism to the Humanities: Education and the Liberal Arts in Fifteenth- and Sixteenth-Century Europe* (Cambridge, Mass., 1986), 1–3, 18–22, and 27–28. For similarly critical appraisals of the classical regimen pursued in the grammar schools of sixteenth-century England and the *gymnasia* of Germany, see R. R. Bolgar, "Classicist Reading in Renaissance Schools," *Durham Research Review* 6 (1955): 18–26, and Gerald Strauss, "Liberal or Illiberal Arts?" *Journal of Social History* 19, no. 2 (1985): 361–67.

17. I included no sample from the Carnegie Specialized Institutions category. These are institutions granting at least 50 percent of their degrees in a single discipline. There are 722 of them and they are mainly professional in nature (e.g., business, law, engineering, health professions, Bible studies).

18. Comparing catalogue descriptions and lists of texts actually assigned for several literature courses at the University of Minnesota in 1992, Will Morrisey, Norman Fruman, and Thomas Short, "Ideology and Literary Studies, Part II: The MLA's Deceptive Survey," *Academic Questions* 6, no. 2 (1993): 46–58 (at 47–48), correctly warn us about the latter possibility.

19. Swarthmore College and Cornell University are both examples of institutions where there were only the most modest changes between 1954 and 1986 both in the overall number of B.A. degrees awarded and in the percentages of arts and sciences degrees conferred; see Turner and Bowen, "The Flight from the Arts and Sciences," 518 (Table 1). And at Swarthmore, for example, the 1969–1970 and 1994–1995 catalogues indicate the persistence of a history department unchanged in size but reveal, nonetheless, roughly a 75 percent increase in the number of history courses listed.

20. I draw these course titles from the 1969–1970 catalogues of The College of William and Mary (in the Carnegie category Doctoral I) and of Butler University (Comprehensive/Masters I), and from the 1994–1995 catalogues of Yale University (Research I) and Wellesley College (Liberal Arts/Baccalaureate I).

21. I proffer the following course descriptions (drawn, it must be confessed, not entirely at random) in order to display the contrast in bold relief:

Amherst College (Liberal Arts/Baccalaureate I), 1969–1970: History 26, "Early Modern Europe": "Studies in the nature of the early modern state 1400–1600."

Cornell University (Research I), 1994–1995: History 454, "The Herodotean Moment: The Uses and Abuses of 'Western Civilization'": "The basic premise of the seminar is that the concept of 'Western Civilization' is a problematic one in need of critical and historical analysis. The course will examine the evolution and transformation of this concept from antiquity to the twentieth century by focusing on selected moments (and texts in which they are represented) of actual and/or perceptual encounters with other civilizations. It will also inquire into the political uses and abuses of the idea of the West, and the literary, psychological, and anthropological dimensions of the idea's history. Readings include selections from Herodotus's *Histories*, Virgil's *Aeneid*, Augustine's *City of God*, *The Song of Roland*, Petrarch, Pico, Machiavelli, Montesquieu, Flaubert, Shelley's *Hellas*, Arnold, Hegel's *Philosophy of History*, James Mill's *History of British India*, and, from the secondary critical literature, Tzvetan Todorov's *The Conquest of America* and Edward Said's *Orientalism*."

22. Thus at Williams College (Liberal Arts/Baccalaureate I) the number of formally established interdepartmental programs went up from three to twelve between 1969 and 1994.

23. Thus, whereas the offering of courses in postcolonial literature currently appears to be the prerogative largely of such leading research universities as Chicago, Cornell, and Yale, the 1994–1996 catalogue of Ball State University (Doctoral I), for example, lists history courses in Russia, Africa, Asia, South and Southeastern Asia, China, the Middle East, and the Caribbean. Similarly, Bergen Community College (Associate of Arts Colleges; 1994–1995) lists courses in Japanese, Korean, and Russian, as well as in French, German, Spanish, and Italian, while Wilkes University (Comprehensive/Masters I; 1994–1995) lists courses in the history of Eastern Europe, Russia, India, China, and Japan in addition to the more traditional American and Western European fare.

24. Thus, for example, Castleton State College (Comprehensive/Masters II) lists courses for 1994–1995 in "Afro-American Literature," "Native American Literature," "Asian Literature and Thought," "Women Writers," and "Women in History"; Texas Lutheran College (Liberal Arts/Baccalaureate II) lists courses for 1994–1995 in "Chicano Literature and History," as well as in Far Eastern, Latin American, African, and women's history; and Butler University (Comprehensive/Masters I) lists courses for 1994–1995 in Buddhism, Islam, "Religions of China," and "Faiths of Russia and Its Neighbors."

25. Thus, for 1994–1995 again, for example, Bergen Community College lists two courses in "Intermediate Italian for Medical Students" designed specifically to help students meet the language requirements for admission to medical schools in Italy. Similarly, the University of Tulsa (Research II) lists two courses for 1994–1995 in the Cherokee language, and Howard University (Research I), blessed by the presence on its faculty of distinguished specialists in the fields involved, has for 1994–1995 been able to offer a classics course on "Blacks in Antiquity" as well as several courses on the history and geography of the black diaspora.

26. One is reminded of the reminiscences of Bliss Perry, one of the literary "generalists" of the turn of the century, who found as a freshman at Williams that "his first Latin lesson, in the preface to Livy" was in 1876 "exactly the same assignment" as his father before him had had in 1848. And it turned out also to be the same as his own son was to have in 1916. Canonicity with a vengeance! See Bliss Perry, *And Gladly Teach* (Boston, 1935), 38–41.

27. See Oakley, *Community of Learning*, 105–6, for a comment on this odd phenomenon.

28. See Arthur Levine and Jeanette Cureton, "The Quiet Revolution: Eleven Facts about Multiculturalism and the Curriculum," *Change* 24 (January-February 1992): 25–29; "Change Trendlines: Signs of a Changing Curriculum," *Change 24* (January-February 1992): 49–52.

29. *Music in the Undergraduate Curriculum: A Reassessment*, Report of the Study Group on the Content of the Undergraduate Music Curriculum, CMS Report no. 7 (Boulder, Colo., 1989); *Survey of the Historical Profession: Academia 1981–82*, Summary Report, American Historical Association (Washington, D.C., 1984), 7–10; Charles B. Harris, "The ADE Ad Hoc Committee on the English Curriculum: A Progress Report," *ADE Bulletin* 85 (1986): 26–29; Bettina J. Huber and David Laurence, "Report on the 1984–85 Survey of the English Sample: General Education Requirements in English and the English Major," *ADE Bulletin* 87 (1989): 30–43; Bettina J. Huber, "Today's Literature Classroom: Findings from the MLA's 1990 Survey of Upper-Division Courses," *ADE Bulletin* 101 (1992): 34–60; Phyllis Franklin, Bettina J. Huber, and David Laurence, "Continuity and Change in the Study of Literature," *Change* 24 (January-February 1992), 42–48; Bettina J. Huber, "What's Being Read in Survey Courses? Findings from a 1990–91 MLA Survey of English Departments," *ADE Bulletin* 110 (1995): 40–48.

30. Huber, "Today's Literature Classroom," 46–58; Franklin et al., "Continuity and Change," 46–48.

31. Levine and Cureton, "The Quiet Revolution," 25–26; "Change Trendlines," 51, Chart 2.

32. "Change Trendlines," 51, Chart 1.

33. Levine and Cureton, "The Quiet Revolution," 29.

34. *Music in the Undergraduate Curriculum: A Reassessment*, especially 50–52 and Charts 14 and 15. For the statistical limitations of the survey data supporting these conclusions, see pp. 25–26.

35. *Survey of the Historical Profession: Academia 1981–82*, 7–10, Tables IA and IB.

36. See note 29.

37. See Morrisey et al., "Ideology and Literary Studies, Part II," 46–58.

38. Ibid., 57.

39. Huber and Laurence, "Report on the 1984–85 Survey of the English Sample," 30–36 and 43.

40. Ibid., 34–36 (especially Table 8) and 43.

41. Harris, "The ADE Ad Hoc Committee on the English Curriculum," 26–29. The year 1965 was the launching date of the National Survey of Undergraduate Programs in English," which was completed in 1970. Its results, which conveyed no sense of great change in the years preceding, were included in Thomas W. Wilcox, *The Anatomy of College English* (San Francisco, 1973).

42. See Robin Wilson, "Bennett: Colleges' 'Trendy Lightweights' Replace Classics with Nonsense," *Chronicle of Higher Education*, February 10, 1988, A27.

43. Huber, "Today's Literature Classroom," especially 39–46, 52–56, and Appendix A. Cf. Franklin et al., "Continuity and Change," 44–46.

44. Morrisey *et al.*, "Ideology and Literary Studies, Part II," 47.

45. See Christopher Clausen, "It Is Not Elitist to Place Major Literature at the Center of the English Curriculum," *Chronicle of Higher Education*, January 13, 1988, A52. This flip comment was picked up and treated as a piece of documented evidence by the *Wall Street Journal*, the *New Criterion*, and Dinesh D'Souza, and it was echoed glancingly or indirectly by others. See Edward Jayne, "Academic Jeremiad: The Neoconservative View of American Higher Education," *Change* 23 (May-June 1991): 30–41 (at 38), and, for the tracking down and demolition of this particular piece of mythology, Graff, *Beyond the Culture Wars*, 17–21.

46. Huber, "What's Being Read in Survey Courses?" 43–46, Tables 4 and 6.

47. Huber, "Today's Literature Classroom," 46–52; Franklin et al., "Continuity and Change," 46–48. There are also some (not very informative) data relating to instruction in music in *Music in the Undergraduate Curriculum: A Reassessment*, 42–46.

48. Huber, "Today's Literature Classroom," 46–50 (especially Tables 17, 19, and 20); Franklin et al., "Continuity and Change," 46–48.

49. This goal was phrased as "helping students to understand how reading exposes the impossibility of deciding whether meaning communicates a reality outside language." Morrisey et al., "Ideology and Literary Studies, Part II," 55, complain that "this last goal is stated in so dogmatic a fashion as must have repelled many who do in fact delight in deconstruction."

50. Huber, "Today's Literature Classroom," 46–50 (especially Tables 18, 21, and 22).

51. Morrisey et al., "Ideology and Literary Studies, Part II," 56–57.

52. Similarly, the prediction of Harold Howe (former U.S. Commissioner of Education) that by the year 2000 "every citizen in the United States [would] have an educational entitlement from the federal government of so many dollars . . . [to be] used any time during a person's life"; see "A Symposium: The State of the Humanities," *Change* 7 (Summer 1975): 70–87 (at 58 and 68). Or, a little earlier, Judson Jerome's dire predictions about the fate that would soon befall the university if it did not commit itself to a radical self-transformation; "The American Academy: 1970," *Change* 1 (September-October 1969): 10–47 (at 13).

53. Geoffrey Barraclough, *Main Trends in History* (New York and London, 1979), especially 1–18, 30–45, and 89–94. "The search for quantity," he says (at 89), "is beyond a doubt the most powerful of the new trends in history, the factor above all others which distinguishes historical attitudes in the 1970s from historical attitudes in the 1930s."

54. On which see Francis Oakley, *Omnipotence, Covenant, and Order: An Excursion in the History of Ideas from Abelard to Leibniz* (Ithaca and London, 1984), 18–40.

55. Thus Alvin Kernan, *The Death of Literature* (New Haven and London, 1990), 213, in the course of arguing more generally that "for all their appearances of being new, the radical criticisms of recent years are in fact only hypertrophied extensions of old literary values."

56. For this last, see the interesting analysis by Lydia Goehr, "Writing Music History," *History and Theory* 31, no. 2 (1992): 182–99.

57. Charles Bernheimer in Bernheimer, ed., *Comparative Literature in the Age of Multiculturalism* (Baltimore and London, 1995), 16. For related cautions from other humanities fields and subfields about any too unreflective an adoption of the contextualist tactic, see Bhikhu Parekh and R. N. Berki, "The History of Political Ideas: A Critique of Quentin Skinner's Methodology," *Journal of the History of Ideas* 34, no. 2 (1973), 163–84; David Boucher, *Texts in Context: Revisionary Methods for Studying the History of Ideas* (Dordrecht, 1985), 255–56; Mark Bevir, "The Errors of Linguistic Contextualism," *History and Theory* 31, no. 2 (1992): 276–98. In any case, one cannot help feeling a twinge of sympathy for Richard Rorty's sense of generational calm about the fate of intellectual trends. See his comments in Peter Conn et al., *Viewpoints*, ACLS Occasional Paper no. 10 (New York, 1989), 12.

Four

Evolution and Revolution

CHANGE IN THE LITERARY HUMANITIES, 1968–1995

MARGERY SABIN

MANY reasonable consultants prescribe more debate as the best treatment for current symptoms of pathology in the humanities.[1] Debate therapy, however, in this case somewhat resembles the old fever cure. Rhetorical techniques such as caricature, imprecation, lament, and dire prophecy all win debate points in the humanities, but only while further raising our collective fever. The degree to which grandiose claims and spectacular accusations have in recent decades infected discussion of change in the humanities is itself a key symptom of a historical disorder that the method of debate can hardly hope to cure.

Any account of this history must, moreover, contend with the bewildering absence of a shared vocabulary among participants within the academy as well as between the academy and the public. Inflammatory reports to the general public often exploit the mystifying language that academics indulge in to impress each other.

Take, for example, the summer 1995 issue of the prestigious academic journal *New Literary History*, which collected a series of commentaries on the humanities under the rubric "Higher Education." Some of the up-to-date language here jumps even ahead of public doubt to discredit the academic enterprise it presumably intends to support. In "The University Without Culture?" Bill Readings starts from the asserted premise that "'Culture' no longer matters as an idea for the [liberal arts] institution. And along with culture goes the hero of the story, the individual intellectual. . . . It is no longer possible for an individual subject to claim to 'embody' the life of the mind—which has major implications for humanities research and teaching." "Indeed!" exclaim the legislator, the dean, the taxpayer, and the poor parent, warily assessing quite contrary claims in the glossy college prospectus.

Speaking the language of "postmodern pragmatism," Readings proceeds as though academic analysis had definitively buried "the individual subject" and decisively demonstrated the thorough subservience of the earlier university to the nation-state (now also declared obsolescent).

Readings's conclusion circles back to his premise: "the modern university is a ruined institution."[2] What differentiates his postmodern pragmatism from conservative hostility to the university is hardly more than a sanguineness of tone. With the help of certain sociologists of postmodernity, such as Jean-François Lyotard,[3] Readings judges the ruins to be habitable, even inviting. In metaphors that are more aesthetic than sociological, he compares the postmodern university to some Italian city: "we cannot seek to rebuild the Italian city-state, nor to destroy its remnants and install rationally planned tower-blocks, only to put its angularities and winding passages to new uses, seek to learn from and enjoy the cognitive dissonances that enclosed piazzas and nonsignifying *campanile* induce—and we have to worry about what our relation to tourism is."[4] The playfulness of the image is almost Jamesian—one thinks of the Prince in *The Golden Bowl*, fitting into the American millionaire Verver ménage like a Palladian church in an Italian town square. Cognitive dissonance in *The Golden Bowl*, however, foreshadows brutal struggles for power.

"After New Literary History and Theory? Notes on the MLA Hit Parade and the Currencies of Academic Exchange," Jonathan Beck's essay at the end of the *New Literary History* volume, construes postmodern pragmatism through metaphors taken from business. "What are today's (and tomorrow's) blue-chip issues?" he coaches students and young scholars to ask. The low market value of traditional scholarship, criticism, and teaching is to Beck a plain fact. Also obsolete is the idea, which he calls an "ideology," of choosing directions of work in the humanities for any other than marketplace reasons. "The ideology formerly dominant in academe sought to banish vulgar considerations of the marketplace to the less noble confines of business. To say 'formerly dominant' is to register the fact that such views today are associated with what are called conservative values."[5]

In the world outside academe, of course, an exclusively marketplace mentality all too precisely identifies currently dominant "conservative" values. Beck's pragmatism reduces academic work to just another fiercely competitive business of profits and promotion. Look sharp, he warns: "As you look ahead to the balance sheets compiled by individuals and committees who count up your production and evaluate your contribution, you would do well to pay more attention—more than previous academics paid, or had to pay—to what it will take, in a changing market with a floating currency, to make your writing count, countable, counted." In a voice that unwittingly echoes the overaccommodating Jesuit priest in James Joyce's ironic story "Grace," Beck's metaphors erase all tension between material and other values. To identify the unabashed embrace of the marketplace in the humanities with radical liberation from "conservative" ideology is political double-talk. Even taken allegorically, an eye focused too sharply on the "currencies of academic exchange" is and always was likely to issue in alienated as well as derivative intellectual work.

In this essay I reassess some of the changes during the past quarter century that have produced our current predicament. The main phases of the sequence have become excessively familiar: radical social protest in the late 1960s; deconstruction in the 1970s; ethnic, feminist, and Marxist cultural studies in the 1980s; postmodern sexuality in the 1990s; and rampant careerism from beginning to end. What else is there to say?

Relying on the interpretation of language that remains the principal expertise of the literary humanities, I have selected a few exemplary texts—from mundane documents such as course catalogues to the more high-flown self-representations offered at institutional gatherings, such as those of the Modern Language Association (MLA)—as markers of the rhetorical and structural changes in the literary humanities during the past twenty-five years. Although some of my examples point to the repudiation of what I will be calling literary reading, I cite at the end two current teaching programs that exemplify how innovation and tradition can be and are being effectively integrated in some current approaches to reading and writing in the humanities. One is the current undergraduate English curriculum at a private, liberal arts college; the other is a basic reading and writing course for underprepared students at a large university. Although not guaranteeing these examples as "blue-chip" stocks, I aim to counter the widespread impression that implacable forces have shattered continuity with the past, like it or not.

First, the perception of ruin. The image of a curricular city-state in ruins might well emerge from contrast between the past and present English major at Amherst College, preeminent among undergraduate colleges at least from the 1940s for the distinction of its English program, before the tumult of the late 1960s began to threaten not only its curriculum but its very identity as an all-male, mostly white and upper-middle-class private college. In the Amherst department of English, the powerful currents of the era gained particular force because of the simultaneous loss (through job shifts, retirements, and death) of faculty leaders, such as Robert Frost, Reuben Brower, and the redoubtable Theodore Baird.

I begin by naming names because the vitality of the old Amherst English, like that of virtually any coherent curriculum, depended on the inspiring conviction of particular individuals rather than on the universal or enduring truth of their ideas. Brower's influence gave New Critical formalism at Amherst a pragmatic flexibility and improvisational flair more indebted to the English models of I. A. Richards, William Empson, and F. R. Leavis than to the American codifications of Brooks and Warren. Robert Frost's force as pedagogical performer as well as poet introduced a distinctively New England tonality: irreverent, colloquial, individualistic.[6] Theodore Baird, who staunchly upheld his individual right to embody the life of the mind, kept the whole college for twenty-five years under the sway of his innovative composition course, in which the only texts were his own elaborate sequence of assignments, designed to develop speculative rigor about the complex relations among language, perception, and the varieties of what we call reality.[7]

The Amherst catalogue of any year from the end of World War II through the late 1960s shows the English department building upon a strong and uniform foundation. In addition to the year-long writing course required of every student, the English major required another two-semester sequence of "critical reading," taught (like the composition course) by both senior and junior faculty with a single syllabus and assignments hammered out together in staff meetings.[8] Contrary to commonplace generalizations about the total split between close reading and literary history, a third two-course survey, "English Literary History," was also required of English majors during some of these years; its reading list followed the chronology of major writers from Chaucer to the early twentieth century.

This model, it should be noted, bears little resemblance to and in some ways directly opposes in content and method the rival idea (equally strong on certain other campuses in this era) of a humanities curriculum in which universal truths are transmitted to students from on high through the great books of Western civilization.[9] Some recent pundits nostalgically forget that their own favorite city-states ruled very limited territories even in their heyday and coexisted with their neighbors in mutual suspicion, if not contempt. Nostalgia also tends to erase the dissidents within each city-state; Amherst alumni continue even now to argue about the merits of the structure they shared, and also about the rifts within it.

The least disputable truth purveyed by the old Amherst English curriculum was that literary study was a "discipline." A two-part comprehensive examination loomed over the senior year: the 1962–1963 catalogue describes Part I as factual, objective, and informational, testing "those regular habits of study through which the student of literature as a matter of course acquaints himself" with matters of fact. Part II was a version of the "sight reading" whose appalling results at Cambridge University in the 1920s had stimulated I. A. Richards's influential pedagogical reforms in *Practical Criticism* (1929). The Amherst catalogue gives no indication of whether its disciplined course of study produced better results. Although the examination expects a daunting degree of literary knowledge (more than most Ph.D. programs in English demand today), a colloquial informality combines threat and reassurance to imply that there is nothing arcane or specialized here, and that only the laziest of dunces will fail:

"The examination as a whole will ascertain whether students of American and English literature know, in the simplest and most obvious terms, where they have been and what they have been reading in their preceding semesters of study."[10]

After twenty-five years of gradual erosion and then eventual collapse, the 1994–1995 Amherst catalogue exemplifies one meaning of "revolution" in literary study during this period, beginning with its disclaimer about "English" as a distinct discipline of study at all: *Major Program. The English Department acknowledges that a variety of interests and motives leads students to declare a major in English and that a variety of disciplines and modes of study intersects within the curriculum of the Department.*" All the requirements are gone, as is the comprehensive examination. Students begin the major with one of ten semester courses. Only three of the ten resemble Amherst's old foundational course in close reading; they are all taught by the surviving older men from the *ancien régime.* The "new" faculty has decisively turned the department toward what is now called cultural studies, which means not only such new curricular content as film, television, advertising, child-rearing manuals, and tutoring at the local high school, but also new oppositional conceptions of the activity of reading itself, as in the course called "Writing and Everyday Reading: The course will approach reading as an act of consumption and appropriation."[11] For students who choose it as their introduction to the English major, literary study begins with a conception of reading itself as a suspect social act.

Before venturing a critique of Amherst's new interdisciplinary English major, I should pause to interject that as an undergraduate in the 1950s, I would not myself have chosen the old version, even if Amherst had admitted women, which it decisively did not. I avoided even the looser (if also more boring and neglectful) English major at Harvard-Radcliffe, repelled by its lists of unfamiliar names, its inert periodization, its tacit message that qualified students already knew where they were going and why. I chose instead the interdisciplinary major of modern History and Literature, a venerable undergraduate program instituted at Harvard back in the 1890s to cut through disciplinary boundaries already at that time regarded as restrictive.

It pains me to emphasize here my own undergraduate preference lest I seem disloyal to my eventual teaching apprenticeship in Humanities 6, the famous close reading course brought by Reuben Brower from Amherst to Harvard, a collaborative teaching experience that launched my career and permanently shaped my commitments as teacher and critic. But History and Literature enjoyed significant ties to the close reading pedagogy that was at that time marginalized in the Harvard English department. Brower was on the governing committee, and my teachers included young members of his staff: Richard Poirier, David Kalstone, Neil Hertz, Paul de Man, and the historian William R. Taylor.

Interdisciplinary study in the History and Literature program conveyed no intrinsic conflict between careful attention to explicit and implicit designs of language in literary and in historical inquiry. French history, as taught to me by Stanley Hoffmann, introduced economic, political, social, and ideological contexts for the great variety of texts in his course, "Modern French Society," but his methods of historical and political analysis were entirely congruent with literary study. At the same time, the interdisciplinary mixture of influences generated less mystique than the old Amherst English major about literary reading as a specialized intellectual operation to be performed on a special class of objects. Certain valuable forms of cognitive dissonance did result from moving between disciplines and across cultural divides. I found that the designs of language in modern French writing, for example, peculiarly resisted the attentiveness to social tone and verbal drama that counted for so much in my English studies. The stimulating suspicion that some English literary values were culture-bound, that French language and literature "worked" by different principles, contributed to the comparative investigation of French and English traditions that dominated my own work for the subsequent twenty years.

Reactions other than nostalgia for a purity that I chose to avoid in my own education thus inform my critique of the revisionary structures that Amherst's current English program exemplifies. The dichotomy between so-called nostalgic conservatism and the so-called radicalism of inter-disciplinarity disables rational discussion by erasing the variegated educational experiences that make up the actuality of so many individual histories, in an earlier generation as well as now.

Returning to the current Amherst English major, there is the conspicuous addition of multicultural literary courses that are the easiest of the new features to endorse, because this change is expansive rather than undermining. The literary curriculum is now richer for including women writers not mentioned in Amherst's old curriculum (Willa Cather, Gertrude Stein, Zora Neale Hurston) as well as the literature of ethnic minorities ("Major African-American Authors," "Jewish Writers in America," "Contemporary Literature by Asian-Americans and Latinos"). Several courses that recognize film as a major contemporary performing art form also enlarge without subverting the English department's traditional curricular commitments. Initial dismay that the proliferation of so many new courses has obliterated earlier literary subjects diminishes somewhat once allowance is made for the oversell of the catalogue's new marketing technique. Four of the eight film courses listed were "omitted" from the curriculum of 1994–1995, as were six of the eight African or African American courses and four of the five other multicultural offerings. The pared-down actuality of the taught curriculum at Amherst in 1994–1995 looks considerably less revolutionary than it did at first glance because of the inflated packaging of the program. *Caveat emptor.*

What then has really been lost? First, there is the virtually total separation between the traditional literary courses taught by the "old" Amherst faculty and the new courses taught by the young. This conspicuous segregation spells trouble for both the present and the future.[12] No collaborative activity appears to be preparing the future faculty to carry forward the literary reading of major writers after the impending retirements of the senior holdovers. Even now, since the old close reading course remains only one of several entirely unrelated introductory courses, the students have no common foundation of skills and the whole curriculum has become in a sense introductory. Regardless of numbering in the course sequence, many of the new course descriptions emphasize their introductory character: "Studies in the Literature of Sexuality: The course aims to introduce students to contemporary discourse concerning the literature of sexuality"; "Native American Expressive Traditions: The course is intended as an introduction to the verbal artifacts in the expressive traditions of several native North American cultures."

Even more striking, the familiar interdisciplinary linkages *within* the humanities—such as those between literature and history, between literature and the other arts, or between one culture and language and another—have given way to connections primarily with the social sciences. Cultural studies derives its self-descriptive vocabulary from poststructuralist sociology, anthropology, neo-Marxism, and neo-Freudian psychoanalysis, often without explicit notice of what relation specific theories or methodologies bear to traditional work in the humanities (or, for that matter, to the social science disciplines themselves). Indeed, the term *interdisciplinary* itself seems a misnomer in courses in which methodologies derived from the social sciences are simply *applied* to cultural artifacts, some of which happen to be from literature.

It takes considerable experience in the close reading of current cultural theory, moreover, to identify the ideological arguments embedded in some course descriptions as premises or established truth, as in the course "British Fiction: Colonialism, Class, and Representation: A study of fiction, in both the novel and film, which seeks to rigorously re-examine the twin conceits of class and empire upon which British identity is built."[13] The rhetoric here promises pedagogical skepticism in the phrase "rigorously re-examine," but the syntax leaves the object of reexamination peculiarly elusive. Grammatically, the object of reexamination is not the provocative assertion that British identity rests on (nothing but?) class and empire, nor is fiction itself the object. In what sense will the "twin conceits of class and empire" be "*re*-examined," since it is this sentence itself that initiates the punning notion of them as "twin conceits"? Does not this language convert an identifiable theory, really an accusation against British culture, into a premise rather than an object of examination?

Whereas the old style of the Amherst catalogue gloved its coerciveness in colloquial language, obscure pseudo-hypotheses more elaborately disguise a new coerciveness in the cultural studies courses; for example: "The Politics of the Gothic in the English Novel: Taking 'the gothic' to mean that moment when human subjectivity is formed under the pressure of being looked at, this course considers the structural and ideological role of the gothic in eighteenth-century English fiction about marriage."[14] What undergraduate (or reader of this essay, for that matter) understands this vaguely Lacanian language well enough to take (or reject) the premise of this course? What secret rhetorical code unlocks the definition of a literary genre as a "moment when human subjectivity is formed under the pressure of being looked at?" Whose idea is that?

The most generous interpretation of the jargon that clots the new cultural studies curriculum is that it resembles (and may in fact be) the language of dissertation abstracts produced for the academic commodities market in accord with Beck's investment counsel. Competition in the academic marketplace presses young scholars to double-market their specialized products; bids for publication double as courses for undergraduates, as young scholars mimic the economies of their graduate school mentors. The scramble for space on the overcrowded cutting edge leaves neither time nor will for a whole staff together to hammer out educational goals and language appropriate to them.

The historical dynamic of this situation involves the undergraduate curriculum in a larger professional situation to be understood only in relation to graduate programs and the official institutions that determine the academic currencies of the moment. Whether in self-congratulation or lament, most observers of our recent history agree that the dramatic shift in the currency for literary study occurred at the end of the 1960s, when political and social protest joined with the importation of continental theory to shatter Anglo-American literary authority. In looking back at the MLA record of this institutional history, the significant revolutionary event occurred not in the glory days of 1968, when a radical professor from MIT was elected to presidential succession after his arrest by police for mounting an antiwar poster at the MLA convention, but the following year, when more lasting barricades were constructed between Old and New, Backward and Advanced, within the academic profession itself. The internal rupture outlasted the precipitating crises of the political moment as well as the also temporary allegiances of many individuals involved. What remains from

the painful confrontations of that era is mainly the structure of confrontation itself and the exaggeration of personal and substantive opposition in
the heat of polarized public debate.

One session at the 1969 MLA featured, among the spokesmen for
radical challenge, the young Frederick Crews, already prominent in his
mid-thirties for writings that included a psychoanalytic study of Hawthorne. The rhetorical question of Crews's title, "Do Literary Studies Have
an Ideology?" mounted the challenge whose unrelenting repetitions and
oversimplifications in the following decades would eventually drive the
mature Frederick Crews across the barricades in disgust. In the bliss of
protest in 1969, however, Crews embraced oversimplification for the sake
of a good cause. "The temptation to self-righteousness on this issue is
strong," he acknowledged at the beginning of his speech, only to quip,
"and after a few precautionary paragraphs I am going to succumb to it."

The form taken by Crews's self-righteousness at the 1969 MLA was a
patchwork of Marxist indictments of so-called capitalist scholarship. Having newly learned that capitalism perverts scholarship for "purposes of
exploitation and conquest," he felt like begging his fellow professors to
"drop the scales from their eyes" and see that the function of "capitalist
scholarship" was to foster "compliance with disguised class governance."
Putting to the side his own considerable professional success through the
unorthodox methodology of psychoanalytic criticism, he generalized the
ideological coerciveness of the profession into "the sweeping imperative to
prostrate ourselves before literature's autonomous emanations of meaning." After a few concessions to the unfortunate reality that the bureaucra-
cies of "present-day socialism" sanctioned only criticism that was "simple-
minded and venal," Crews nevertheless went on to disparage all "the old
legitimations for conventional work—objectivity, neutrality, humanistic
values, 'culture'" and predicted that "the best critics in the immediate
future will reject such escapism and demand that works be understood,
not as transcendent icons and refuges from the world, but as contingent,
imperfect expressions of social and mental forces."[15]

Whatever the accuracy of Crews's (after all, moderate) prediction for
the future, it is his distortion of the present that stands out with irony in
relation to the occasion itself. For the president of the MLA in 1969,
official guardian of what Crews called capitalist scholarship's "sweeping
imperative," was no New Critical formalist or conservative philologist, but
Crews's own older colleague at Berkeley, Henry Nash Smith, the progressive critic whose compelling and influential book, *Virgin Land: The American West as Symbol and Myth* (1950), had brought him recognition as
one of the founders of interdisciplinary American studies.[16] Far from
prostrating himself before "literature's autonomous emanations of meaning," in Crews's phrase, Smith had two decades before virtually invented

the technique of examining social ideology through the juxtaposition of subliterary material, such as the "Dime Novel," and canonical literature and historiography.[17] His career exemplified precisely the kind of criticism that Crews was stridently demanding; recognition of his contribution had been honored, moreover, through his election to the presidency of the MLA.

The presidency of the MLA in 1969 was, to be sure, a dubious prize. Turning to Smith's presidential address, the question shifts to why such a veteran progressive could not effectively defuse the dynamic of confrontation. The complexity of his own allegiances comes across as a confession of ineffectuality in the circumstances. As leader of an organization that he was himself willing to criticize, and in a profession that he valued short of idealization, Smith tried to respond to the radical challenge with good will, relying on a number of tactics that would become familiar among beleaguered liberals in subsequent years: concessive humor, in taking the title of his speech from a Bob Dylan song, "Something Is Happening But You Don't Know What It Is, Do You, Mr. Jones?"; deflationary wryness in the suggestion that maybe what looked like part of a "worldwide revolution against capitalism and technology" would turn out to be only "a pressure group of younger members." Most significantly, he did not dismiss as ludicrous the questioning of "received ideas." He discriminated, however, between justified criticism of the official literary institution and sweeping radical repudiation of "objectivity" in scholarship and teaching. He defined his own position as somewhere in the hapless middle of "inglorious liberalism," which he elucidated by remarking that "neither the conventional claim to disinterestedness nor the radical claim to superior morals and definitive insight can be accepted at face value." Far from claiming heroic force for his liberalism, he apologized for "the platitudes" in the truth that "all political activity involves some degree of guilt. Absolute purity is unattainable; but to fail of perfection is not necessarily to accept total corruption."

The failure of Smith's speech, at least in the professional debate as it was already becoming structured, may be summarized as the polemical weakness of complexity in a dynamic of confrontation. In response to radical demands for "action," Smith reflected on the complex relations between different kinds of "action" and the study and teaching of literature. He enacted in his own language the tensions between scholarship and social reform.

Perhaps the most painful and representative consequence of Smith's honorable refusal to meet self-righteousness on its own ground was the way his "inglorious liberalism" left the rhetorical field open to simpler polarizations. Before his speech was done, Smith himself got trapped in the polarization of radicals against "the Establishment," for example when he made the error of giving over the responsibility for change to the other side: "in challenging the Establishment the radicals incur an obligation to propose" solutions, he said, and then again, "the critics of conventional procedures seem to me to owe us more explanation than they have so far provided."[18] Out of fatigue, or irritation, or perhaps accurate recognition that he could not possibly reshape the debate at that time from such a platform, what should have been a strong voice for reform on the basis of a complex understanding of the relations between literature and politics ended up sounding too much like a defensive apology for "conventional procedures" and the official Establishment ("us"). As in so many areas of national life since the 1960s, the energy of liberalism fell short at a crucial moment of conflict.

Impatience with the seeming ineffectuality of complexity as an intellectual value pervades the issue of the *PMLA* reporting the 1969 convention. A letter from an instructor of English at Youngstown State University complained that "the experience of literature is used to reinforce a sense of helpless awe before the complexity of our culture."[19] Even the advertisers in the *PMLA* had gotten wind of the diagnosis that English literary study induced passivity and prostration. Many of the new textbooks of 1969 quickly adopted the tonic of revolutionary confrontation. Macmillan, for example, offered *The Rhetoric of Revolution*, a composition text with selections "chosen to motivate the student" by pitting revolutionary against contrarevolutionary polemic. Contrarevolutionaries are at least activists. Even textbooks and anthologies without identifiable political topics capitalized on activist rhetoric by calling themselves revolutionary. More disturbing than the frequently lamented politicization of literature, these advertisements began the emptying out of political meaning from political language that is now endemic in the profession.

What is most revolutionary in the rhetoric of 1969 is the model it promotes of thought and language itself: instead of encouraging qualified differentiation and attention to dilemmas warranted by conflicting values or complex realities, critical thinking itself becomes a version of activist confrontation. Thus, from the Free Press there is the anthology *From Left to Right*, whose aim is "to present, as it were, three minds in collision . . . a series of confrontations of first-rate thinkers."[20] Confrontation became established as advanced intellectual style in 1969, and it has survived many permutations, from antiwar protest to deconstructionist *aporia* (not an ambiguity or a tension but an internal collision of meanings) and the *alterity* of postcolonial cultural theory.

Aggressive and adversarial gestures of language came to dominate competition within "advanced" critical discourse in the 1970s, especially in combination with new collective alliances and repudiations. Thus in his preface to a volume entitled *Literature and Society*, drawn from English

Institute papers in 1978, Edward Said struck out a set of new positions with a scorched earth strategy. After describing the previous decade's successful displacement of primary literary texts by metacritical speculation, Said simultaneously affiliated himself with deconstruction and already repudiated it as a new orthodoxy, "mindlessly followed by a whole band of academic enthusiasts" writing "a highly rarified jargon." Although echoing the objections to deconstructionist theory made by many literary critics and scholars all through the 1970s, Said extended no olive branch to what he called the "rather empty standpoint of 'humanistic' scholarship." On the contrary, the one unqualified accomplishment of deconstruction for Said was that it knocked "humanistic" criticism out of the field. Said repeated the aggressive gestures of repudiation so conspicuous at the 1969 MLA meeting: he dismissively caricatured all earlier literary scholarship and criticism as nothing but "a discredited conservative philosophy of gentlemanly refinement, or sensibility." His English Institute volume, he insisted, was the very opposite of "backward-looking." His polarization disallowed any qualities from the past to help against the drive to new orthodoxies; he was bent on carrying the cultural revolution further through a new "collective act of critical consciousness."[21]

Editors of the annual English Institute papers from before the revolutionary era tended to disavow collectivity, even while they sought principles of coherence for the separate papers in their volumes. In 1968, although the Berkeley Renaissance scholar, Norman Rabkin, tentatively organized the essays in his volume, *Reinterpretations of Elizabethan Drama*, around one new phrase of the moment, "reader response," he also quickly backed off to remark on "the horror" his contributors would have in being lumped together for a "manifesto."[22] Reuben Brower, in the crisis year of 1969, insisted almost obsessively that the only commitment shared by the contributors to his volume, *Forms of Lyric*, is to "flexibility of approach" and "immediacy of response to the poems." He even dropped the abstracting and collectivizing definite article from the original conference session, "Forms of *the* lyric," in order to guard against "the possibility that we may freeze the life of the poem into lifeless formula."[23] In Said's volume, the self-conscious individuality of editors such as Rabkin and Brower gives way to the solidarity defined by one of his contributors, Terry Eagleton, as the struggle between "dominant and oppositional ideologies."[24]

The aggressive shift from individual to collective projects in literary criticism paradoxically marks its least oppositional feature, despite the Marxist flavor of its rhetoric. In our competitive society, the ethos of group power increasingly dominates every area from business to medicine to myriad self-help groups. The anomaly has until recently been the unaffiliated scholar-critic in the humanities, nurturing the luxury of independence from oppressive group conformity; one of my older colleagues in his youth returned to the academy from a foray into corporate engineering, in order to be "alone in a room with a book," as he likes to say.

Upon closer inspection, to be sure, this myth of independent reading and writing proves almost as much of an exaggeration as the contrary claim that collective acts of consciousness in the humanities represent radical novelty. Even James Joyce, in his courageous exile, promoted his literary power through the formation of critics, journals, and publicists into a group around him. Many supporters of literary values have been slow to overcome their phobia of group activity. The daunting challenge for any new groups—there are signs of several—will be how to avoid entrapment in the reductive dichotomy between Old and New, Backward and Advanced, that has heretofore kept independent-minded scholars and critics in their private studies, alone or with the consolation of a few friends. This lockout is itself a trap that can be sprung only through persistent, energetic collaborations to redefine the essential features of literary study in fresh terms. The difference between collaborative and collective activity is itself a distinction that needs further comment as we describe the relations among writers in the past, and even among ourselves. It is precisely the kind of distinction that can free us from dead-end debates between defenders of the individual and champions of the group.

My concluding examples of collaborative teaching efforts display two models of effective adaptation to change without inflated and self-destructive calls to arms. First, the English curriculum at Williams College, a private liberal arts college occupying a spot virtually identical to that of Amherst in the structure of higher education, but interesting for the conspicuous difference of response to the same current pressures and opportunities.

Comparison of the current to the past structure of the curriculum in English at Williams shows much less drastic change than at Amherst. The 1971 catalogue rather blandly proposed a curriculum that "enables students to explore English and American literature from a variety of perspectives." The very looseness of the old Williams program perhaps facilitated change in a department whose earlier identity was less distinctive, less coherent than that of Amherst. For better and worse, there seems to have been less to defend in Williams's old English curriculum, so that change could occur with less trauma. Already by 1971, a smattering of the new subjects of film, African American literature, and cultural criticism had entered the English department. Currently, an expanded literary canon, theory, and cultural criticism coexist within what is still a recognizably literary program, beginning with a required semester introduction to "the close reading of poetry, prose fiction, and drama through the study of several major writers." Descriptions of traditional courses in literary interpretation show a visible effort to sustain literary values without being backward, as in one of the seminars for majors: "Renaissance Lyric Dialogues; Donne, Shakespeare and Herbert: Whereas modern poets such as Eliot encourage us to think of the lyric as 'the voice of the poet speaking to himself or nobody,' these three great English Renaissance love poets all use poetry as a means of communicating their most private thoughts to friends, lovers or a very intimate God—and as a way of contributing to passionate political debates over courtship, worship, gender, and power."

This associate professor has made interesting choices of language. She holds on to "great," but does not force the opposition between evaluative judgment and political debates in and about poetry. Explicit acknowledgment that conceptions of poetry change coexists with continuing enthusiasm for the poetry written in the past, and not merely to provide an exercise in opposition to dead white males. The poets survive by name, moreover, and as contributors not only to political debate but also to a literary category called "lyric." Neither poets nor poems have been displaced to the undifferentiated and anonymous category of "texts." At the same time, the description accepts responsibility for stimulating fresh interest in these poems, rather than relying on legislated requirements. She stoops to advertise, but in language that in itelf suggests complexity to be part of what this course offers: "Witty, erotic, exalted, and political, Donne's *Songs and Sonnets*, Shakespeare's *Sonnets*, and Herbert's *The Temple* comprise some of the most highly wrought and fascinatingly elusive lyrics in the English language."

Equally impressive as the renovation of traditional literature courses at Williams (taught by both junior and senior faculty) is the English department's success in adapting current topics in cultural studies to the conceptual framework of literary study. One among many striking examples is another seminar for majors, called "Violence and Narrative":

> Postmodern, anti-humanist theorists are now saying these inflammatory things about narrative itself: that it is death-oriented (Peter Brooks), violence-driven (Leo Bersani), given over to control and domination (D. A. Miller, Nancy Armstrong). Two critics, using Jane Austen as their counter-intuitive example, go so far as to venture that violence outside of texts (such as warfare) cannot be distinguished from the violence *of* texts. This is not to say that some texts are violent; it is to say that writing and reading are necessarily violent. We shall test this set of notions. Readings will include essays by the theorists just mentioned and a few theorists of violence and control *per se* (Clausewitz, Foucault, Scarry). The primary texts will include a few chosen for their violence . . . and a few chosen for their apparent tranquility (by Henry James and Jane Austen).[25]

What keeps this interdisciplinary inquiry within the purview of the humanities is the way the course assigns human authorship to theory as much as to lyric poetry and narrative fiction. The attribution of controversial propositions to named critics and theorists introduces them while delimiting the authority of mystifying theorized language. Literary theorists offer not scientific models to *apply* to texts, but controversial and sometimes deliberately inflammatory propositions. Clearly differentiated readings in both primary and theoretical texts prepare the student to "test" theoretical ideas, rather than merely submitting in advance to obscure pseudo-hypotheses. These descriptive principles appear so consistently within the Williams catalogue that they amount to a departmental policy. The result is a literary program crowded with names, titles, and controversies. "Struggles" refer not only to collisions between minds, or between dominant and oppositional ideologies, but also to a variety of mental activities within individual minds and the language of particular writings.

One would need of course to unwrap the attractive packaging of such courses to assess them. What is the actual quality of the readings taught and learned? Students will be able to test difficult critical theories on primary works of literature only if they have supple and subtle reading habits, an accomplishment that depends more on the quality of their professors' talent, graduate training, and methods of teaching reading than on the course description or syllabus. If new faculties of literature have in their own graduate education been directed to invest most of their time in mastering property law, the economics of Victorian publishing, and Lacanian psychoanalysis, their own literary knowledge and skill in reading poems, plays, and novels will remain crude, as any reader of current job applications can testify is ever more the case. Young literary scholars are cruelly caught between the pressure to rush into print with their amateur forays into economics, psychology, anthropology, and so forth and their need—possibly even their desire—to advance their reading of literature beyond its undergraduate limits. The students of this poorly educated faculty, in turn, will be inevitably deprived of the literary experience necessary to test the hostility to literature promulgated by much advanced theory.[26] Nevertheless, the catalogue itself at Williams represents an impressive integration of old and new, as does the spread across the faculty of responsibility for teaching literature as well as theory and cultural texts.

The "Basic Reading and Writing Course" (BRW) at the University of Pittsburgh, invented and described by David Bartholomae and Anthony Petrosky, shifts attention to an entirely different area of the humanities and to a different institutional and demographic situation. It would take more than an essay to represent the structural changes of the past decades that have in many cases detached expository writing from its former caretakers in English departments. A separate, huge industry, with its own new graduate degrees, journals, conferences, and profitable publishing contracts, now carries on its own debates between old and new, backward and advanced. Although expository writing is the fastest-growing area of instruction in the humanities, its faculty suffers more than the rest from the oppressive conditions now spreading through the whole American labor force: part-time work, low benefits, low pay, subjection to mechanical measurements of productivity. And at the bottom of the hierarchy in expository writing is the basic writing course, a euphemism for the structure assigned to carry the ever-growing population of underprepared students into the democratic promise of higher education made by liberals and radicals twenty-five years ago.

The low status of basic writing in the university has resulted in peculiar if predictable incongruities. The natural alliance between the writing faculty and the students based on their shared class consciousness often breaks down because of divergent aspirations. Short of taking to the streets together, the routes out of oppression for the radical wing of the writing movement and the students it serves point in different directions. For the faculty, professional success means investing in the same stocks of avant-garde radicalism—poststructuralism, social constructionism, and cultural materialism—that have brought such profitable returns to their prosperous colleagues elsewhere in the humanities. The students, no less legitimately seeking prosperity, know that they need to develop the skills to succeed in the academic tasks demanded for their degree, to say nothing of the work world outside academe. But neither the "expressive" pedagogies notably associated with Peter Elbow in the 1970s nor the more recent neo-Marxist disclosure of academic writing as hegemonic cultural appropriation offers a conceptual basis for effective training in the writing required for academic work.[27] In the rest of the university, even the most radical professor of oppositional theory (or, more likely, the teaching assistant who does the grading) complains if student essays fail to demonstrate skills of analysis and sequential argument in grammatical prose.

David Bartholomae has persuasively argued out these issues in public debates and, with Anthony Petrosky and the staff of the writing course at Pittsburgh, in the compelling book, *Facts, Artifacts, and Counterfacts.* Bartholomae and Petrosky assert their primary commitment to student aspirations in strong terms: their course is "designed to give students access to the language and methods of the academy. It is not a course designed to make the academy—or its students—disappear."[28] This pragmatic position becomes controversial only in the shadows of extreme expressivist or oppositional dogma. Theories of the writing course as a "site" of either personal or collective insurrection often do seem intent upon erasing the university, or at least they abrogate responsibility for preparing their students to survive in such an oppressive place.

"Basic Reading and Writing" at Pittsburgh starts from the courageous recognition (pertinent to increasing numbers of students who are not classified as "remedial") that students trying to acquire some authority in their new roles as academic writers may need to begin from the beginning by inventing themselves as readers and writers. Bartholomae differentiates the reader as "composer" from a "decoder" who receives fixed transmitted meanings (such as "the main idea"). A reader, in this pedagogy, is a person who is composing and recomposing the text by selecting details, para-phrasing, translating, generalizing, organizing a new narrative, and recog-nizing relationships with other authorities who have written and read in the same field. An elaborate structure of assignments, exercises, discus-sion, and readings of progressive complexity turns the entire course into a laboratory of investigation into the nature of authority in language.

Resemblances between the theory and organization of "Basic Reading and Writing" at Pittsburgh and Baird's old Amherst course become less surprising in light of I. A. Richards's influence on both.[29] Bartholomae departs from both Richards's and Baird's speculative investigation of meaning in language, however, by staying focused on the pragmatic and social conditions of making meaning in language. With the help of theo-rists such as Hans-Georg Gadamer and Paulo Freire, in addition to Richards, he develops a model of authority in language that is another version of postmodern pragmatism: eclectic, skeptical, practical, bent on using inquiry into the nature of authority in language for the purpose of developing the authority of students themselves as writers. "Who speaks such words," the course keeps asking of published writing as well as of student work, "and why is it that he would want to talk to the rest of us in those terms?"[30]

Under the pressure of debate with Elbow, Bartholomae classifies himself with the radical opposition, teaching students "the power politics of discursive practice," while he places Elbow with "traditional humanism" in his ideal of "independent, self-creative, self-expressive subjectivity."[31] In the details of the teaching project, however, this exaggerated dichotomy disappears. As at Williams, the essentially literary and humanistic nature of Bartholomae's approach to reading and writing is in the emphasis on authorship in language: who chooses to speak certain words and why. Authors make meanings through their choice and arrangement of words.

From 1968 until recently, ambitious, aggressive energies in the human-ities fed on the perception of a monolithic traditional structure, which served as a kind of backboard for the play of challenge and protest. That structure, never as firm or uniform as portrayed, has now crumbled from neglect as much as from battering. Left to market forces alone, mergers and acquisitions by the social sciences to which the humanities has itself yielded authority will continue to erode the intellectual, the aesthetic, and (not least) the professional identity of literary study.[32] New energy for reconstruction thus seems more important at this time than the sharpening of conflict within a shrinking and weakened territory. Although no single authority may any longer lay total claim to the definition of literary study, more agreement would likely follow upon adequate realization that the continuing life of the entire field depends on what it offers as a discipline in itself and as a contribution to interdisciplinary study. In the current configuration of dominant and oppositional forces in academe, argument on behalf of literary study has become the subversive position, especially for young aspirants to a career, requiring of them independence and risk. Those in a position to influence academic currency now have the obligation to reconsider the distinctiveness of humanistic reading and writing that can no longer be taken for granted.

Notes

1. See Gerald Graff, *Beyond the Culture Wars: How Teaching the Conflicts Can Revitalize American Education* (New York: Norton, 1992); William Cain, ed., *Teaching the Conflicts: Gerald Graff, Curricular Reform, and the Culture Wars* (New York: Garland, 1994); Francis Oakley, *Community of Learning: The American College and the Liberal Arts Tradition* (New York: Oxford University Press, 1992), 159–65.

2. *New Literary History* 26 (1995): 465–92 (at 467 and 480).

3. Jean-François Lyotard, *The Postmodern Condition: A Report on Knowledge*, tr. Geoffrey Bennington and Brian Massumi (Minneapolis: University of Minnesota Press, 1984) and *Political Writings* (Minneapolis: University of Minnesota Press, 1993); Readings also cites Samuel Weber, *Institution and Interpretation* (Minneapolis: University of Minnesota Press, 1989).

4. Readings, "The University Without Culture?" 480.

5. *New Literary History* 26 (1995): 695–709 (at 706–7, 702, and 706).

6. See Richard Poirier, *Poetry and Pragmatism* (Cambridge, Mass.: Harvard University Press, 1992), 186–93.

7. See Walker Gibson, "Theodore Baird," in *Traditions of Inquiry*, ed. John Brereton (New York: Oxford University Press, 1985), 136–52, and William Pritchard, *English Papers: A Teaching Life* (St. Paul, Minn.: Graywolf Press, 1995), 21–26.

8. Pritchard, *English Papers*, 114–22.

9. The model of the great books curriculum at the University of Chicago informs Alan Bloom's ideal of a humanities curriculum in *The Closing of the American Mind* (New York: Simon & Schuster, 1987). Pritchard, *English Papers*, 18–20, describes the great books course included in Amherst's "New Curriculum," instituted in 1947, which was a humanities course separate from the English department. Famous curricular variants of great books courses continue at Columbia College and St. Johns College.

10. *Amherst College Bulletin, 1962–63* (Amherst, Mass., 1962), 83.

11. *Amherst College Bulletin, 1994–95* (Amherst, Mass., 1994), 132 and 135.

12. Pritchard, *English Papers*, 172–77, comments on this division.

13. *Amherst College Bulletin, 1994–95*, 145.

14. Ibid., 138.

15. *PMLA* 85 (1970): 423, 426, and 428. Crew's study of Hawthorne was *The Sins of the Fathers: Hawthorne's Psychological Themes* (New York: Oxford University Press, 1966). Crews reassesses his own earlier psychoanalytic criticism in relation to his current critique of the literary academy in the afterword to the 1988 reprinting of *The Sins of the Fathers*, also reprinted in *The Critics Bear It Away: American Fiction and the Academy* (New York: Random House, 1992), 3–15. His conception of "truly liberal criticism" in the introduction to *The Critics Bear It Away* comes very close to Henry Nash Smith's position in 1969.

16. Posthumous recognition of Smith's influence appears in Beverly R. Voloshin, ed., *American Literature, Culture, and Ideology: Essays in Memory of Henry Nash Smith*, American University Studies, series 24, vol. 8 (New York: Peter Lang, 1990).

17. Henry F. May, "The Rough Road to Virgin Land," in Voloshin, *American Literature, Culture, and Ideology*, 1–23.

18. Smith, *PMLA* 85 (1970): 417 and 421.

19. Mark J. Curran, *PMLA* 85 (1970): 306, 342, and 359.

20. *PMLA* 85 (1970): 342, 359.

21. Edward W. Said, preface to *Literature and Society: Selected Papers from the English Institute 1978*, ed. Edward W. Said, new series, no. 3 (Baltimore, Md.: Johns Hopkins University Press, 1980), ix and xi.

22. Norman Rabkin, foreword to *Reinterpretations of Elizabethan Drama: Selected Papers from the English Institute 1968*, ed. Norman Rabkin (New York: Columbia University Press, 1969), vii.

23. Reuben A. Brower, foreword to *Forms of Lyric: Selected Papers from the English Institute 1969*, ed. Reuben A. Brower (New York: Columbia University Press, 1970), viii and vii.

24. Terry Eagleton, "Text, Ideology, Realism," in Said, *Literature and Society*, 172.

25. *Williams College Bulletin, 1994–95* (Williamstown, Mass., 1994), 163, 172, and 173.

26. See Margery Sabin, "The Debate: Seductions and Betrayals in Literary Study," *Raritan* 12, no. 3 (1994): 123–46; "Literary Reading in Interdisciplinary Study," *Profession 95* (1995): 14–18.

27. Lillian Bridwell-Bowles, in her 1994 chair's address to the Conference on College Composition and Communication, discusses the professional advantages and the pedagogical problems associated with "professionalizing and theorizing" composition studies by aligning it with such theoretical developments as "feminist theory, multicultural and postcolonial theory, poststructuralism." See Bridwell-Bowles, "Freedom, Form, Function: Varieties of Academic Discourse," *Journal of the Conference on College Composition and Communication* 46 (1995): 46–61; see also James Berlin, "Composition Studies and Cultural Studies: Collapsing

Boundaries," in *Into the Field: Sites of Composition Studies*, ed. Anne Ruggles Gere (New York: Modern Language Association, 1993), 99–116.

28. See David Bartholomae, "Writing with Teachers: A Conversation with Peter Elbow," *Journal of the Conference on College Composition and Communication* 46 (1995): 62–71; Peter Elbow, "Being a Writer vs. Being an Academic: A Conflict in Goals: A Conversation with Peter Elbow," *Journal of the Conference on College Composition and Communication* 46 (1995): 72–83; and "Interchanges: Responses to Bartholomae and Elbow," *Journal of the Conference on College Composition and Communication* 46 (1995): 84–107. See also Bartholomae, *Facts, Counterfacts, and Artifacts: Theory and Method for a Reading and Writing Course* (Portsmouth, N.H.: Boynton/Cook–Heinemann, 1986), 9.

29. See Ann E. Berthoff, "I. A. Richards," in *Traditions of Inquiry*, 50–80.

30. Bartholomae, *Facts, Counterfacts*, 34.

31. Bartholomae, "Writing with Teachers," 64.

32. John E. Bassett presents a more optimistic version of this loss of boundaries between the humanities and social sciences in "Confronting Change: English as a Social Science?" *College English* 57 (1995): 319–32.

BOOKS, LIBRARIES, READING

Five

Humanities and the Library in the Digital Age

CARLA HESSE

Libraries at the Crossroad

THE earliest evidence of library formation is a collection of Babylonian clay tablets from the twenty-first century B.C. But libraries have probably existed from the very moment humans began to make marks durable enough to be conserved. The fixing of significations in some durable material form made it possible for them to transcend the immediacy of experience, for them to be suspended above the flow of time in order to be revisited later, grouped and compared, reflected upon at greater length, or shared with people not immediately present. Inscription itself, of course, is not a mode of signification, but a mode of deferring the apprehension of signs by representing them in a fixed form. Library formation—the compilation of meaningful signs into larger and larger fixed groupings—is a logical extension of the impulse to transcend the immediacy and transparency of speech through forms of representation that make deferral possible.

The future of humanities scholarship in the twenty-first century A.D. will be intimately linked with the fate of our research libraries. This is so because from the very beginnings of human history libraries have been the principal repositories of the record of human knowledge and experience. They are our laboratories. And it is now clear that the modern research library is at a critical crossroad. The conjuncture is at once economic and technological. How our libraries emerge from this conjuncture will be as crucial as decisions about classroom curricula in shaping both the content and the form of humanities scholarship in the future.

Since the early 1970s research libraries have been caught ever more painfully between the two blades of an economic scissors: rapidly increasing production of printed matter and the spiraling increase in its costs on the one hand, and steady decline in both public and private funding for library acquisition budgets on the other. The rate of growth in scholarly production and in the forms of documentation that sustain it are exceeding, at an ever-increasing rate, the ability of even the largest and best-funded libraries to acquire these materials, or to store and sustain their use.[1] Moreover, research libraries are commanding a smaller and smaller percentage of the general budget of universities.[2]

These general trends are deeply troubling for the future of research in all fields of inquiry, but their impact has been most acute for the humanities disciplines. Increasing publication costs and declining library acquisition rates have resulted in a significant internal shift in the allocation of library funds from the acquisition of book monographs to that of serial publications. This shift has had a hidden differential impact on humanities scholarship because of all the forms of scholarly inquiry it is the one traditionally most wedded to the book as the principal mode of inquiry and exchange. More disconcerting still, the data concerning scholarly book publication and library acquisition by discipline reveal that humanities subjects have declined in comparison to subjects in the hard sciences, business, law, and technology.[3]

These economic and institutional indicators of the diminishing presence of libraries within the university and of humanities scholarship in the library should be cause for serious reflection among humanities scholars not merely because they are evidence of increasing economic constraint, but more significantly because they suggest that the scholarly and educational priorities of modern universities are shifting away from the institutions and forms of communication that have traditionally sustained the humanities, and humanities subjects themselves, in favor of the laboratories of the hard sciences and the professions. They offer evidence, as do the data on university degrees (discussed elsewhere in this volume), that the humanities disciplines are coming to be perceived as increasingly less relevant and less necessary to modern life than other forms of knowledge. The data betray the fact that if forced to choose which forms of knowledge to conserve and facilitate, the humanities are increasingly seen as more expendable than other disciplines.

The past thirty years have at the same time witnessed the evolution of electronic digital technology into powerful new media for the production, conservation, and exchange of texts, images, and sounds. The introduction of electronic media of communication has opened up exhilarating possibilities for reconfiguring intellectual life. At the same time it has thrown into question some of our most cherished assumptions about the nature and the aims of scholarly inquiry in modern democratic societies.

Can Digitalization Save the Humanities from the Downsizing of Libraries?

The conversion, conservation, production, and circulation of texts, images, and sounds in electronic media may well make it possible for research libraries to escape from the economic and material constraints of mechanical print culture. The recent flurry of debate among scholars, librarians, economists, computer scientists, and public policymakers about the future of libraries has focused almost exclusively on this question. And with good reason. Digital technology holds out the hope that the economic and material constraints libraries now face may be solvable without requiring any serious reassessment of the value of humanities scholarship to society at large. Digital technology may make it economically affordable to escape from the hard choices research libraries have had to make over the past several decades.

Current experiments in the digitalization of textual and visual materials offer the hope that we may be able to break free from the economic and material limits of print culture through the conversion of the publication and the conservation of texts and images via electronic media. Two characteristics of the electronic medium are especially relevant to the problems currently facing research libraries: demassification and interconnectivity. The conversion of text and images into digital form makes it possible for them to shed unprecedented amounts of mass. The entire contents of the *Oxford English Dictionary*, to take a commonly cited example, can now be stored on two thin CD-ROMs, yet read in a normal or even limitlessly enlarged typeface. And there is every reason to expect that our technical ability to reduce the ratio of data to matter will increase dramatically in the coming decades.[4] The implications of this dramatic demassification of data for library storage problems are already quite evident: the card catalogues are gone and the conversion of large numbers of government records and reference works to CD-ROM has already liberated huge amounts of space within libraries, relieving pressing storage problems.

The potential cost savings to libraries of conversion to digital media are not limited to issues of storage. As the production and publication of texts moves increasingly toward the adoption of electronic technologies there will be, it is predicted, considerable cost savings in the production of documents, and consequently in the purchase price and the conservation costs of texts and images.

Currently, the most significant factors behind price increases by publishers are spiraling paper and labor costs. The deterioration of paper and bindings is the most significant cost factor in conservation as well. In the digital environment, where each reader will be able to consult his or her own unique copy (ideally a facsimile produced through imaging), deterioration of the original document through reader use will also disappear, as will the need to store multiple copies of heavily used texts. Other very expensive aspects of library maintenance (reshelving, for example) will be eliminated, or at least radically diminished as readers simply call up documents on their screens and log off when finished.

Along with demassification, conversion to electronic media also opens up unprecedented possibilities for enhancing the interconnectivity of research libraries throughout the nation, and even the globe. One of the largest areas of increase in library budgets has been the growth in demand for interlibrary loan services as library acquisition rates decline.[5] Huge sums have been spent in recent years to coordinate regional and national collection development to reduce redundancy and enhance cooperation and interlibrary exchange. The development of the Internet and the World Wide Web will soon make it possible to link up library collections and data bases and transmit them at unprecedented speeds among user sites on the globe and beyond. It will soon be technically possible to have access to the collections of the Bibliothèque Nationale de France at any major library in the United States. No single library will be required to acquire materially the documents that it can make available.

Demassification, however, is not dematerialization. Digitalization has radically reduced the mass of the material support needed for documents, but it has not made it disappear. As a researcher at the Xerox Palo Alto Research Center, Paul Duguid, has recently observed, digital data, at bottom, still require material support, albeit much less and in new forms. Plastic, wire, and glass fiber are replacing paper, cloth, and glue. Digital media are evolving rapidly, and the conservation and maintenance costs of these new material supports are not yet fully calculable. Moreover, the reallocation of library resources from acquisition and conservation to access services may in fact result in a shift, rather than a real reduction, in costs. The initial capital investment in the conversion of documents into electronic media will be great. Systems maintenance may prove as costly as the conservation or building and collection maintenance of print-based libraries.

Computer scientists, engineers, publishers, librarians, and economists are rapidly making progress in resolving these technical issues related to the conversion of our communications infrastructure into digital forms.[6] And there seems to be good reason to be cautiously optimistic that digitalization may provide libraries with a pathway out of the economic scissors of the past several decades. It is now possible to conceive not only that research libraries will soon be able to recover the hope of keeping up with the continuously accelerating rate of the production of knowledge, but that we may be able to exceed the abilities of earlier generations to create knowledge and to make it universally available.

Through demassification and interconnectivity, digitalization could make it possible to have more documentation available, faster, cheaper, at any time, and in any place. These aspects of digitalization promise to help us to continue to realize one of the most cherished ideals of modern democratic polities and the libraries they have created: universal access to all forms of human knowledge. Indeed, the history of the organization and growth of modern research libraries has in fact had more to do with the progressive demands for democratization of American society and culture than it has with the history of our technological ability to achieve that ideal.

The founding of our great libraries, and their growth in number and scale, have been a result, not of the advent of new technologies of communication, but rather of the great waves of democratization in our national history: the founding of the Library of Congress in 1800, the great takeoff of public libraries in the 1890s, and the exponential growth of university research libraries in the postwar period (1945–1975). Modern libraries embody and put into practice our ideals of universal access to knowledge and its maximum accumulation and circulation in order to facilitate its growth and progress. The current material and economic pressures facing our libraries are the result of our desire to maintain and further these ideals in the face of the massive democratization of educational and scholarly institutions since the 1960s. Electronic technologies hold out the hope that it will be possible to sustain and to facilitate the further realization of these ideals into the next century. But with what consequences for the ways in which we organize and conduct scholarly research, and public cultural life more generally?

The Consequences of Electronic Textuality for Human Communication and Humanities Scholarship

To arrive at an adequate answer to this question requires that we shift our attention from the instrumental questions—What can we do? What is technically and economically possible?—to more foundational ones— What do we want to do? The questions are: What kind of public scholarly and intellectual life do we seek to create in the digital age? What place will the humanities have within it?

Much confusion has been created in current discussions of the future of libraries in the electronic age owing to a persistent failure to distinguish clearly between two different, though clearly interrelated, levels of analysis: the history of communications *media* (clay tablets, printing presses, networked computers) and the history of *modes* of communication (the codex book, the newspaper, the bulletin board) as well as the legal and institutional modes of configuring human communication (copyright law, public libraries, parliaments, and universities). Careful discrimination between the means and the mode of communication, and consideration of the nature of their interrelation, are critical to our comprehension of both the complexities and the possibilities that the advent of electronic media presents to the library and the forms of knowledge that are sustained by them. New media may open up new possibilities for human communication, but they do not determine how we use them, or how we collectively organize their use.

Libraries have a long history—one that begins with recorded human history itself. But the evolution of the earliest institutions in Babylon into the research libraries of the late twentieth century A.D. has been a result not of changing media (the shift from tablet to papyrus or the shift from script to print) but of changing notions of how collective intellectual life should be organized. The history of modern libraries, as I have previously suggested, has been shaped more by the history of our democratic ideals than by the history of the technologies that our polity has employed.

It is nonetheless true that our modern cultural ideals and the legal and institutional forms that have ensured their realization evolved during an era in which the printed word was the dominant medium for the public exchange of ideas and information. Our legal and institutional ability to ensure the prevention of injury, freedom of expression, and the furtherance of public good—and to mediate the tensions between these three ideals—has been thrown into question by the advent of electronic modes of textual production and exchange. This is occurring, as we know, because the regulatory environment and institutional forms of configuring public intellectual life that have been elaborated since the democratic revolutions of the eighteenth century were based upon a mechanical model of textual production and exchange—let us call it "print culture" or, following Walter Benjamin, the "age of mechanical reproduction"—that is not fully capable of grasping what is happening on the terrain of electronic texts, images, and sounds. I suggest that the reason that electronic modes of signification and representation seem to elude the current regulatory environment is that they were based upon a set of assumptions about the fixity of forms that are no longer self-evident in the electronic age.

Despatialization and the Loss of Mechanical Forms

As Howard Bloch and I have argued in our book *Future Libraries*, the current debate about the consequences of electronic libraries is haunted by a deep anxiety over the loss of fixed cultural forms. Images of the metaphorical and literal decorporealization of texts, and of the spaces in which they are located, abound. In the world of the Web we have gained an unprecedented power to access and to connect up massive amounts of text, images, and sounds of all kinds, but the points of origin and end of these materials have been rendered uncertain; borderlines delimiting texts, or groups of texts, have become porous and infinitely malleable. The possibility of boundless textual promiscuity and miscegenation is attended by feelings of both liberatory exhilaration and terror. We seem to have left the terrain of the beautiful and entered that of the sublime.

The boundlessness of electronic texts has led in recent years to a despatialization of our conception of libraries and of the rhetorical construction of the knowledge that will no longer lie within but rather circulate through these nonspatial mechanisms of accessing, producing, and reconfiguring textual and visual material. In fact, as Howard Bloch and I have written, "Knowledge is no longer conceived and construed in the language of forms at all ('bodies of knowledge,' or a 'corpus,' bounded and stored), . . . no longer that which is contained in space, but something that passes through it, like a series of vectors, each having direction and duration, yet without precise location or limit."[7] The very means of distinguishing different forms of knowledge and the boundaries of different scholarly fields of inquiry—"literature," "history," "political science," and so forth—in this environment is difficult to ascertain.

But one thing seems clear. The electronic library is rapidly recasting our understanding of the key institutions of modern literary culture—the book, the author, the reader, the editor, the publisher, and the library—in terms of time, motion, and modes of action, rather than space, objects, and actors. The designers of the work stations for the new Bibliothèque Nationale de France, for example, define readers in terms of the kind of reading they practice (long- versus short-term readers). Gone are the social (learned and popular), political (public and private), or economic (fee-paying versus non-fee-paying) categories that once described the constituents of spatial libraries.[8] The reader is thus now conceived as an independant navigator in a continuous textual flow.

What appears to be emerging from the digital revolution is the possibility of a new mode of temporality for public communication, one in which public exchange through the written word can occur without fixity or deferral, in a continuously immediate present. This is a world in which we are all, at least potentially, continuously present to one another through electronic writing, and at the same time not really located anywhere at all. There is something unprecedented in this possibility of the escape of writing (and other modes of signification and representation as well) from fixity. What digitalization seems to have opened up is the possibility for writing to operate in a temporal mode hitherto exclusively possible in speech—for writing to operate, in the terms of structural linguistics, as *parole* rather than *langue*.

New modes of reading-writing are emerging: e-mail communication in "real time," the on-line public forum, certain forms of interactive hypertext, the development of dynamaps for weather forecasting or genetic and bibliographic research, and so forth.[9] The implications of these performative modes of electronic writing for humanities scholarship, and public culture more generally, are profound. Writing, like reading, is being reconceived as performance rather than composition.[10] These developments make it possible to imagine a world in which writing loses its particular relation to time, in which the space created by the structure of deferral gives way to pure textual simultaneity, to what I have elsewhere called "scripted speech."[11]

The escape of writing and imagemaking from fixity in the electronic environment has also opened up radical possibilities for boundless individuation in human meaning-making and communication. Without fixity, the determinacy of any given signification is rendered uncertain, or at least optional rather than given. The social consequences of this development are profound. In principle, electronic text is infinitely reproducible and infinitely malleable. The material limits of print culture imposed social constraints upon the power of the individual to acquire a text (you had to purchase or borrow a copy), to modify it (you had to own it to mark it or cut it up), and, especially with a text not cheaply available on the market, to share its use (either by borrowing and lending or by reading aloud).

Electronic libraries, in which any document is available at any time and copies can be infinitely reproduced and modified, are leading to the possibility of modes of communication that are not only performative but also entirely asynchronous.[12] There are no longer any material guarantees that two or more individuals will ever be reading the same text, nor that they will need to coordinate their writing-reading practices with others. At a minimum, electronic texts and images are producing a dramatic desocialization of meaning-making. (A single individual can now do on a home computer what ten years ago required a significant coordination of social resources.) The risk is that performative modes of textuality will not increase communication but rather encourage solipsism. Readers and writers, past, present, and future, will have less reason to take one another into account, or to be accountable to one another.

Although digitalization holds out the promise of unprecedented possibilities for the expansion of knowledge and our power to access it, it has also introduced a new mode of textuality that calls into question some of our most basic assumptions about the forms of human meaning-making and communication that fixed inscription made possible. Performative modes of textuality awaken the hope of infinite, immediate, transparent, and universal communication. But at the same time they threaten us with a loss of synchronous community, individual accountability, and, most profoundly, the space of reflexivity that the logic of deferral through fixity made possible.

From a Spatial to a Temporal Theory of Literary Forms

How can we begin to conceptualize modes of textuality in temporal rather than spatial terms? Rethinking libraries and their institutional forms after digitalization will require us to move from a structural to a performative theory of literary relations.[13] Here, I think, historians of the book may be of some help. And so I turn for a moment to one instance in the history of publishing in modern France. On the eve of the French restoration of the Bourbon monarchy in 1814 the liberal political philosopher Benjamin Constant observed that

> All enlightened men seemed to be convinced that complete freedom and exemption from any form of censorship should be granted to longer works. Because writing them requires time, purchasing them requires affluence, and reading them requires attention, they are not able to produce the reaction in the populace that one fears of works of greater rapidity and violence. But *pamphlets*, and *handbills*, and *newspapers*, are produced quickly, you can buy them for little, and because their effect is immediate, they are believed to be more dangerous.[14]

It is significant to note here that what Constant sees as the critical distinction between "the book" and other forms of printed matter is not the physical *form* of the printed word, nor the implicit set of social actors that it requires (author, printer, publisher, and reader) but rather the *mode of temporality* that the book form establishes between those actors. The book is a *slow* form of exchange. It is a mode of temporality that conceives of public communication not as action but rather as reflection upon action. Indeed, the book form serves precisely to defer action, to widen the temporal gap between thought and deed, to create a space of reflection and debate. It is a fulcrum that fixes both author and reader in a given relation for the duration of the text. The book, as Marcel Proust recognized, is a fulcrum that creates space out of time. Recall our synecdochial experience of reading, in *Swann's Way*, about little Marcel reading in the garden, or more vividly still, the image of his guppy-catching glass cup plunged into the stream, at once containing and contained by the flow.[15] The book then is not so much a material object as a mode of textuality that stands at the opposite end of the temporal discursive field from real time. It is a mode of deferral that makes representation possible rather than a mode of immediacy that renders experience transparent. Deferral makes the apprehension of experience possible.

The library before the advent of electronic media, as I suggested at the outset of this essay, has functioned as a multiplier of the logic of deferral sustained by the book. The book is a slower and longer form of expression than a pamphlet or a broadside. Libraries, the places of many books, are modes of configuring reading that are slower and longer still. Libraries composed of fixed forms of signification are not simply points of access for documents, they are places of deep investigation, concentration, reflection, and contemplation. Victor Hugo was perhaps wrong when, in the famous passage in *Notre Dame de Paris*, he has the archdeacon cry out: "This will kill that. The book will kill the building."[16] He would have better written: "This will become that." Libraries *are* the cathedrals of the modern secular world. They are our most cherished spaces of contemplation and reflection upon human experience.

This is why humanities scholarship, more than any of the other forms of modern human inquiry, has remained wedded to the book form and to the libraries that have been composed of books. This logic of deferral through fixed representation is the essence of both the sources and the aims of humanities scholarship. It is the essence of its sources because fixity is precisely what makes it possible for us to have access to the diversity and complexities of human experience over time and space. And it is essential to the aims of humanities scholarship because giving durable form to human experience is what makes it possible to examine and reflect upon how humans have constituted themselves, individually and collectively, and how they have constituted their relations to the world around them. The capacity for representation is essential to human self-constitution and to human self-governance. The aim of the humanities is to understand these processes in all their depth, complexity, and diversity.

But faced with the advent of electronic textuality, we should hesitate to commit the same error as Victor Hugo by proclaiming that "This will kill that. The networked computer will kill the book." The book as a cultural form was not the inevitable consequence of print culture; it emerged long before the advent of mechanical print, and its preservation as our most cherished cultural form, in modern market-oriented liberal democratic societies, has been the work of a very elaborate legal, institutional, and administrative framework that has aimed to ensure a particular vision of cultural life that embodies the ideals of the autonomous, self-creating and self-governing, property-owning individuals; universal access to knowledge; and the assurance of cautious public reflection and debate. Indeed, the model of knowledge acquisition and exchange that the book embodies and makes possible is precisely the one that Thomas Jefferson described in his *Notes on Virginia:* "A patient pursuit of facts, and cautious combination and comparison of them, is the drudgery to which man is subjected . . . if he wishes to attain sure knowledge."[17] It is a salutary drudgery because many of the issues facing humanity are too complex and too fraught with potential danger to be fully apprehended, or to be acted upon, instantaneously.

What we must confront, then, in the remaking of the library in the electronic age, is our choice either to challenge or to affirm these ideals through the legal, political, economic, and institutional policies we implement. We must determine what kind of cultural agents we envision for the future. To put the question somewhat tendentiously, are we to sustain self-constituting and accountable citizens of a democracy or are we going to advance a future of continuously and spontaneously recomposing postmodernist subjectivities, inhabiting an increasingly imaginable, technocratically managed empire? An account of what is at stake in these choices, in my opinion, is more adequately expounded in the *Late Histories* of Tacitus, which chart the transition from republican to imperial Rome, than in the descriptions to be found in recent publications concerning hypertext, cyberspace, or virtual reality.

Flow, Friction, and Deferral

Reconfiguring textual practices and relations in the electronic library will entail letting go of our current spatial notions of the library and the forms of documentation that comprise them. The library, rather, will be a nexus for configuring the flow of texts, images, and sounds through the elaboration of a temporal ethics of intellectual community that makes human self-constitution and self-governance possible. We should not be asking the questions "Who should read and write?" and "To what should they have access?" (the answers are obvious: anyone, anything), but rather when and how.

In elaborating a temporal ethics of human communication, two concepts may be useful: friction and deferral. Modes of friction and deferral in the electronic library might be thought of, following the literary critic Gérard Genette, as "thresholds," or fulcrums that require readers and writers to pass through gates of entry and exit in order to enter the flow of communication and that determine the duration of an encounter or exchange and the participants in the exchange.[18] How can one enter into the flow? When? For how long? And in what ways? These questions may lead us to rules of friction and deferral that will make it possible for us to give sustaining form to human experience, to continue to investigate the nature and value of the forms we create, and to remain accountable to one another in the process. The economic ideal of "friction-free" market relations in cyberspace, recently celebrated by Bill Gates in *The Road Ahead*, would undoubtedly benefit the commercial life of our nation, but it is not an adequate model for the furtherance of knowledge, nor for public self-governance.[19] The book, the classroom, and the scholarly conference—frictious modes of exchange—should not give way entirely to the on-line correspondence course. Nor should the library as a mode of reflexivity give way to the on-line forum.

Scholars in the humanities are already active in attempting to elaborate these rules. A significant beginning has been made by the report on *Humanities and Arts on the Information Highways*, issued by the Getty Foundation, the American Council of Learned Societies, and the Coalition for Networked Information, for the elaboration of paratextual mechanisms within the digital environment. If human experience is not to dissolve into a pure memory flow of continuous on-line exchange, they rightly suggest, we will need to evolve standards and tools to ensure the preservation of the integrity of textual and visual artifacts as they are converted into digital form. We will also need to ensure a record of their provenance and their survival in their original form over time, as well as standards of verification and rules of use that are commensurate with our civic ideals. Imaging techniques that create electronic facsimiles of original texts and artifacts, being developed by Xerox Corporation in collaboration with the Cornell University Library, are especially promising in this regard.[20]

Conclusion: Transparency and Representation in Human Communication

Of all the forms of human inquiry, electronic textuality poses its greatest challenges to scholars in the humanities because the initial impulses behind the development of electronic communications technologies (military and commercial in their origin) were aimed, for the most part, at two goals:

   1. To diminish reaction time, to close the gap between reader and writer, and to erase the space of deferral that mechanical forms of inscription could not transcend (lock on the target and shoot; see the object and buy).
   2. To dodge attacks and evade detection.

This means that the electronic modes of textuality tend, almost inherently, toward a public culture of mutability, immediacy, and transparency rather than deferral and determinacy.

For many it has reawakened a utopian dream of a world in which we are all always present to one another. This dream of transparency is one that deeply threatens what I take to be the essence of liberal democratic culture and the humanities scholarship that has sustained it, that is, a culture that constitutes public life *through* determinate representations, through the public constitution of collective and individual identities and the reasoned public discourse that modes of deferral make possible. The role of the humanities in shaping the libraries of the twenty-first century A.D. should be that of reinventing modes of friction and deferral in electronic media that will thicken the possibilities of representation—poetic, historical, and ethical—rather than promise us, or threaten us with, a collapse of representation into the transparency of pure duration.

The advent of electronic texts has opened up the possibility of a collapse of *langue* into *parole* that would spell the end of both libraries and the humanities as we know them. But it does not mean that such a collapse is inevitable. Rather it means that what were once the material limitations upon which modern literary culture and its key institutions have been based will now have to be understood as cultural choices that we must opt for or against. The library will be a key site of struggle over how we reconstitute public cultural life in the wake of digitalization, because it is through this institution that we configure collective cultural life independently of the interests of state security on the one hand, and the drives of commerce on the other.[21]

Electronic textuality has made it necessary to reexamine the foundational assumptions of the humanities and the nature of the libraries that sustain them. But there is good reason to believe that libraries, books, and the scholars in the humanities who study them will remain not only a relevant but also a necessary element of our educational institutions and our public culture more generally. As long as we are a society that remains interested in making things of sustained value, and of reflecting upon the value of the things that we create, the humanities will remain an essential, indeed a core, element of educational and scholarly life. It is not insignificant, I think, to our future that at the heart of the Xerox Corporation's Palo Alto Research Center—the birthplace of the mouse—there lies a traditional library composed of tables and chairs, as well as book and serial stacks, so that researchers can engage in long, silent reading and reflection on where they are going and what they are doing. Nor is it incidental that even the CEO of Microsoft Corporation, Bill Gates, recently felt compelled to retreat from the flow of life to his wilderness cabin, like Hans Castorp to his *Magic Mountain*, in order to take stock of where he has come from and where he is going. *The Road Ahead* is a book, even if you can also read it on CD-ROM.

Notes

1. For the most current assessment of the economic trends in scholarly publication and library acquisitions see, in particular, Anthony M. Cummings, Marcia L. Witte, William G. Bowen, Laura O. Lazarus, and Richard H. Ekman, *University Libraries and Scholarly Communication: A Study Prepared for The Andrew W.*

Mellon Foundation (Princeton, N.J.: Andrew W. Mellon Foundation, 1992); and Richard H. Ekman and and Richard E. Quant, "Scholarly Communication, Academic Libraries, and Technology," unpublished working paper prepared for The Andrew W. Mellon Foundation and made available by the Association of Research Libraries, February 1994.

2. Cummings et al., *University Libraries and Scholarly Communication*, xvii.

3. See Cummings et al., *University Libraries and Scholarly Communication*, xviii–xix, and Chapters 5 and 6. See also Sandra B. Freitag, "The Endangered Monograph," *Perspectives: American Historical Association Newsletter* 33, no. 7 (October 1995): 3–4; and Sandra B. Freitag, "Publishing, Copyright and 'Scholarly Communication,'" *Perspectives: American Historical Association Newsletter* 33, no. 8 (November 1995): 3–4.

4. On demassification see Paul Duguid, "Material Matters: The Past and Futurology of the Book," in *The Future of the Book*, ed. Geoffrey Nunberg (Berkeley and Los Angeles: University of California Press, 1996); and Bill Gates, *The Road Ahead* (New York: Viking, 1995), especially 116–26.

5. See Martha Kyrillidou, "Trends in Research Library Acquisitions and Interlibrary Loan Services," Association of Research Libraries Report no. 180 (Washington, D.C.: Association of Research Libraries, 1995).

6. On the economic and technical complexities and possibilities of document conversion from print to electronic media see Duguid, "Material Matters," and William G. Bowen, "JSTOR and the Economics of Scholarly Communication," report to The Andrew W. Mellon Foundation, October 4, 1995; and Ekman and Quant, "Scholarly Communication, Academic Libraries, and Technology."

7. R. Howard Bloch and Carla Hesse, eds., *Future Libraries* (Berkeley and Los Angeles: University of California Press, 1995), 11.

8. See Gérard Grunberg and Alain Giffard, "New Orders of Knowledge, New Technologies of Reading," in *Future Libraries*, ed. R. Howard Bloch and Carla Hesse (Berkeley and Los Angeles: University of California Press, 1995), 80–93.

9. On new modes of writing see Pierre Levy, "The Electronic Book or Navigation in Hyperspace? Toward Virtual Worlds of Shared Meanings," and Jay David Bolter, "The Architecture of Electronic Writing," papers delivered at the workshop "The Electronic Book: A New Medium?" Xerox PARC, Grenoble, France, September 9–10, 1993.

10. The university librarian at the University of California at Berkeley, Peter Lyman, for example, has recently compared computer literacy to competence in playing a musical instrument; see "What Is Computer Literacy and What Is Its Place in Liberal Education?" *Liberal Education* 81, no. 3 (Summer 1995): 8–10. The semiotician Umberto Eco likens hypertextual reading practices to improvisational jazz; see his afterword to *The Future of the Book*, ed. Geoffrey Nunberg (Berkeley and Los Angeles: University of California Press, 1996).

11. Carla Hesse, "The Book in Time," in *The Future of the Book*, ed. Geoffrey Nunberg (Berkeley and Los Angeles: University of California Press, 1996).

12. The liberatory possibilities of asynchronous communication are celebrated as a "killer application" by Gates in *The Road Ahead*, 65–68; for a more cautious assessment of the consequences of asynchronicity for public culture see Monore

Price, "Free Expression and Digital Dreams: The Open and Closed Terrain of Speech," *Critical Inquiry* 22, no. 1 (Autumn 1995): 64–89.

13. Interestingly, though perhaps not surprisingly, it has been the lawyers who have been the first to seize upon the social implications of this development and who have begun to advance new regulatory models for electronic reading-writing-publishing as performance and service rather than commodity. See Czeslaw Jan Grycz, ed., *Economic Models for Networked Information*, a special issue of *Serials Review* 18, no. 1–2 (1992); Jane C. Ginsburg, "Copyright Without Walls?: Speculations on Literary Property in the Library of the Future," in Bloch and Hesse, *Future Libraries*, 53–73; and Eric Schlachter, "Cyberspace, the Free Market and the Free Marketplace of Ideas: Recognizing Legal Difference in Computer Bulletin Board Functions," *Comm/Ent: Hastings Communications and Entertainment Law Journal* 16, no. 1 (Fall 1993): 87–150.

14. Benjamin Constant, *De la liberté des brochures, des pamphlets et des journaux* (Paris, 1814), 1.

15. Marcel Proust, *Swann's Way*, vol. 1 of *In Remembrance of Things Past*, tr. C. K. Scott Montcreiff (New York: Random House, 1961), 63–68 and 129–130.

16. Victor Hugo, *Notre Dame de Paris*, tr. John Sturrock (New York: Penguin, 1978), 188.

17. Cited in Cummings et al., *University Libraries and Scholarly Communication*, xxviii.

18. Gérard Genette, *Seuils* (Paris: Seuils, 1987).

19. Gates, *The Road Ahead*, 157–83.

20. *Humanities and Arts on the Information Highways: A Profile, Summer 1994*, a national initiative sponsored by the Getty Art History Information Program, the American Council of Learned Societies, and the Coalition for Networked Information (Santa Monica, Calif.: Getty Foundation, 1994), especially 31–32. On the collaboration between Xerox Corporation and Cornell University, as well as other promising projects, see also Ekman and Quant, "Scholarly Communication, Academic Libraries, and Technologies," and Steven J. DeRose, "Structured Information: Navigation, Access, and Control," paper presented to the Berkeley Finding Aid Conference, April 4–6, 1995.

21. On the possibilities of reshaping computer command language toward scholarly rather than military or commercial ends see Lyman, "What Is Computer Literacy," 4–15.

Six

The Practice of Reading

DENIS DONOGHUE

IT MAY be well to speak to a text. I have chosen *Macbeth* for reasons that hardly need to be explained. I will quote two or three passages of literary criticism, directed upon a few speeches from the play, to indicate what close, patient reading of the play has been deemed to entail. But I must approach these passages by a detour, to indicate why I am citing them in an essay on current practices of reading. I confine myself to *Macbeth* and its attendant commentaries, but I assume that similar problems of reading are encountered in the humanities generally. Reading a painting must be just as arduous—and as pleasurable—as reading a poem, play, or novel.

In the fall of 1946 I. A. Richards spoke at a conference in Princeton on "The Humanistic Tradition in the Century Ahead." The occasion, Richards recalled in an essay in the *Journal of General Education* for April 1947, "was felt to be challenging." The conference had been preceded by one on nuclear physics and another on the social sciences: "it was hardly possible throughout the discussion not to wonder where—in the balance of forces that are shaping the future—the humanities did come in." Richards noted some of the conditions in which the question was necessarily raised: the enormous and still increasing population of the world, 700 million in 1840, 2.2 billion in 1947; the rise of mass education and the hopes and fears it provoked; and the exposure of minds to "a range and variety and promiscuity of contacts unparalleled in history." Finally he emphasized the juncture of the sciences with the humanities:

> What are meeting now head on are two unreconciled ways of conceiving man and his good and how to pursue it. Both wish him well, but they differ radically as to how he can be helped. The physical and social sciences alike—being applications of methods of observation and calculation—conceive men as units subject to forces playing upon them *from without*. . . . Thus a man's desires and opinions and beliefs, the springs of his action and sources of his triumphs or sufferings, are likewise, for science, to be studied from without. . . . In contrast,

the humanities pin a faith, which is experimentally still ungrounded, on the ideal autonomy of the individual man.[1]

It will not be supposed that I regard Richards's account of these matters as definitive. It is no longer true that the main opposition to the humanities comes from the sciences: it comes from the humanities themselves and takes the form of "techniques of trouble"—R. P. Blackmur's designation of the ways in which we make trouble for ourselves, doubting our purposes. As humanists—in the special and limited sense in which we are teachers of the humanities—we are unable or unwilling to say what we are doing, or why our activities should receive support in the form of salaries, grants, and fellowships. We are timid in describing the relation between training in the humanities and the exercise of the moral imagination. We have largely given up the claim that one's reading of, say, *Little Dorrit* has any bearing, however tenuous or oblique, on the exercise of one's informed sympathies at large. Other aspects of Richards's commentary, too, may be questioned. It is astonishing that he spoke with such confidence of the "ideal autonomy of the individual man." It is now widely if not universally believed that, far from being, even ideally, autonomous, everyone is socially constituted. The view of mankind that Richards ascribed to scientists is now commonly held by humanists: that each of us is a consequence of extraneous and contingent forces. A claim for one's autonomy, however modestly expressed, is rarely heard.

But Richards's comments are still useful, even if they chiefly provide opportunities for disagreement. When we put his sentences beside other descriptions of the cultural conditions that obtain in the humanities—I am thinking of Blackmur's *Anni Mirabiles* and of several more recent interventions—we gain a sense, good enough for most purposes, of our hopes and fears. For the moment I would add only this: that those hopes and fears turn upon the question of reading. What we fear is that our students are losing the ability to read, or giving up that ability in favor of an easier one, the capacity of being spontaneously righteous, indignant, or otherwise exasperated. We fear, too, that the impatience our students bring to the slow work of reading literature is a symptom of more drastic trouble, the general decline of literacy in the United States, and the increase in the number of those who are literate but choose not to read. What we hope is that we may still be able to show our students the keener pleasure of reading in a more exacting spirit.

I must be summary at this point. I believe that the purpose of reading literature is to exercise or incite one's imagination, specifically one's ability to imagine being different. "What must it be to be different?" Hopkins asked himself in one of his journals. Reading a poem or a novel, attending a play, looking at a painting, listening to music—these experiences should provoke me to imagine what it would mean to have a life different from my own. A good reading is in that sense disinterested, as we used to say. I know that disinterestedness is commonly denounced as just another interest, flagrantly masked, so I use the word only in a limited sense. But it is possible to distinguish a reading more or less disinterested from one demonstrably opportunistic.

I begin with D. W. Harding's commentary—amplified by a paragraph of scholarship from Helen Gardner—on the "Pity, like a naked new-born babe" passage. Macbeth is trying to talk himself out of murdering Duncan:

> Besides, this Duncan
> Hath borne his faculties so meek, hath been
> So clear in his great office, that his virtues
> Will plead like angels, trumpet-tongu'd, against
> The deep damnation of his taking-off;
> And Pity, like a naked new-born babe,
> Striding the blast, or heaven's Cherubins, hors'd
> Upon the sightless couriers of the air,
> Shall blow the horrid deed in every eye,
> That tears shall drown the wind.   (I.vi.16–25)

Harding believes that most poets bring language to bear upon their thinking at a notably early stage of its development. He has explained this idea in an essay on the poetry of Isaac Rosenberg:

> Usually when we speak of finding words to express a thought we seem to mean that we have the thought rather close to formulation and use it to measure the adequacy of any possible phrasing that occurs to us, treating words as servants of the idea. "Clothing a thought in language," whatever it means psychologically, seems a fair metaphorical description of much speaking and writing. Of Rosenberg's work it would be misleading. He—like many poets in some degree, one supposes—brought language to bear on the incipient thought at an earlier stage of its development. Instead of the emerging idea being racked slightly so as to fit a more familiar approximation of itself, and words found for *that*, Rosenberg let it manipulate words almost from the beginning, often without insisting on the controls of logic and intelligiblity.

So, too, with Shakespeare, allowing for differences in the scale of genius between him and Rosenberg. In "The Hinterland of Thought" Harding returns to the idea and associates it with Susanne K. Langer's distinction, in *Philosophy in a New Key*, between presentational symbolism and

discursive thinking, the latter coming later in cognition than the former.
Harding writes:

> A half-way house between presentational symbolism and discursive statement is
> to be seen in some of the torrential passages of Shakespeare where half-activated
> images succeed one another with great rapidity and gain their effect through not
> being brought to the full definition of an exact metaphor. The *Macbeth* passage
> about Pity like a naked new-born babe is an obvious example. The sense of the
> passage is that in spite of the seeming helplessness of any protest against the
> horrors perpetrated by unscrupulous power, the decent human emotion of pity
> can in the end mobilize enormous strength. But Shakespeare stopped long
> before this stage of discursive statement. He had in mind presumably a mass of
> items and associations related to the central theme: the new-born babe as an
> example of extreme helplessness, the cherubs on maps blowing the winds, the
> immense power of the wind and the fact that it brings tears to the eyes—and
> they could be tears of pity—especially if it blows something into them, the way
> it rushes all over the world like an invisible messenger carrying heaven's protest
> against the crime, in other words carrying pity, which in spite of being a helpless
> infant is now in charge of the tremendous strength of divine as well as human
> condemnation of the crime.[2]

There is indeed more to be said about this famous speech. Helen
Gardner has explicated it further in reply to Cleanth Brooks's analysis of it
in *The Well Wrought Urn*. Brooks did not know enough about angels,
apparently; he thought cherubims must be avenging angels. Not so: they
are "angels of the presence of God," standing above the throne, "contem-
plating the glory of God." It is not their task to act upon God's will:

> The babe, naked and new-born, the most helpless of all things, the cherubims,
> innocent and beautiful, call out the pity and the love by which Macbeth is
> judged. It is not terror of heaven's vengeance which makes him pause; but the
> terror of moral isolation. He ends by seeing himself alone in a sudden silence,
> where nothing can be heard but weeping, as, when a storm has blown itself out,
> the wind drops and we hear the steady falling of the rain, which sounds as if it
> would go on for ever. The naked babe "strides the blast" because pity is to
> Shakespeare the strongest and profoundest of human emotions, the distinctively
> human emotion. It rises above and masters indignation.[3]

The next passage I choose is from F. R. Leavis's *Education and the University:
A Sketch for an "English School"* (1943), the chapter called "How to Teach
Reading." The lines he is reading are the "temple-haunting martlet" speech
of Banquo to Duncan under the battlements at Dunsinane:

DUNCAN: This castle hath a pleasant seat; the air
                Nimbly and sweetly recommends itself
                Unto our gentle senses.
BANQUO: This guest of summer,
                The temple-haunting martlet, does approve,
                By his loved mansionry, that the heaven's breath
                Smells wooingly here: no jutty, frieze,
                Buttress, nor coign of vantage, but this bird
                Hath made his pendent bed, and procreant cradle:
                Where they most breed and haunt, I have observed
                The air is delicate.   (I.vi.1–10)

Leavis's commentary reads, in part:

> We note the insistence, throughout the passage, of the element represented by
> "pleasant," "sweetly," "gentle"; it is so insistent that it appears even in a place
> so apparently inappropriate (on editorial inspection) as to elicit from the *Arden*
> editor the comment: "probably a proleptic construction." But
>
>   The air
>   *Nimbly* and sweetly recommends itself,
>
> and the set of associations represented by "nimbly" is equally important on the
> whole: we are in hill air, which is not only sweet but fresh and vital—a sharp
> contrast to the smothering sense, already evoked, of the "blanket of the dark."
> But that is not all; every word in the passage contributes. Why, for instance,
> "temple-haunting"? It co-operates with "guest" and "heaven" to evoke the
> associations belonging to the "sanctity of hospitality": for "heaven," reinforced
> by "temple," is not merely the sky where the fresh winds blow. Nevertheless the
> suggestion of altitude is potent:
>
>   No jutty, frieze,
>   Buttress, nor coign of vantage, . . .
>
> —"above the smoke and stir of this dim spot." But why "martlet"? The bird,
> with its swift vitality and exquisite frail delicacy, represents a combination
> analogous to "nimbly and sweetly." But more; its "pendent bed," secure above
> the dizzy drop, is its "procreant cradle"; and "procreant" is enforced by
> "breeds": all these suggestions, uniting again with those of "temple" and
> "heaven," evoke the contrast to "foul murder"—life springing swift, keen and
> vulnerable from the hallowed source.

Leavis's analysis of the passage was meant to support his claim that
"attention directed upon 'character' and 'psychology' is not favourably
disposed for doing justice to the kind of thing Shakespeare does here with
words."[4] The words are spoken by Banquo, indeed, but Leavis does not
make much of that fact; he discourages the reader from valuing the speech

as evidence of Banquo's character rather than for its bearing upon the play as a poetic whole and upon Shakespeare's particular way of using words. I find no contradiction between these interests. It is important, for the reasons Leavis offers, to have Banquo's words spoken at this point in the play: important, too, to have them spoken by him. There is no discrepancy between Shakespeare's inventive genius among the words and the enabling propriety of his assigning them to Banquo.

I shall give another example of close reading in response to the first part of Macbeth's speech at the beginning of act 1, scene vii. William Empson's analysis concentrates on the first four lines, in which he finds "a resounding example" of the ambiguity by which two or more alternative meanings are resolved into one:

> If it were done, when 'tis done, then 'twere well
> It were done quickly:

(Double syntax since you may stop at the end of the line)

> If th' assassination
> Could trammel up the consequence, and catch
> With his surcease success; that but . . .

Words hissed in the passage where servants were passing, which must be swaddled with darkness, loaded as it were in themselves with fearful powers, and not made too naked even to his own mind. *Consequence* means causal result, and the things to follow, though not causally connected, and, as in "a person of consequence," the divinity that doth hedge a king. *Trammel* was a technical term used about netting birds, hobbling horses in some particular way, hooking up pots, leveling, and running trolleys on rails. *Surcease* means completion, stopping proceedings in the middle of a lawsuit, or the overruling of a judgment; the word reminds you of "surfeit" and "decease," as does *assassination* of hissing and "assess" and, as in "supersession," through *sedere*, of knocking down the mighty from their seat. *His* may apply to Duncan, *assassination* or *consequence*. *Success* means fortunate result, result whether fortunate or not, and succession to the throne. And *catch*, the single little flat word among these monsters, names an action: it is a mark of human inadequacy to deal with these matters of statecraft, a child snatching at the moon as she rides thunderclouds. The meanings cannot all be remembered at once, however often you read it; it remains the incantation of a murderer, dishevelled and fumbling among the powers of darkness.[5]

I have been going back to these and other critics—notably G. Wilson Knight, John Crowe Ransom, and L. C. Knights—to rehearse the purposes to which they turned their readings of *Macbeth* in particular, of Shakespeare more generally, and of other writers in relation to Shakespeare. Up to a point (and despite Ransom's belated appreciation of Eliot's early poems) the critics might be called the School of Eliot: their critical essays were impelled by his early poetry and *The Sacred Wood*. The motive I find in common among these critics is Eliot's, that of gaining, against increasing difficulty, an intelligent readership for literature. Leavis is most explicit on that issue, just as the considerations that led to his explicitness are most clearly indicated by Q. D. Leavis's *Fiction and the Reading Public* (1932). In that book Mrs. Leavis studies the rise and the disintegration of such a readership, the development of journalism, the book market, advertising, economic considerations, and the significance of best-sellers in relation to serious fiction. The place to start, in the work of cultivation, was clearly the school, the college, the university: the crucial discipline was a revised "English School." In schools and colleges, F. R. Leavis reiterates, the critical study of literature must involve "a training of intelligence that is at the same time a training of sensibility." Furthermore, "If literature is worth study, then the test of its having been so will be the ability to read literature intelligently, and apart from this ability an accumulation of knowledge is so much lumber." Again: "By training of reading capacity I mean the training of perception, judgment and analytic skill commonly referred to as 'practical criticism'— or, rather, the training that 'practical criticism' ought to be."[6] That last qualification put a certain distance, however cordially, between Leavis's program and Richards's: the distance need not concern us here.

The critics I have referred to worried about the fate of intelligent reading in conditions of mass society, the resurgence of logical positivism, and the dominance of science. They argued that a work of literature differs from a scientific treatise in not being a sequence of discursive statements. A poem, as Brooks said in *The Well Wrought Urn*, does not properly eventuate in a proposition, and even if it is grammatically divisible into sentences, a proper reading of those sentences takes them as actions—symbolic actions, Kenneth Burke called them—performed in a certain hypothetical context. They are to be questioned not for their truth but for their direction and force within the poem. The "To-morrow and to-morrow and to-morrow" speech is not a philosophy of life, Shakespeare's or Macbeth's, but a sequence of statements issuing from Macbeth's sense of himself at that moment.

It is not true, therefore, as John Guillory has claimed, that the method of close reading, practiced by the New Critics, was in the cause of a conservative ideology of the self. The method was used by critics on the left and on the right: it is enough to name, indicating the left, Empson's *Some Versions of Pastoral*, Burke's *The Philosophy of Literary Form* and *Permanence and Change*, and L. C. Knights's *Drama and Society in the Age of Jonson*. Nor is it true, as Guillory has maintained, that the practice of the New Critics in purging political considerations from the study of literature "has a tendentially conservative effect, conservative by default."[7] When we read a work of literature as a symbolic action, we indeed purge the political, but we also purge the metaphysical, the religious, the economic, the historical, or any other ideological discourse. We give none of these any privilege, for the simple reason that we pay attention not to propositions that might be extracted from the work but to statements made under the pressure of the context; and we attend to these not as independent truths or falsehoods but as things said in that context. I have made what may seem to be another detour, but it enables me to say that in recent commentaries on *Macbeth* what is repeatedly ignored is precisely the distinction between a proposition and an action. The homework I have been doing on these commentaries has led me to think that we are in the presence of a New Thematics, which represents itself as literary criticism, or as something else than literary criticism. Over the past fifteen years or so a consensus on *Macbeth* has emerged that I shall delineate in a moment: it satisfies the interests of social science, apparently, rather than those of criticism. By that difference I mean that the commentaries issue not in analyses of the language of the play but in a diagnostic account of the ideology the play allegedly sustains: for that purpose, a close reading of the play in the detail of its language is thought to be a nuisance.

The critics of *Macbeth* I have been reading include Peter Stallybrass, Marilyn French, Dennis Biggins, Terry Eagleton, Jonathan Goldberg, Madelon Gohlke, Lisa Jardine, Catherine Belsey, Malcolm Evans, Janet Adelman, and Garry Wills. Why these? It would be sufficient reason that they reveal what is happening in criticism, even more clearly than what happens in *Macbeth*. Many of them embody the consensus by citing one another. There is common cause between them, or most of them.

It is my understanding that the new reading of *Macbeth* was stimulated by the publication of Alan Macfarlane's *Witchcraft in Tudor and Stuart England* (1970) and Keith Thomas's *Religion and the Decline of Magic* (1971). Scholars have continued to read the play in terms of the Gunpowder Plot, the Gowrie Conspiracy, Scottish conventions of monarchy, and Shakespeare's need to gratify James I. But these books by Macfarlane and Thomas drew new attention to witchcraft and fears about it in the sixteenth century and prompted critics to interpret *Macbeth* afresh, making much of the witches and of Lady Macbeth in relation to them. Dennis Biggins's "Sexuality, Witchcraft, and Violence in *Macbeth*"[8] and Peter Stallybrass's "*Macbeth* and Witchcraft"[9] mark the first phase of the consensus. Terry Eagleton's *William Shakespeare* (1986) gave it a stirring conceit:

> To any unprejudiced reader—which would seem to exclude Shakespeare himself, his contemporary audiences and almost all literary critics—it is surely clear

that positive value in *Macbeth* lies with the three witches. The witches are the heroines of the piece, however little the play itself recognises the fact, and however much the critics may have set out to defame them. It is they who, by releasing ambitious thoughts in Macbeth, expose a reverence for hierarchical social order for what it is, as the pious self-deception of a society based on routine oppression and incessant warfare. The witches are exiles from that violent order, inhabiting their own sisterly community on its shadowy borderlands, refusing all truck with its tribal bickerings and military honours.[10]

But the consensus was in place before Eagleton's book was published.

The gist of the consensus is that *Macbeth* is Shakespeare's fantasy of male self-begetting and immortality, without recourse to women. It is crucial to the new reading to bring Lady Macbeth and the witches together as sisters in subjection. They are not forces of evil or the uncanny, but victims of male oppression; they testify to every value a society governed by men excludes. The earliest essay in this vein, so far as I can discover, is Madelon Gohlke's "'I wooed thee with my sword': Shakespeare's Tragic Paradigms" (1980):

> The world constructed by Macbeth attempts to deny not only the values of trust and hospitality, perceived as essentially feminine, but to eradicate femininity itself. Macbeth reads power in terms of a masculine mystique that has no room for maternal values, as if the conscious exclusion of these values would eliminate all conditions of dependence, making him in effect invulnerable. To be born of woman, as he reads the witches' prophecy, is to be mortal. Macbeth's program of violence, involving murder and pillage in his kingdom and the repression of anything resembling compassion nor remorse within, is designed, like Coriolanus's desperate militarism, to make him author of himself.[11]

Jonathan Goldberg took up the theme in "Speculations: *Macbeth* and Source":

> The hypermasculine world of *Macbeth* is haunted . . . by the power represented in the witches; masculinity in the play is directed as an assaultive attempt to secure power, to maintain success and succession, at the expense of women. . . . Macbeth looks in the mirror and sees his reflection in the line that extends to James; not in the mirror is Mary Queen of Scots, the figure that haunts the patriarchal claims of *Basilikon Doron*, the mother on whom James rested his claims to the throne of England—and whom he sacrificed to assure his sovereignty.

But in the end "all masculine attempts at female deprivation—including Lady Macbeth's desire to unsex herself—are robbed of ultimate success. . . . What escapes control is figured in the witches."[12]

Perhaps the most thoroughgoing version of the consensus is found in Janet Adelman's "'Born of Woman': Fantasies of Maternal Power in *Macbeth*" (1987)[13] and *Suffocating Mothers: Fantasies of Maternal Origin in Shakespeare's Plays: "Hamlet" to "The Tempest"* (1992). She writes of "the decisive masculine act as a bloody rebirth, replacing the dangerous maternal origin through the violence of self-creation," and of the play as representing "both the fantasy of a virtually absolute and destructive maternal power and the fantasy of absolute escape from this power."[14]

These versions of the new reading are not of course identical: we would not expect them to be, coming as they do from exponents of feminism, psychoanalytic criticism, and new historicism. But they are at one in interpreting the play as a fantasy of self-begetting and immortality. They differ in determining whether or not the fantasy is fulfilled. Some critics see the end of the play as restoring the old masculine values; others think the forces embodied in the witches are still creatively at large, on the margin of the society they at any moment are capable of threatening. But we have a consensus of alleged fantasy and diagnosis, nonetheless.

It would be helpful if I could quote a few passages of close reading of *Macbeth* from adepts of the New Thematics. Not surprisingly, I cannot. Close reading is not what they do. Several reasons suggest themselves. The first is that these critics are queering one discipline—literary criticism— with the habits of another—social science. Their métier is not verbal analysis but the deployment of themes, arguments, and diagnoses: hence the only relation they maintain to the language of *Macbeth* is a remote one. A second consideration: these critics evidently think that Shakespeare's language is transparent to reality, and that the reality it discloses can be represented without fuss in political and psychoanalytic terms. This is a strange assumption, after many years of deconstruction in which we have been admonished that language is constitutionally opaque and its meanings undecidable. The new readers of *Macbeth* are not impeded by these considerations. They take language for granted as providing direct access to reality and to fantasy. Acting upon this assumption, they also take for granted what Geoffrey Hill has called, with rebuking intent, "the concurrence of language with one's expectations."[15] These critics have no sense of the recalcitrance of language, specifically of Shakespeare's English: they think that in reading his words they are engaging with forces and properties indistinguishable from their own. In philosophic terms, they practice the most blatant form of idealism, even though they profess—many of them—to be materialists.

It follows that when such critics quote, they do so merely to illustrate a theme, a discursive claim, or a diagnosis they have already produced. Eagleton quotes part of the "To-morrow and to-morrow and to-morrow" speech, but only to say that it shows Macbeth "reduced to a ham actor, unable to identify with his role."[16] That is not what the lines do. The reductive nature of Eagleton's comment may be shown by quoting, as an example of responsible interpretation of the lines, L. C. Knights's comment that "Macbeth is groping for meanings, trying to conceive a time when he might have met such a situation [as his wife's death] with something more than indifference."[17] Lisa Jardine, much in Eagleton's style, quotes Lady Macbeth's "Come you spirits / That tend on mortal thoughts, unsex me here" speech, but says of it merely that it represents "this steady misogynistic tradition" in which Lady Macbeth and other women "are represented as 'not-woman' at the peak of dramatic tension before committing 'unwomanly' acts—generally murder." When Jardine quotes Lady Macbeth's challenge to Macbeth, "What beast was't then / That made you break this enterprise to me?" she remarks only that it is yet another instance of "threatening womanhood."[18] In *The Subject of Tragedy* Catherine Belsey quotes the "Pity" speech and makes no literary comment upon it, but uses it to reproach "Liberal Humanism" for finding "its own reflection, its own imaginary fullness everywhere," in this case by constructing "the feeling, self-conscious, 'poetic' Macbeth, a full subject, a character."[19]

To what desires in contemporary literate society does the New Thematics correspond? A new form of reading, or a relapse into an old form, is interesting only if it exhibits such correspondence.

My sense of the matter comes back to the notion of transparency. I find a suggestive passage, bearing upon this motif, in Matei Calinescu's *Rereading*, where he writes about the general move from intensive to extensive reading; from the slow reading of a few texts, sacred or profane, to the skimming of many books, magazines, and newspapers: "With the growth of 'extensive reading,' the growing prestige of science, and the rise of political democracy, modernity has fostered a powerful longing for transparency doubled by a hostility to those forms of secrecy that were traditionally claimed as a prerogative of power, whether supernatural or human. But the modern ideal of transparency does not apply to the personal secrets of individuals, which, again reversing a long-standing tradition, should from now on be protected by the modern 'right to privacy.'"[20] This desire for transparency takes many forms, all reductive. It shows itself in the determination to construe every work of literature—a play about kings, treason, murder, and equivocation, for instance—as a simple parable, invidiously recited, of men and women. More clamorously, it presents itself as a desire to find great literature rotten with fantasy and

corruptly in league with men of power. "There is no document of civilization," we hear Walter Benjamin alleging, "that is not at the same time a
document of barbarism."[21]

The broad background to these desires is the assumption that all knowledge is socially constructed and that sociologists of knowledge are fully
equipped to understand the processes of this construction. The authors of
The Social Construction of Reality (1966) tell us that "it will be enough,
for our purposes, . . . to define 'knowledge' as the certainty that phenomena are real and that they possess specific characteristics."[22] Even with the
weasel qualification "for our purposes," this definition of knowledge is
scandalously loose, but it serves the purposes of those who for one reason
or another want to suppress metaphysical, religious, or visionary experience. What sociologists offer, to prove the social constitution of knowledge,
is a simplified account of particular social practices. Their definitions are
useless in trying to explain how the same material and social conditions
produced Shakespeare and Webster, or why Blake's art differs so radically
from Sir Joshua Reynolds's. As Michel Serres has remarked: "You can
always proceed from the product to its conditions, but never from the
conditions to the product."[23]

These factors, along with more obvious considerations such as film,
television, and video, explain why there has been a palpable loss or lapse
of interest in verbal culture by comparison with the culture of visual
images and artifacts. Guillory has argued, with E. D. Hirsch's *Cultural
Literacy* in mind, that "if Americans are 'culturally illiterate,' this fact is
evidence of the educational system's failure to install a motive for reading
in a nominally literate population."[24] What would such a motive be?
Pleasure, I hope: but pleasure of a distinctive kind. There is no point in
offering our students the experience of reading works of literature as if it
could compete with more mundane felicities. A different experience is
entailed, not an immediate gratification. I'll try to say what it involves, by
way of an attempted sketch of an English school.

The pleasure of reading literature arises from the exercise of one's imagination, a going out from one's self toward other lives, other forms of
life, past, present, and perhaps future. This description denotes its relation
to sympathy, fellowship, the spirituality and morality of being human. It is
certainly not a substitute for anything else—for one's commitments in
religion or politics, for instance. It is what it is. The reading of literature
may be taken as exemplary of artistic experience in general, without
implying that literature is superior to any other form of art. It may be true,
as Walter Pater maintained, that all the arts constantly aspire toward the

condition of music. But in literature that aspiration is qualified by the writer's more fundamental desire to explore and extend the resources of language. It is once again necessary to assert, in the face of much dissent, that literature exists; that it is not just a form of discourse like any other. By saying this, I may be thought to be endorsing some version of essentialism and claiming that every work of literature embodies some universal essence that floats entirely free of the conditions of its production. I make no such claim. But I assert, provoked by the opposite claim now more commonly heard, that a work of literature is accompanied by the circumstances and forces of its production, pressed upon by them, but it is not determined by them. Indeed, Shakespeare's achievement in *Macbeth*, the powers of invention and discovery he put to work in that play, are such as to make me entertain the conceit that the play was written in almost complete freedom. Still, there is no merit in countering one extravagance with another.

If literature exists, it is necessary to say in what respect it exists. I agree with Paul de Man on this matter: "For the statement about language, that sign and meaning can never coincide, is what is precisely taken for granted in the kind of language we call literary. Literature, unlike everyday language, begins on the far side of this knowledge; it is the only form of language free from the fallacy of unmediated expression. All of us know this, although we know it in the misleading way of a wishful assertion of the opposite. Yet the truth emerges in the foreknowledge we possess of the true nature of literature when we refer to it as *fiction.*"[25] The fallacy to which de Man refers is much in evidence in recent commentaries on *Macbeth:* the critics have not considered what mediation entails in Shakespeare's language or how one's reading should engage with that force.

What, then, are we to ask our students to read? Life, being short, is better spent reading great works rather than mediocre ones. If it is alleged that critical adjudication between one work and another has invariably been effected by men, and that masculine values have been enforced in those decisions, we now have the pedagogical conditions—classes, seminars, conferences, journals—under which an alternative canon, or additions to the canon, may be tried out. I would be surprised to see many works of literature, now deemed canonical, dislodged by this process. But I recognize certain troubling signs, such as the inclination of many students to read only modern if not contemporary works, and among those to prefer prose fiction to poetry. A bad sign; we find in poems more exactingly than in novels the qualities of language that give point to de Man's emphasis on mediation. But it is hardly likely that the question of merit in a particular work will gain much of a hearing, silenced as it is likely to be by questions of topical relevance and diagnostic availability. There are works of literature that answer to local interests and may be quoted to illustrate a theme or a set of cultural forces. That is probably the readiest use to which teachers are inclined to put them. But a great work of literature, like *Macbeth*, is one that answers to a remarkably wide range and pressure of interests. It is also, like the world according to Whitehead's sense of it, "patient of interpretation in terms of whatever happens to interest us."[26]

Nevertheless it is sometimes maintained that we should not prescribe great works of literature for students who come from a different cultural setting than our own. In "The Function of Literary Theory at the Present Time" (1989) J. Hillis Miller denounced as "repressive" the practice of "forcing a Latino or Thai in Los Angeles, a Puerto Rican in New York, an inner city African-American in either city to read only *King Lear*, *Great Expectations*, and other works from the old canon."[27] Miller's sentence is bizarre. "Forcing" is an exaggeration, the proportion of required to elective courses in American colleges and universities being as concessive as it is. "Only" is also a wild exaggeration: no such prescription ever arises. These are details, but on the substantive issue I see no reason whatever for not asking Latino, Thai, or Puerto Rican students who have chosen to read English for a degree to read *King Lear*, *Great Expectations*, and other works from the old canon. If these students were reading French or German or Italian for a degree, they would expect to read major works in the old canon of that literature and would regard themselves as cheated if they did not receive good teaching in the mysteries of that language and its literature. Miller is patronizing those students by claiming that they are not to be asked to read great literature or to be taught how best to read it.

Indeed, my disagreement with him on this issue impels me to claim that the best way to read English, under present circumstances, would be to read it as a second language and a second literature. Most of the defects of our reading and teaching arise from the fact that we are reading and teaching English as though our students were already in command of the language. We assume that they know the language well enough and are qualified to move to a study of the literature. We would not make this assumption if we were teaching a foreign language. If we taught English as a second language and a second literature, we would become more responsible to the mediating character of the literary language, the opacity of language as such: we would not assume that the language is transparent to our interests.

Surely I am forgetting the expository writing programs (EWPs) that take up so much time and energy in our colleges and universities? No: EWPs exist because so many junior school and high school teachers work under conditions in which it is impossible to teach their students how to read and write. If the conditions were propitious, EWPs would happily cease, and their teachers would be employed teaching the literature they entered the profession hoping to teach. Instead, they find themselves helping their students to become functionally literate, a process for which the reading of great literature is generally considered unsuitable. No student in an EWP class is obliged to read *King Lear.* As Edward Corbett has written, "literary texts will more often than not serve as a distraction from, rather than a promoter of, the objectives of a writing course."[28]

A latecomer to the United States, I have never taught a class in expository writing, so I must quote what other teachers report of the experience. In *The Culture of Literacy* Wlad Godzich gives convincing evidence that only a restricted notion of literacy obtains in EWPs: they "provide for competence in a specific code, with little, if any but the most rudimentary, awareness of the general problematics of codes and codification in language." I do not warm to this talk of codes; it does not answer to my sense of the reading of literature, the activity in which we have seen Harding, Leavis, Empson, and other critics engaged. But Godzich's general argument is persuasive: "It is not an exaggeration to state that the effect of the new writing programs, given their orientation, is not to solve a 'crisis of literacy' but to promote a new differentiated culture in which the student is trained to use language for the reception and conveyance of information in only one sphere of human activity: that of his or her future field of employment."[29]

Guillory's reflections on the EWP are even more pointed; they bear on the civic aim of such a program. He refers to

> a new kind of "oral performance" on the basis of the new kind of writing practice inculcated in the compositional syllabus. We will have no difficulty in recognizing what this speech sounds like: it is the speech of the professional-managerial classes, the administrators and bureaucrats; and it is employed *in its place*, the "office." It is not "everyday" language. The point of greatest historical interest about this speech is that its production bypasses the older literary syllabus altogether. Students need no longer immerse themselves in that body of writing called "literature" in order to acquire "literary" language. In taking over the social function of producing a distinction between a basic and a more elite language, composition takes on as well the ideological identity of that sociolect, its pretension to universality, its status as the medium of political discourse.[30]

Leavis's aim was to train students to form an intelligent reading public: his ideal student might well become a man of letters or, as in the case of Q. D. Leavis, a woman of letters. The aim of EWPs is to train students to take part in the decorum of social and public life. The divided forces of a plural society—ideologies of race, class, gender, creed—are meant to be reconciled in offices of management and the corporations. Meanwhile the study of literature is confined to a relatively small part of the English school, and its aims are regularly alleged to be elitist.

Not that literature needs to be defended; it merely needs to be read, intensively. I cannot regard recent readings of *Macbeth* as intensive; they exhibit that premature recourse to the political and the psychoanalytic that is one of the banes of contemporary practice. But I should emphasize, even in a mere sketch of an English school, that a theory of communication is not adequate to the reading of literature. No matter how elaborately such a theory is proposed, as by Richards or by Roman Jakobson, it does not answer the requirements of reading literature. Pierre Bourdieu has argued that "utterances are not only (save in exceptional circumstances) signs to be understood and deciphered; they are also *signs of wealth*, intended to be evaluated and appreciated, and *signs of authority*, intended to be believed and obeyed."[31] I would add: some words and sentences are also tokens of largesse, acts of grace and flair, to be appreciated as such. So a theory of performance, not of communication, is required. Performance is the larger motive, within which the secondary motive, communication, can be housed comfortably enough. What we find in *Macbeth* is Shakespeare's performance in the modes of language and theater, copiousness of expression far beyond the requirements of communication though still compatible with those. The speeches analyzed by Leavis, Empson, Harding, and Knights would be largely redundant, their inventive eloquence quite exorbitant, if the local requirements of communication were primary.

Performance and therefore form: bringing words, gestures, and actions to the condition of form. This is the most complex issue in literary criticism: how to divine the form of a work as distinct from the object of reference when we recite the plot of a novel or count the lines of a sonnet. It is a serious limitation in the "close reading" practiced by Leavis's colleagues that it had little or no purchase on the form of a work of literature. Except in their readings of short poems, the New Critics could indicate the form of a work only by delineating its structure of images, as in *The Well Wrought Urn* or Mark Schorer's essays on English fiction. Form is achieved content, Schorer said: true, and his phrase recognizes the work of performance, but it does not say enough to be useful beyond that. In *The Aesthetic Dimension* Herbert Marcuse argues that Marxist critics have been misguided in attacking formalism in criticism: of many works of literature it may be shown that it is by virtue of its form that a work of art is genuinely revolutionary. The form of *Macbeth* is not indeed its five-act structure, though it is related to that. Form is the embodiment, first word to last, of a principle, a source of energy, or—in Aristotle's sense—a human action that is the animating motive of the play.

The first requirement, if we are to read literature in the spirit indicated by my approved instances, is a recovered disinterestedness. If we cannot or will not sequester our immediately pressing interests, put them in parentheses for the time being, we have no hope of reading literature. If we read merely to have our political or other values endorsed, or to find them abused, by the work of literature, the situation is vain. Received wisdom would have it that disinterestedness is a cloak at once to conceal and to reveal economic capital: to conceal it by making its signs a matter of tone and gesture; to reveal it by showing it in a sublimed transformation. The only person who can be disinterested, we are told, is someone who has enough money, leisure, and freedom to enjoy the experience. That is not true, or not entirely true. The few years that Miller's Latino, Thai, and Puerto Rican students spend in college or university taking a degree are designed to provide them with conditions of relative freedom under which they can study. During those years, unless the system of higher education has already broken down, these students have the opportunity of standing apart, at least to some extent, from the primary interests that beset them—jobs, money, responsibilities. They ought to be helped to take pleasure in reading great literature by having them read it a little apart from the culture that otherwise governs them. They might also be helped to enjoy for a while a quality Blackmur found in Marianne Moore's poems: the perfection of standing aside. If that is not possible, then the system has already failed.

The word I have not used, which seems to trouble many critics and teachers, is "aesthetics." It is thought to denote moral lassitude, political irresponsibility, decadence. The troubling is unnecessary. But in any case I have been heartened recently, reading certain critics who might be thought to be entirely "political" and finding them coming around again to the recognition of aesthetics as a necessary discipline of attention. Edward Said in *Culture and Imperialism* and George Levine in *Aesthetics and Ideology* are willing to recognize "the aesthetic" as providing what Levine calls "a space where the immediate pressure of ethical and political decisions are [sic] deferred." Levine also recognizes "how difficult it is to resist or qualify in any way the primacy of the ideological project of criticism."[32] That recognition is enough for my purpose. But some critics remain invincibly hostile to aesthetics. I can only note that aesthetics means perception, the practice of paying attention to objects that ask only to be perceived. If the word offends, I would be pleased to replace it by "poetics," which I take to mean the inductive study of works of literature with a view to understanding—but only late in the day—the principles of their working. That, it seems to me, is what an English school should take as its goal.

Notes

1. I. A. Richards, *Speculative Instruments* (Chicago: University of Chicago Press, 1955), 63.

2. D. W. Harding, *Experience into Words* (Cambridge: Cambridge University Press, 1982 reprint of 1963 edition), 99 and 181–82.

3. Helen Gardner, *The Business of Criticism* (Oxford: Clarendon Press, 1959), 59–60.

4. F. R. Leavis, *Education and the University: A Sketch for an "English School"* (London: Chatto & Windus, 1943), 123–24.

5. William Empson, *Seven Types of Ambiguity* (New York: New Directions, 1955), 59–60.

6. Leavis, *Education and the University*, 68 and 69.

7. John Guillory, *Cultural Capital: The Problem of Literary Canon Formation* (Chicago: University of Chicago Press, 1993), 156.

8. *Shakespeare Survey* 8 (1975), 255–77.

9. In John Russell Brown, ed., *Focus on "Macbeth"* (London: Routledge & Kegan Paul, 1982), 188–209.

10. Terry Eagleton, *William Shakespeare* (Oxford: Basil Blackwell, 1986), 1–2.

11. Madelon Gohlke: "'I wooed thee with my sword': Shakespeare's Tragic Paradigms," in *Representing Shakespeare: New Psychoanalytic Essays*, ed. Murray M. Schwartz and Coppelia Kahn (Baltimore, Md.: Johns Hopkins University Press, 1980), 176.

12. Jonathan Goldberg, "Speculations: *Macbeth* and Source,": in *Shakespeare Reproduced: The Text in History and Ideology*, ed. Jean E. Howard and Marion F. O'Connor (New York and London: Methuen, 1987), 259–60.

13. Janet Adelman: "'Born of Woman': Fantasies of Maternal Power in *Macbeth*," in *Cannibals, Witches, and Divorce: Estranging the Renaissance*, ed. Marjorie Garber (Baltimore, Md.: Johns Hopkins University Press, 1987), 90–121.

14. Janet Adelman, *Suffocating Mothers: Fantasies of Maternal Origin in Shakespeare's Plays: "Hamlet" to "The Tempest"* (New York: Routledge, 1992), 130 and 146.

15. Geoffrey Hill, "Style and Faith," *Times Literary Supplement*, December 27, 1991, 4.

16. Eagleton, *William Shakespeare*, 3.

17. L. C. Knights, *Some Shakespearean Themes* (Stanford, Calif.: Stanford University Press, 1959), 141.

18. Lisa Jardine, *Still Harping on Daughters: Women and Drama in the Age of Shakespeare* (Sussex, U.K.: Harvester Press, 1983), 94–95 and 97.

19. Catherine Belsey, *The Subject of Tragedy* (London: Methuen, 1985), 51.

20. Matei Calinescu, *Rereading* (New Haven, Conn.: Yale University Press, 1993), 265.

21. Walter Benjamin, *Illuminations*, tr. Harry Zohn (New York: Schocken, 1969), 256.

22. Peter L. Berger and Thomas Luckmann, *The Social Construction of Reality: A Treatise in the Sociology of Knowledge* (New York: Doubleday, 1966), 1.

23. Michel Serres, *Hermes: Literature, Science, Philosophy*, ed. Josué V. Harari and David F. Bell (Baltimore, Md.: Johns Hopkins University Press, 1992), 106.

24. Guillory, *Cultural Capital*, 35.

25. Paul de Man, *Blindness and Insight: Essays in the Rhetoric of Contemporary Criticism*, 2d rev. ed. (Minneapolis: University of Minnesota Press, 1983), 17.

26. Quoted in Frank Kermode, *The Genesis of Secrecy: On the Interpretation of Narrative* (Cambridge, Mass.: Harvard University Press, 1979), xi.

27. J. Hillis Miller, *Theory Now and Then* (Durham, N.C.: Duke University Press, 1991), 391.

28. Edward Corbett, "Literature and Composition: Allies or Rivals in the Classroom?" in *Composition and Literature*, ed. Winifred Bryan Horner (Chicago: University of Chicago Press, 1983), 180. Quoted in Guillory, *Cultural Capital*, 80.

29. Wlad Godzich, *The Culture of Literacy* (Cambridge, Mass.: Harvard University Press, 1994), 5.

30. Guillory, *Cultural Capital*, 79–80.

31. Pierre Bourdieu, *Language and Symbolic Power*, tr. Gino Raymond and Matthew Adamson, ed. John B. Thompson (Cambridge, Mass.: Harvard University Press, 1991), 66. Quoted in Jonathan Loesberg, "Bourdieu and the Sociology of Aesthetics," *ELH* 60, no. 4 (Winter 1993): 1042.

32. George Levine, ed., *Aesthetics and Ideology* (New Brunswick, N.J.: Rutgers University Press, 1994), 15 and 17.

THEORY

Seven

"Beyond Method"

GERTRUDE HIMMELFARB

> Dewey and Foucault make exactly the same criticism of the tradition. They agree, right down the line, about the need to abandon traditional notions of rationality, objectivity, method, and truth. They are both, so to speak, "beyond method."
>   *Richard Rorty*[1]

FOR THE journalist, the medium is the message. For the scholar, the method is the message. On this one proposition, traditional and nontraditional scholars may agree. Methodology does not dictate the conclusions that any particular study may come to, but it does dictate the parameters of the study: the way the research is conducted, how the findings are presented, even what are suitable subjects for study. A revolution in methodology is, therefore, of more than "academic" interest, as the invidious phrase has it—more than a technicality or formality. And it is all the more momentous if it affects a wide variety of disciplines throughout the university.

We have recently experienced such a revolution. The dominating force in that revolution is postmodernism, an omnibus term for poststructuralism, deconstruction, new historicism, semiotics, and the like. These, in turn, give philosophical credibility and legitimacy to such other movements as feminism and multiculturalism. The effect, on both the subject matter and the methodology of the humanities, has been nothing short of revolutionary. This is not just another "revisionism" of the kind that has always been the lifeblood of the academy. A revisionist thesis about the origin of World War II or the meaning of *Huckleberry Finn* offers a new interpretation of that particular event or work occasioned by new evidence, a new insight, or a new theory. Postmodernism is a new way of thinking about all subjects and all disciplines.

Imported from France (which had acquired it from Germany), postmodernism made its appearance in the United States in the 1970s, first in departments of literature and then in other disciplines of the humanities.[2] Its forefathers are Nietzsche and Heidegger, its fathers Derrida and Foucault. From Jacques Derrida postmodernism has borrowed the vocabulary and basic concepts of deconstruction: the "aporia" of discourse, the indeterminacy and contrariness of language, the fictive and duplicitous nature of signs and symbols, the nonreferential character of words and their dissociation from any presumed reality, the "problematization" of all subjects, events, and texts. From Michel Foucault it has adopted the idea of power: the power structure immanent not only in language—the words and ideas that "privilege" the "hegemonic" groups in society—but in the very nature of knowledge, which is itself an instrument and product of power. Thus traditional discourse and learning are impugned as "logocentric," "phallocentric," and "totalizing."

In literature, postmodernism entails the denial of the fixity of any text, of the authority of the author over the critic or reader, of any canon of great books, and of the very idea of greatness. In philosophy, it is a denial of the constancy of language, of any correspondence between language and reality, indeed of any essential reality or any proximate truth about reality. In history, it is a denial of the objectivity of the historian, of the factuality or reality of the past, and thus of the possibility of arriving at any truths about the past. And so with the other disciplines: it induces a radical skepticism, relativism, and subjectivism that denies not this or that truth about any subject but the very idea of truth—that denies even the *ideal* of truth, truth as something to aspire to even if it can never be fully attained.

If literary critics have been in the forefront of the postmodernist movement, it is in the field of history that its revolutionary effects may be seen most clearly. For postmodernism reverses two centuries of scholarship designed to make of history a "discipline"—a rigorous, critical, systematic study of the past, complete with a methodology designed to make that study as objective as possible. Before there was postmodernist history, there was "modernist" history, as it may be called—the discipline as it evolved in the past two centuries under the influence first of Enlightenment rationalism, then of Germanic scholarship, and in this century of academic professionalism. Modernist history is not, *pace* its present critics, positivist history. It does not profess to be a science (although some early enthusiasts occasionally fell into that rhetoric). On the contrary, precisely because it is not a science, its practitioners have felt it all the more necessary to devise a methodology that compensates for its inherent weaknesses, that makes it a discipline in spite of the fact that it is not a science.

Modernist history may be understood as an attempt to resolve the ambiguity in the word *history*: history in the sense of the past, and history meaning the writing about the past ("history" and "historiography," or "history-as-actuality" and "history-as-record," as they are sometimes distinguished). For the modernist, the ambiguity itself, the fact that the word encompasses both meanings, suggests that there is an inherent, if only proximate, relation between them. To bring the historical work into the closest correspondence with the past requires a conscious effort of self-discipline on the part of the historian. And it is this self-discipline that is the basis of the "discipline" of history.

This is the meaning of Leopold von Ranke's famous and much-derided phrase: to know the past as it "actually happened." It now sounds like a vainglorious boast, but in its context it was modest enough. Distinguishing his own work from that of his more ambitious contemporaries, Ranke wrote: "To history has been assigned the office of judging the past, of instructing the present for the benefit of future ages. To such high offices this work does not aspire: It wants only to show what actually happened." Ranke himself had no illusions about the ease of that task or his own success in realizing it. "I know to what extent I have fallen short of my aim. One tries, one strives, but in the end it is not attained."[3]

The present-day modernist is even more painfully aware of the vulnerability of the historical enterprise: the fallibility and deficiency of the historical record, the fallibility and selectivity inherent in the writing of history, and the fallibility and subjectivity of the historian. As long as historians have reflected upon their craft, they have known that the past cannot be recaptured in its totality, if only because the remains of the past are incomplete and are themselves part of the present, so that the past itself is, in this sense, irredeemably present. They have also known that the writing of history necessarily entails selection and interpretation, that there is inevitable distortion in the attempt to present a coherent account of an often inchoate past, that, therefore, every historical work is necessarily imperfect, tentative, and partial (in both senses of the word).

Historians have also known—they would have to be extraordinarily obtuse not to—that some of the ideas and assumptions they bring to history derive not only from their own culture and place in society, but also from the ideas and beliefs to which they are committed. A century ago, the lead article in the first issue of the *American Historical Review* informed the profession: "History will not stay written. Every age demands a history written from its own standpoint—with reference to its own social condition, its thought, its beliefs, and its acquisitions—and therefore comprehensible to the men who live in it."[4] Relativism in this sense, however, was not taken to absolve historians from the duty of being as objective as they could be. On the contrary, it obliged them to make the most strenuous efforts to be as objective as possible, to rise above their natural conditions and inclinations. A few years after that issue of the *Review*, the annual report of the American Historical Association explained that "the principle of historical relativity" meant that events and actions should be placed in their historical contexts rather than in accord with any "latter-day ideals."[5] This caution became immortalized in Herbert Butterfield's dictum about "the Whig fallacy": the fallacy of present-mindedness, of projecting the present upon the past.[6]

So, too, historians have always known what seems to have come as a revelation to some scientists: that historical discoveries, like the scientific revolutions described by Thomas Kuhn, often originate in "flashes of intuition" that suggest new "paradigms," new ways of looking at reality.[7] But historians, like scientists, also know that those intuitions and paradigms have to be supported by hard evidence, that they require not less but more rigorous scholarship if they are to become the accepted paradigm or consensus.

Until recently, the discipline of history was epitomized by the required course on "methodology" (sometimes called "historical method") that was the keystone of every graduate program in history and even of the more ambitious undergraduate programs.[8] The immediate purpose of the course was to prepare students for the writing of their dissertations, the larger purpose to teach them the craft of history. The course covered such topics as the tools of research, the distinction between primary and secondary sources, the authenticity of documents and reliability of witnesses, the verification of evidence and the search for countervailing evidence, the alertness to bias (on the part of the researcher as well as the documents and sources), and the perils of present-mindedness.

Students were also introduced to the myriad rules governing footnotes and bibliography. Those who were inclined to dismiss these as trivial or arbitrary were soon disabused of that notion. The documentary apparatus, they were told, had two purposes: to bring to the surface the infrastructure of the historical work, thus exposing it to criticism and correction (the prescribed footnote forms, for example, made the sources easily identified, located, and checked), and to encourage the historian to a maximum exertion of objectivity, in spite of all the temptations to the contrary. There were also discussions of such more elevated questions as whether history is an art or a science; whether the historian can be truly objective or has to be content with "verisimilitude"; whether "counterfactual" history (the "ifs" of history) is a legitimate part of the historical enterprise; what the ethical obligations of the historian are; and how the narrative (it was assumed that history is primarily a narrative) can accommodate the ambiguities, complexities, and contradictions of the historical record.

But the more important part of the course was the exercises designed to implement the methodological principles. In the year-long course I took under Louis Gottschalk at the University of Chicago, there were two principal assignments tailored to the student's field of specialization. Since mine was the French Revolution, I was asked to determine the hour of sunrise on a particular day during the Revolution. I do not now remember the day (to say nothing of the time), nor do I remember how I solved the problem. But I do recall, after my initial resentment at having to devote so much effort to so trivial a matter, becoming conscious of the importance of determining that fact (it turned out to be crucial to some event) and also taking pride, even pleasure, in the practical experience of research.

That was a minor chore. The major assignment was a paper based upon the detailed examination of a few pages from the most reputable, recent work in our field. The charge was simple, or so it seemed until we tried to carry it out. We were to examine every published source cited (manuscript sources were excepted only because they were unavailable to us), first to see whether the quotations and footnotes were accurate, and then, more important, to see whether each quotation or paraphrase was faithful to the sense and context of the source; whether the source itself was trustworthy and impartial (or, if not, whether that was taken into account by the author); whether the author drew the proper inferences from the sources; whether every significant or controversial fact in the text was based upon relevant and reliable sources; and whether there were other relevant and reliable sources that were not cited and that might have supported other facts and conclusions.

It was a challenging exercise and a salutary experience. In my case, I discovered several errors in quotations and citations and one serious discrepancy between the source and the deductions drawn from it. This was my initiation into the discipline of history—a painful initiation, because it made me acutely sensitive to the rigors and difficulties of scholarship (and because my own half-written thesis had drawn heavily upon that book, and I had to go back to check all the facts and quotations I had borrowed from it). At the same time it was an exhilarating experience, rather like a game of chess. And like a good game of chess, it gave me a great respect for the craft of the discipline, a craft that was patently not infallible but that did aspire to high standards and could be tested against those standards. (I later discovered that this was essentially the exercise, on a much larger scale obviously and with access to the primary documents, that Forrest McDonald performed when he refuted Charles Beard's *An Economic Interpretation of the Constitution of the United States.*)

Such required courses on methodology are now relatively rare. Although modernist history continues to be practiced by a good many historians, it no longer has the credibility and authority to sustain a mandatory course of this kind. For the postmodernist the very idea of a "discipline" of history, let alone of a methodology, is regarded as specious, even fraudulent. Where the modernist tries to overcome the ambiguity of "history" and bridge the gap between the past and the writing about the past, the postmodernist insists upon its radical, immutable ambiguity, the absolute disjunction between the past and any work about the past. Where the modernist, aware that there is no absolute truth, tries to arrive at the closest approximation to truth—to modest, contingent, tentative, incremental, proximate truths—the postmodernist takes the denial of truth as a deliverance from any kind or degree of truth. Where the modernist makes every effort to avoid present-mindedness, the postmodernist happily acquiesces in it, declaring the "Whig fallacy" itself, the pretense of past-mindedness, to be the ultimate fallacy. Where the modernist is challenged to try to achieve as much objectivity as possible, the postmodernist discredits the very idea of objectivity.[9] Where the modernist, in short, tolerates relativism and tries to limit and control it, the postmodernist celebrates and exploits it.

For the postmodernist, there is no truth to be derived from the past because the past is only a "social construct" devised by the historian. The events of the past are "texts," much as poems are, and the historian has the same authority over the past as the literary critic has over the poem. Nor is there any more "truth" or "objectivity" or "factuality" (these words now habitually appear in quotation marks) in history than in poetry. Moreover, the idea of a "discipline" of history is not only delusory, it is tyrannical. Just as Foucault exposed the prison and asylum as institutions designed to "discipline" society, so the postmodernist seeks to "demystify" and "demythicize" the discipline of history, to show up the methodology as a specious show of objectivity intended to privilege a hegemonic ideology.

The liberation from the tyranny of the discipline takes many forms. At the simplest level, it is a liberation from footnotes (or endnotes, as is now commonly the case). Not only is there no longer any consensus about the form of notes; there is no longer any presumption in favor of notes in any form, so that a good many scholarly books are being published, even by university presses, without any notes at all.[10] Arno Mayer, the author of a controversial and unfootnoted book on the Holocaust, explained to an interviewer that footnotes are "a fetish [that] very often interferes with careful intellection and rumination."[11] Another historian, William Appleman Williams, presenting a revisionist view of American Cold War policies, says that footnotes and bibliographies are "poor jokes" for a book like his, because the source of any quotation is meaningless except in relation to all the other documents and to the author's "process of reflection." If the reader, he argues, trusts the author because the source of the quotation is cited, there is no reason to distrust him because it is not.[12] This claim, that the historian need not prove himself to the reader, takes on a special meaning in the context of multiculturalism. The authors of a book on Native Americans find the very idea of footnotes demeaning: "It is our culture and history and we do not have to prove it to anyone by footnoting."[13]

While some historians protest against the fetish of footnotes, others object to the "fetish of archival research"—the study of original or primary documents.[14] Still others deplore the emphasis upon documentary evidence in general; this objection applies especially to political and constitutional history, which are most reliant upon such documents.[15] When the English historian Geoffrey Elton assumed the chair of English Constitutional History at Cambridge in 1968, he defended both the subject and the methodology implicit in it: constitutional history because it represents the efforts of a nation to organize itself as rationally as it can; and documentary history because it represents the efforts of the historian to discover as objectively as possible the truth about the past.[16] The documents, to be sure, have to be interpreted and reinterpreted, amplified and modified by other kinds of evidence, but they cannot be denied or falsified. It is precisely this last claim that is now rejected, for the documents themselves are deemed to be as problematic and indeterminate as any other source. Indeed they are more so, because they embody all the rationalist, elitist, and sexist ideas that distort the past.

The liberation from the fetish of footnotes, archives, and documents has as its corollary a liberation from the fetish of facts—or "facticity," as is said pejoratively.[17] If everything about history is problematic, including facts (in quotation marks), there is little reason to fuss about such trivia as misstatements, misquotations, or miscitations. When the work of one young historian was criticized for numerous errors in transcription and deductions from the sources, some eminent historians rallied to his defense. One historian chastised those old-fashioned, naive scholars who believe in "the absolute certitude of historical fact." Historians, he explained, are more than the "tenured custodians of facts." They require a "historical imagination," an effort of "imaginative creation," that goes well beyond documents and facts. "Young historians," he warned his colleagues, "will never learn their craft if their elders become fact fetishists."[18]

Even before postmodernism became fashionable, Theodore Zeldin proposed a still more radical mode of liberation: the abandonment of narrative history, which relies upon the "tyrannical" concepts of causality, chronology, and collectivity (the latter referring to class and nationality). To free history from these constraints, historians should adopt the model of a pointillist painting composed entirely of unconnected dots. This would have the double advantage of emancipating the historian from the tyrannies of the discipline and emancipating the reader from the tyranny of the historian, because the reader would be free to make "what lines he thinks fit for himself."[19]

The objection to narrative history—"narrativity," as it is called—is at the heart of the postmodernist opposition to traditional history. Narrative, one historian explains, is a "coercive category, one that by its normative inclusive character denies its own fictionality and instability and thereby distorts the creative possibilities of the present and future."[20] Any narrative is "coercive" because it presents "facts" as if they were true, imposing upon the past a logical, coherent structure, a story that does not reflect the indeterminate nature of the past. It is also fallacious because it is "logocentric," assuming a specious rationality of language and thought.

One of the many ironies in the critique of narrative history—apart from the fact that the critique itself is rational, coherent, and "logocentric"—is the partiality of postmodernists for a new kind of narrative: "microhistory" or "micronarrative." Unlike traditional narrative history, which relates a series of public events over the course of time, this new genre focuses upon a small episode involving a single individual or community, sometimes in the briefest span of time, and often with no pretense of being typical or representative. Among the best-known exemplars of this kind of narrative are Natalie Zemon Davis's *The Return of Martin Guerre*, the story of a peasant of Languedoc in the mid-sixteenth century who suddenly disappears and of the imposter who is accepted by his wife as the long-lost husband; Jonathan Spence's *The Death of Woman Wang*, about a seventeenth-century Chinese peasant woman who is killed by the husband to whom she has been unfaithful, climaxed by her last dream revealing her intimate feelings and thoughts; Simon Schama's *Dead Certainties (Unwarranted Speculations)*, including a "demythologized" (and decidedly unheroic) account of the death of General Wolfe during the Battle of Quebec in 1759; and John Demos's *The Unredeemed Captive*, the story of an English girl captured by Iroquois Indians who eventually marries into the tribe, refusing the appeals of her family to return.

These works, all by distinguished historians, not only read more like fiction than history but actually are, to one degree or another, fictionalized—not historical fiction à la Walter Scott, but fictionalized history, which is quite another thing. All the authors admit the intrusion of fictional elements into their work, but Schama gives the most elaborate defense of it.[21] In an "Afterword" and "A Note on Sources," he explains that whereas he follows "the documented record with some closeness," his essays are "historical novellas," "works of the imagination, not scholarship," including some passages that are "pure inventions," "purely imagined fiction." (These "passages" include four pages of the most dramatic part of the book: a fictional soldier's account, related in the first person, of Wolfe's death.) It is a "banal axiom," Schama says, that all historical knowledge is "fatally circumscribed by the character and prejudices of its narrator," so that even the most scholarly work necessarily relies upon the "inventive faculty—selecting, pruning, editing, commenting, interpreting, delivering judgments."[22] Elsewhere Schama assures us that he is not a "deconstructionist" and does not "scorn the boundary between fact and fiction."[23] Yet the effect of his work, as of the others, is to blur that boundary, to do, perhaps unwittingly, what the deconstructionist does deliberately. The "banal axiom" of the traditional historian is not that history is "fatally circumscribed"—only that it is "circumscribed." With the addition of that adverb the axiom ceases to be banal and becomes fatal—fatal, at least, to the traditional conception of history as a search for facts however uncertain, rather than fiction however "inventive."

So far, few historians have ventured into the new genre of fictionalized history, although those who have are among our most eminent and gifted historians. But many more historians, freed from the fetishism of truth, factuality, and objectivity, feel released from the coercive conventions of scholarship. It might be said that the brilliant historian can flout these conventions with impunity, much as a talented writer can occasionally (but only occasionally, without nullifying the effect) violate the precepts of grammar. But it is quite a different matter if the exception is made the rule—if, as one postmodernist puts it, all of history is regarded as a form of "historiographic metafiction."[24]

The most fashionable words in the profession now are *imagined, invented, constructed, created.*[25] Where once historians were exhorted to be accurate and factual, they are now urged to be imaginative and inventive. Instead of "recreating" the past, they are told to "create" it; instead of "reconstructing" history, to "construct" or "deconstruct" it. Formerly, when historians invoked the idea of imagination, they meant the exercise of imagination required to transcend the present and become immersed in the past: "empathy, imagination, the attempt to place oneself in an historic situation and into an historic character without pre-judgment."[26] For many historians today it means exactly the opposite: the imagination to create a past in the image of the present.

The challenge to modernist history comes not only from postmodernism but also from the several varieties of "new history" (some no longer so new). These histories are defined by their subjects rather than their methods: social history, feminist history, multiculturalist history, the race-class-gender modes of history. But methodologically they have much in common with postmodernism. Social history—"history from below," the history of ordinary people in their daily lives—is in principle consistent with the older methodology. It becomes less so, however, when it departs from documentary evidence (parish rolls, court records, memoirs) and relies upon oral interviews, fiction, psychoanalytic concepts, the "ideal types" of sociology, or the "thick description" of anthropology. These do not lend themselves to the kind of scrutiny—for accuracy, reliability, impartiality, relevancy, representativeness—that would satisfy the traditional rules of evidence.

Feminist history, too, as it was originally conceived—as the history of women in particular historical periods and events—was entirely compatible with the traditional methodology. It was only when feminists began to reject not only women's history in this sense but also the "mainstreaming" of women's history into general history—the "add women and stir recipe," as it is invidiously called[27]—that the modernist methodology was discarded together with its ideology. The new feminist history calls for the "reconceptualizing" of all of history from a "consciously feminist stance," a "feminist perspective," so that it may be "seen through the eyes of women and ordered by values they define"[28]—the eyes and values of the historian rather than of the women who are the subjects of history. Some feminists reject the very mode of discourse of modernist history, logic, reason, and coherence being said to reflect a logocentric, patriarchal, hegemonic ideology. A leading feminist historian, Joan Scott, explains the affinity between feminist history and postmodernism: "A more radical feminist politics (and a more radical feminist history) seems to me to require a more radical epistemology. Precisely because it addresses questions of epistemology, relativizes the status of all knowledge, links knowledge and power, and theorizes these in terms of the operations of difference, I think poststructuralism (or at least some of the approaches generally associated with Michel Foucault and Jacques Derrida) can offer feminism a powerful analytic perspective."[29]

All modes of multiculturalist history thrive in this postmodernist atmosphere. Although the race-class-gender trinity is ultimately deterministic, assuming that individuals are defined by these categories and their actions, feelings, and beliefs determined by them, the trinity itself derives from an initial indeterminacy, a *tabula rasa*, which permits the historian to construct or create a past in accord with one or another of these categories. Some historians have begun to worry about the resulting "balkanization" of history, the lack of coherence, focus, and continuity.[30] American historians are concerned that the *unum* is in danger of disappearing from the *E pluribus unum* that has traditionally defined the American people and polity. For postmodernists, this is all to the good. The *unum* is precisely the kind of privileged, hegemonic, absolutistic, totalizing history that is anathema to them. "We require a history," Hayden White, the philosopher of history, announces, "that will educate us to discontinuity more than ever before; for discontinuity, disruption, and chaos is our lot."[31]

White's dictum about history applies all the more to literature. Where postmodernist historians emphasize the discontinuity between the past and the writing about the past, postmodernist literary critics emphasize the discontinuity between the literary work and the reading or interpretation of that work. And where these historians assert their dominance over the past by rejecting the idea of objectivity and affirming their own creativity, literary critics assert their dominance over the "text" by rejecting the "authority" of the author and exalting that of the reader. In literature as in history, truth is a casualty. "Criticism," Roland Barthes explains, "is not an 'homage' to the truth of the past or to the truth of 'others'—it is a construction of the intelligibility of our own time."[32] So, too, reading is said to be "a kind of rewriting" rather than "an attempt to mirror the text read."[33] And "rewriting" means altering the very words of the text by introducing hyphens, slashes, parentheses, quotation marks, visible deletions, and additions, thus creating puns, paradoxes, ambiguities, antitheses, and "differences," all of which make the text very different from what the author made of it.

If the deconstructionist rewrites the text by "intertextualizing" it—relating it to others remote from it in time, place, and even subject—the "new historicist" rewrites it by "contextualizing" it: converting it into an economic, social, or cultural event, an event rooted as much in the present as in the past. Thus *The Tempest* may appear as a "post-colonial historical text," or *Don Quixote* as a "twentieth-century mediator of Spanish literary identity."[34] Stephen Greenblatt, the most skillful and learned practitioner of this art, creates a Renaissance literature replete with evocations of latter-day imperialism, colonialism, capitalism, and authoritarianism.[35]

Just as the postmodernist historian dissolves the connection between the past and the writing about the past, or the postmodernist literary critic the connection between literature and criticism, so the postmodernist philosopher annuls the relationship between reality and language—denies, indeed, the "essential" nature of reality. "There is no way," Richard Rorty declares, "to get outside our beliefs and our language so as to find some test other than coherence."[36] Like Derrida, for whom "metaphysics is nothing more than mythology,"[37] Rorty derides the "real live metaphysical prig" who still believes in reality and truth, who thinks that there is some essence or foundation in reality from which truths can be deduced: "You can still find philosophy professors who will solemnly tell you that they are seeking *the truth*, not just a story or a consensus but an honest-to-God, down-home, accurate representation of the way the world is. A few of them will even claim to write in a clear, precise, transparent way, priding themselves on manly straightforwardness, on abjuring 'literary' devices."[38] Philosophy, Rorty insists, should not be "taken seriously" because it teaches neither wisdom nor virtue. The proper role of philosophers is to cultivate a "light-minded aestheticism, . . . dream up as many new contexts as possible, . . . be as polymorphous in our adjustments as possible, . . . recontextualize for the hell of it."[39] Echoing those historians who would fictionalize history, Rorty pays tribute to the "wisdom of the novel," because the novel, unlike philosophy, is not burdened by "transcultural notions of validity."[40]

The effect of postmodernism has been to create a genuinely interdisciplinary academic culture—or not so much interdisciplinary in the old sense, in which one discipline inspires and vivifies another, as transdisciplinary, in which each discipline loses its distinctive character and all become indistinguishable. "The historicity of [literary] texts and the textuality of history,"[41] "the historical text as literary artifact,"[42] the aestheticization and fictionalization of both philosophy and history, the problematization and feminization of all the disciplines—this confusion and amalgamation of genres is the hallmark of postmodernism and, perhaps, its greatest triumph. And it is here that one can see most clearly the methodological implications of postmodernism. For the loss of a distinctive disciplinary character necessarily involves the loss of a distinctive methodology—or of any methodology.

Feminism, for example, not only transcends the disciplines; in its more radical form it transcends the principles and methods upon which all the disciplines traditionally rest. There are feminist philosophers who regard truth, reason, and logic as "logocentric" and "phallocentric," violating women's natural mode of thought and imposing upon them an alien "logos";[43] feminist historians who find the language and concepts of political history—power, empire, sovereignty, leadership—"gender-laden" and repressive; feminist scientists who complain that Newton's *Principia* is suffused with "gender symbolism, gender structure, and gender identity" and his laws tantamount to a "rape manual";[44] feminist literary critics who resurrect forgotten (often deservedly so) women writers while exposing the patriarchal rhetoric of the "canonical" male writers; feminist musicologists who "engender" the musical conventions (cadences, tonality, major and minor modes), charging that they perpetuate masculine and feminine stereotypes;[45] and so with feminist art historians, legal theorists, theologians, and social scientists who reject both the subjects and the methods traditionally associated with their fields. Not all feminists share this radical critique of their disciplines, but all do subscribe to what Paul Ricoeur calls the "hermeneutics of suspicion."[46]

"Cultural studies" is similarly interdisciplinary, in both its subject and the resources it commands. One of the newer entries into the academy, it is now a flourishing field, with its own departments, centers, journals, societies, and all the other professional appurtenances. The subject—popular culture broadly understood—covers a wide range of themes: television and movies, the press and popular literature, communication and consumption, sex and life-styles. And it draws upon materials from every field: literary, artistic, historical, sociological, anthropological, multicultural, feminist, linguistic, psychoanalytic. Because it is so egalitarian (all subjects are equally worthy of study) and so eclectic (all modes of study can be utilized and combined in any fashion), it obviously defies any methodological prescriptions or restrictions. Even J. Hillis Miller is moved to demur to a field so amorphous that it lacks any "common methodology, goal, or institutional site"—characteristics that might be thought to endear it to a deconstructionist. What is really objectionable to Miller is its lack of "theory"—that is, postmodernist theory—which, in his view, mires it down in "pre-critical, pre-theoretical" assumptions.[47]

The most recent interdisciplinary trend is subjectivism, or the "*nouveau solipsism*," as it has been called.[48] (Among French historians, it is known as "*égo-histoire.*")[49] In this country, it has been adopted mainly by feminists who have made it part of their methodology. It does not merely "engender" scholarship; it personalizes it. "The I's Have It" is the apt title of a recent article describing this tendency.[50] The approach to any subject is insistently personal, dwelling upon the feelings, emotions, beliefs, and personal experiences of the scholar. The point is not that professors have taken to writing their autobiographies, nor that they are indulging themselves in occasional reminiscences or personal reflections. What is new is the dominating presence of the author in the scholarly enterprise itself: in a study of Japanese society, or a comparison of primitive and Western culture, or the life of a Mexican peddler, or the analysis of a French painter.[51] The traditionally impersonal, objective voice of the scholar—the "footnote voice," as it has been disparagingly called[52]—is replaced by the "I," the triumphal personal voice of the author. "George Eliot, *c'est moi*," declares a biographer of the great Victorian novelist.[53]

It is hard to assess just how far and how deeply these new (or no longer so new) developments have penetrated into the study of the humanities. It may well be that traditional scholars still outnumber the nontraditional. But intellectual life cannot be quantified; Marxists in the 1930s and 1940s constituted a small proportion of the professoriate, yet they were influential far beyond their numbers. It may also be true that in their own research and writing a good many scholars continue to adhere to traditional methods and standards (although not, perhaps, as rigorously as they might once have done). But they are often unable to translate their own practices into their teaching, to transmit to their students methods and standards that are no longer observed in the profession as a whole.

At the very least one can say that the spectrum has shifted, so that what would once have been unacceptable is now acceptable, and what was once taken for granted is now widely challenged. Some years ago one might have been inclined to describe the conflict between the old modes of scholarship and the new as generational. Now, as succeeding generations

of students have been brought up on the new and as youthful revolutionaries have become elder statesmen, that generational difference is no
longer so marked. The heresies of yesteryear have become the orthodoxies
of today. And the old revolutionaries are firmly entrenched in the establishment; three leading postmodernists—J. Hillis Miller, Richard Rorty,
and Natalie Zemon Davis—are past presidents of their professional associations. Moreover, the associations themselves are more or less committed
to the new modes: the Modern Language Association most conspicuously,
but also the more staid American Historical Association, which celebrated
the centennial issue of its journal with ten articles on the present state of
the discipline, all but one of which was postmodernist in spirit.[54]

American academics draw sustenance from their colleagues abroad. At
the 1995 meeting of the International Congress of Historical Sciences, fifty
scholars from sixteen countries applied to attend one of the most popular
sessions, on "Fictionality, Narrativity, Objectivity." Not one of them, reported the organizer, "expressed any real nostalgia for life before semiotics, deconstruction, and subjectivity." All the papers accepted the basic
precepts of postmodernism, with the occasional reservation that "history
should not fall into total subjectivity, but should reflect some kind of
historical reality." The organizer summed up her impression of the meeting: "A middle ground appears to be emerging between discredited positivism and nihilistic postmodernism."[55]

As postmodernism makes its way through the disciplines, with some
scholars finding ever newer and bolder ways to apply it, others are being
drawn to the idea of a "middle ground," to the reassertion of some kind of
truth, reality, even objectivity. So far, however, that idea has been more a
pious wish than a realistic position, for it is generally accompanied by an
unqualified repudiation of the traditional disciplines (modernist history,
for example, is denigrated as "positivist"), and a renewed commitment to
the relativism, subjectivism, and multiculturalism that militate against
any idea of truth, reality, and objectivity.[56] Yet the wish itself for a "middle
ground" is significant, suggesting a dissatisfaction with what is increasingly perceived as a "nihilistic" tendency. The formation of new associations of scholars pursuing more traditional modes of scholarship (one has
already been founded by literary critics and others are being planned by
historians and art historians) also points to the beginning of something
like a countermovement in the humanities.

Countermovements, like counterrevolutions, never return to the status
quo ante. Certainly the new subjects, which now have so much institutional as well as ideological support—African American, ethnic, cultural,
multicultural, feminist, and gender studies—will not disappear. What is
not clear is whether these subjects (and the old ones as well) lend themselves to some methodological "middle ground," or what such a method-

ology might look like. In the meantime, traditionalists and postmodernists alike will have to tolerate and be civil to each other. The real challenge is to do so while understanding the full import of the scholarly revolution that has affected all the humanities.

Notes

1. Richard Rorty, *Consequences of Pragmatism* (Minneapolis, 1982), 204.

2. Occasional usages of *postmodern* appeared in the 1950s and 1960s (for example, in vol. 9 of Arnold Toynbee's *Study of History*, published in 1954). Robert Lifton claims to have used the word *postmodern* in the late 1960s in *The Protean Self: Human Resilience in an Age of Fragmentation* (New York, 1993), 8. But *postmodernism* became common only in the late 1970s. One commentator takes as a decisive date in the emergence of that term the publication in 1979 of Jean-François Lyotard's *La condition postmoderne*, which was translated into English five years later (Steven Connor, *Postmodernist Culture: An Introduction to Theories of the Contemporary* [Oxford, 1989], 6). *Deconstruction* is generally associated with Jacques Derrida (see Paul de Man, *Allegories of Reading: Figural Language in Rousseau, Nietzsche, Rilke, and Proust* [New Haven, Conn., 1979], x).

3. Leopold von Ranke, "Histories of the Latin and Germanic Nations," in *The Varieties of History*, ed. Fritz Stern (New York, 1957), 57.

4. William M. Sloane, "History and Democracy," *American Historical Review* (October 1895): 5.

5. Gordon S. Wood, "A Century of Writing Early American History: Then and Now Compared; Or How Henry Adams Got It Wrong," *American Historical Review* (June 1995): 679.

6. Herbert Butterfield, *The Whig Interpretation of History* (London, 1931).

7. Thomas Kuhn, *The Structure of Scientific Revolutions* (Chicago, 1962).

8. This is not the same as a course, also frequently required, on "historiography," which dealt with great historians of the past. Nor is it to be confused with courses on "theory" offered today, which deal with neither methodology nor historiography but with "metahistory" or the philosophy of history, almost always from a postmodernist perspective.

9. For an extended critique of the idea of objectivity, see Peter Novick, *That Noble Dream: The "Objectivity Question" and the American Historical Profession* (New York, 1988).

10. See Gertrude Himmelfarb, "Where Have All the Footnotes Gone?" in *On Looking into the Abyss: Untimely Thoughts on Culture and Society* (New York, 1994), 122–30.

11. Lucy S. Dawidowicz, *What Is the Use of Jewish History?* ed. Neal Kozodoy (New York, 1992), 123.

12. William Appleman Williams, *The Contours of American History* (Cleveland, 1961), 491.

13. Wilcomb E. Washburn, quoting the introduction to Allen P. Slickpoo, Sr., and Deward E. Walker, Jr., *Noon Nee-Me-Poo* (1973), in *Idaho Yesterdays: The Quarterly Journal of the Idaho Historical Society* (Summer 1974): 30.

14. Dominick LaCapra, *History and Criticism* (Ithaca, 1985), 20 and 92.

15. There are repeated assertions of a movement back toward political history, but these may be exaggerated. The editor of the recently revised *Guide to Historical Literature* says that the majority of entries for political history are twenty years old, and that many of the newer entries were written by journalists and political scientists rather than historians; *The Chronicle of Higher Education*, April 14, 1995, A8.

16. G. R. Elton, *The Future of the Past* (Cambridge, 1968), 4.

17. Carl Schorske, quoted by Novick, *That Noble Dream*, 620.

18. Thomas Bender, "'Facts' and History," *Radical History Review* (March 1985): 81–83. Henry Ashby Turner, Jr., David Abraham's main critic, anticipated that he himself would be accused of being a "vulgar factologist"; Turner, *German Big Business and the Rise of Hitler* (Oxford, 1985), 357.

19. Theodore Zeldin, "Social History and Total History," *Journal of Social History* (Winter 1976): 242–44. Yet the following year, Zeldin published the second volume of his *France 1848–1945*, whose title comprises two of those "tyrannical" categories, nationality and chronology. Five years later he published *The French*, testifying to the enduring power of one of those categories. More recently, Zeldin has gone so far by way of liberation as to liberate himself from history itself. "Free history," he now finds, can only take the form of fiction—in testimony to which he has written a novel entitled *Happiness*. See *London Review of Books*, September 1, 1988.

20. Dorothy Ross, "Grand Narrative in American Historical Writing: From Romance to Uncertainty," *American Historical Review* (June 1995): 673.

21. When the essay on Wolfe was originally published in the English journal *Granta*, the "Afterword" and "A Note on Sources" were omitted, so that the reader would have been unaware that some parts were fictional.

22. Simon Schama, *Dead Certainties (Unwarranted Speculations)* (New York, 1991), 320, 322, and 327. For a critique of Schama, see Gordon S. Wood, *New York Review of Books*, June 27, 1991, 12–15.

23. Interview with Richard Bernstein, *New York Times*, May 15, 1991, C18.

24. Linda Hutcheon, "The Postmodern Problematizing of History," *English Studies in Canada* (December 1988), 371; reprinted in *A Poetics of Postmodernism: History, Theory, Fiction* (New York, 1988).

25. In a memorial address honoring Paul de Man, Derrida observed that *invention* has become a popular category in intellectual discourse; Werner Sollors, "The Idea of Ethnicity," in *The Truth About Truth: De-Confusing and Re-Constructing the Postmodern World*, ed. Walter Truett Anderson (New York, 1995), 59. These words now appear so commonly in the titles of books that there is hardly a university press catalogue or academic journal that does not feature a few of them.

26. J. H. Plumb, *The Death of the Past* (Boston, 1970), 135.

27. Novick, *That Noble Dream*, 496.

28. Joan B. Landes, *Women and the Public Sphere in the Age of the French Revolution* (Ithaca, 1988), 1–2; Joan Wallach Scott, *Gender and the Politics of History* (New York, 1988), 3 and 6; Bonnie S. Anderson and Judith P. Zinsser, *A History of Their Own: Women in Europe from Prehistory to the Present* (New York, 1988), xviii. See also Philippa Levine, "When Method Matters: Women Historians, Feminist Historians," *Journal of British Studies* (October 1991). Peter Novick, *That Noble Dream*, 496, says that by the late 1970s the idea that history could legitimately be written from a feminist perspective "was no longer being argued; it was a settled question, beyond argument."

29. Scott, *Gender and the Politics of History*, 4. Yet even this radical epistemology is not always radical enough. It is an embarrassment to feminists that Foucault, having exposed the fallacy of "sexual essentialism," persists in using traditional masculine language; Irene Diamond and Lee Quinby, *Feminism and Foucault: Reflections on Resistance* (Boston, 1988), xv–xvi. One commentator (a man, as it happens) apologizes for retaining in his translations Foucault's "relentlessly masculine forms" of pronouns, including the use of *homme* to mean "humanity"; James Miller, *The Passion of Michel Foucault* (New York, 1993), 389.

30. See, for example, Carl N. Degler, "In Pursuit of an American Dream," *American Historical Review* (February 1987); Bernard Bailyn, "The Challenge of Modern Historiography," *American Historical Review* (February 1982); John Higham, epilogue to *History: Professional Scholarship in America* (Baltimore, Md., 1983); Arthur M. Schlesinger, Jr., *The Disuniting of America* (New York, 1992).

31. Hayden White, *Tropics of Discourse: Essays in Cultural Criticism* (Baltimore, Md., 1978), 50.

32. Roland Barthes, "What is Criticism," in *Critical Essays*, tr. Richard Howard (Evanston, Ill., 1972), 260.

33. Donald Davie, "The Gayety of Nations," *Times Literary Supplement*, July 15, 1994, 8.

34. Mario J. Valdès and Linda Hutcheon, *Rethinking Literary History—Comparatively*, ACLS Occasional Paper no. 27 (New York, 1994), 11.

35. Stephen Greenblatt coined the term *new historicist* in "Towards a Poetics of Culture," in *The New Historicism*, ed. H. Aram Veeser (London, 1989), 1.

36. Richard Rorty, *Philosophy and the Mirror of Nature* (Princeton, 1979), 178. Rorty prefers to call himself "post-philosophical" or "pragmatic"; "Comments on Castoriadis's 'The End of Philosophy?'" *Salmagundi* (Spring-Summer 1989): 26.

37. Jacques Derrida, "White Mythology: Metaphor in the Text of Philosophy," *New Literary History* (Autumn 1974), 11.

38. Richard Rorty, *Essays on Heidegger and Others*, Philosophical Papers, vol. 2 (Cambridge, 1991), 86.

39. Richard Rorty, *Objectivity, Realism, and Truth*, Philosophical Papers, vol. 1 (Cambridge, 1991), 110 and 194.

40. Richard Rorty, "Truth and Freedom: A Reply to Thomas McCarthy," *Critical Inquiry* (Spring 1990), 638–39. See also Rorty, "Comments on Castoriadis's 'The End of Philosophy?'" 27.

41. Stephen Greenblatt, *Learning to Curse: Essays in Early Modern Culture* (New York, 1990), 3 (quoting Louis A. Montrose).

42. This is the title of an essay in Hayden White's *Tropic of Discourse*, 81.

43. A recent issue of the feminist newsletter published by the American Philosophical Association criticizes the principle of *modus ponens* ("If P, then Q; P, ergo Q") as a peculiarly masculine way of thinking, "formal symbolic systems" being alien to women. Another article in the same issue rejects the Aristotelian syllogism because it demeans women by separating the form of an argument from its material content, women being traditionally associated with matter rather than form; see Martha Nussbaum, "Feminists and Philosophy," *New York Review of Books*, October 20, 1994, 59. Nussbaum is critical of this kind of feminist philosophy, although in a subsequent reply to her critics, she retreats somewhat from her earlier sharp judgments; *New York Review of Books*, April 6, 1995, 48–49.) See also Sandra Harding and Merrill B. Hintikka, eds., *Discovering Reality: Feminist Perspectives on Epistemology, Metaphysics, Methodology, and Philosophy of Science* (Boston, 1983); and Louise M. Antony and Charlotte Witt, eds., *A Mind of One's Own: Feminist Essays on Reason and Objectivity* (Boulder, Colo., 1993). Both books contain essays on both sides of the issue.

44. Sandra Harding, *The Science Question in Feminism* (Ithaca, 1986), 47 and 113.

45. Susan McClary, *Feminine Endings: Music, Gender, and Sexuality* (Minneapolis, Minn., 1991).

46. Paul Ricoeur, *Freud and Philosophy: An Essay on Interpretation*, tr. Denis Savage (New Haven, 1970), 26–36.

47. J. Hillis Miller, "Return, Dissenter," *Times Literary Supplement*, July 15, 1994, 10.

48. Daphne Patai, "Sick and Tired of Scholars' Nouveau Solipsism," *Chronicle of Higher Education*, February 23, 1994, A52.

49. Jeremy D. Popkin, "The American Historian of France and the 'Other,'" in *Objectivity and Its Other*, ed. Wolfgang Natter, Theodore R. Schatzki, and John Paul Jones III (New York, 1995), 106. See also Pierre Nora, "Entre mémoire et histoires: La problématique des lieux," in *Les Lieux de Mémoire*, vol. 1 (Paris, 1984), xxxiii; *Essais d'égo-histoire*, ed. Pierre Nora (Paris, 1987).

50. Adam Begley, in *Lingua Franca* (March-April 1994), 54–59. See also Ruth Behar, "Dare We Say 'I'?" *Chronicle of Higher Education*, June 29, 1994, B1–B2; Liz McMillen, "Don't Leave Out the Juicy Things," *Chronicle of Higher Education*, Febuary 9, 1994, A18–A19.

51. Cathy N. Davidson, *36 Views of Mount Fuji* (New York, 1993); Marianna Torgovnick, *Gone Primitive: Savage Intellects, Modern Lives* (Chicago, 1990); Ruth Behar, *Translated Woman: Crossing the Border with Esperanza's Story* (Boston, 1993); Eunice Lipton, *Alias Olympia* (New York, 1992). See also *Perspectives* [the American Historical Association Newsletter], October 1995, 23, 25, and 30.

52. McMillen, "Don't Leave Out the Juicy Things," A18.

53. Phyllis Rose, "Confessions of a Burned-Out Biographer," *Civilization* (January-February 1995), 72.

54. *American Historical Review*, June 1995. The exception is the article by Gordon Wood, "A Century of Writing Early American History: Then and Now Compared; Or How Henry Adams Got It Wrong."

55. *Chronicle of Higher Education*, September 22, 1995, A10. (The comments were by Nancy Partner, a professor of history at McGill University.)

56. See, for example, Joyce Appleby, Lynn Hunt, and Margaret Jacob, *Telling the Truth about History* (New York, 1994).

Eight

Changing Epochs

FRANK KERMODE

SINCE the topic of changing cultural epochs, ends and beginnings, is in the fin de siècle air, it might be worth asking whether the one we may conceivably be experiencing is of a kind that will permit the survival of literary studies, a term I use in a sense that the sequel should make clear, or indeed of literature, a term I use in a sense that will still seem innocent to some, though condemned by many others as tainted by nostalgia for the aesthetic, redolent of a hateful elitism, an instrument of ideological oppression.

In Alain Robbe-Grillet's novel *Les Gommes*, published in 1953, there is a celebrated moment when the detective Wallas contemplates a tomato. Cut into quarters by a machine, it is, thinks the detective, "truly without flaw" ("en vérité sans défaut"), but then he notices that it does have a flaw: "un accident à peine visible," a barely perceptible unevenness, has occurred. An irregular piece of skin raised above the surface of the tomato now becomes its most interesting feature. Some suggest that it has been added in the act of description, that it is in the writing and not in the tomato; but the tomato is equally in the writing.

It may be relevant that *Les Gommes* genuinely was, in its way, an epoch-making novel; also that the criticism of the time, including Robbe-Grillet's own, found new ways of talking about fiction, about literature, attending very closely to the text—a practice much less usual now, as we shall see. Robbe-Grillet hated metaphor and would have objected to the use of this passage for purposes smacking of allegory.[1] Nevertheless I shall treat it as a motto for an essay that asks certain questions about mechanical *coupures*, which will to some extent dwell lovingly on the still perceptible irregularity, the accident of recalcitrant skin. The question is, shall we—I mean students and lovers of literature—survive a change of epoch, if only as an accident of that sort?

Does epistemic change come in different sizes or is it always catastrophic and total?

For a long time Hercules was represented in Arab star maps as wearing a short jacket and breeches rather than a lion's skin, and carrying a scimitar rather than a club. But in 1515 Albrecht Dürer published the first modern star map. It still depended to some extent on its Arab precursors, but Dürer's Hercules carried a club in his right hand and wore a lion's skin on his left shoulder. In much the same way he transformed an Arab Perseus, restoring his winged feet and making sure that the head the hero was carrying had been detached not from some medieval demon but from the classical Medusa; indeed Dürer went out of his way to avoid misinterpretation by adding, in the appropriate position, the words "caput Medusae." He had restored to Hercules and Perseus their original iconographic attributes, and in doing so revived "the life and breath of paganism."

The gods had somehow survived through the long interval between antiquity and the fifteenth century, but they had lost their classical forms (Hercules became a monk with a tonsure). Now they were again as they had been originally, though incorporated in a modern—"state-of-the-art"—star map. "To recover the forms used by the ancients as well as their learning, their poetic imagination, and their knowledge of the universe—to reconcile, as they did, mythology and geometry—such was to be the dream of the greatest spirits of the Renaissance."

Jean Seznec, from whose book I borrow these examples, boldly concludes that "we can speak of a Renaissance from the day Hercules resumed his athletic breadth of shoulder, his club and his lion's skin." Indeed, we can speak of "*the* Renaissance."[2] Then began a new epoch, consciously modern, aware that the achievements of the immediately preceding age were henceforth to be scorned and discounted, while the relics of antiquity, ever more anxiously sought out, were to stand as models, as examples, as guides though not as commanders, to the exponents of a self-proclaimed modernity. These were the materials chosen for a new age to fashion itself, once it had cut itself off from the in-between age, the *medium aevum.* The slicing was, we may say, mechanical, with seemingly little recalcitrant skin left over to call into question the efficacy of the machine that made the great *coupure.*

But we know well enough that the cut was not as clean as it looked to those who assumed and exulted in its cleanness. The Renaissance was in some perspectives an extension of the medieval it believed it was rejecting, although its self-conscious modernity derived, paradoxically, from *sacrosancta vetustas*, from a revival of the classic beginning with Petrarch. On further examination the cut left quite a lot of skin visible. Then was the Renaissance after all *sui generis* and a new age? There was a nineteenth-century tendency to continue its celebration as exactly that, but since then, and to this day, doubts persist about its extent, neatness, and uniqueness. A truly cardinal moment in history, a phenomenon so distinctive that we can confidently use it to take our historical bearings on Western culture—or simply one of a number of untidy, somewhat random cultural changes that could not be soberly thought of as catastrophic upheavals?

After all, there are other rather similar cultural manifestations on record. Considering this possible objection, Erwin Panofsky distinguished between *Renaissances* and *Renascences*, using the latter term for less notable or less universal revivals of the antique, such as those of the Carolingian period and the twelfth century. He decided that *the* Renaissance *can* be quite sharply distinguished from the Renascences. It was different in that it manifested itself so generally, in so many areas of culture. It was different in that it was more fully conscious of historical perspective. It took some account of the gulf of time that separated it from the admired ancients. And although proudly inspired by the ancient world it was self-consciously "modern." Vasari, who celebrated a rebirth in painting (calling it *la rinascità*) praised Leonardo da Vinci for having "laid the foundations of that third style which I will call the modern"—so distinguishing it from the first style (Botticelli, Ghirlandaio) and the second (Perugino, Francia). *Modern* was not, as it happens, an exclusively modern word; like *new*, it could refer to something already rather old, as in *devotio moderna*, which was thriving around 1400. And it always seemed to carry the implication "with regard to an understood past." Perhaps what is genuinely modern always has a novel but powerful relationship with a past, preferably (my preference, at any rate) a relationship dialectical rather than abolitionist.[3]

Although it is mostly in respect of classical scholarship, literature, painting, sculpture, and architecture that these developments occupy the attention of cultural historians, we take it for granted when we talk about a new epoch or a new age that they were related to great changes in other departments of life—radical innovation and conflict in political thought; new technologies, including printing; explorations, so damaging to received notions, of new worlds on earth and in the heavens (though these modernities also had their remembrances of appropriate pasts). Life in cities—directly involving the arts—was being transformed by changes in the social order, by new international trade and new money; this was the onset of the first age of capitalism. There were catastrophic religious conflicts, also affecting society and the arts, in which modern ideas of history and philology, individuality and rationality played their part. We can be sure not only that there was, cumulatively and generally, a great change in the times, but also that some people were aware that it was happening, without necessarily understanding what it was and meant.

It is of some importance that an epochal alteration can be announced, whether with pleasure or (as sometimes happened) with anxiety. However wrong they might have been about the details, some people knew that for good or ill they were living in a new age and said so. In this sense the Renaissance was not only a period but also a movement. E. H. Gombrich distinguishes between periods, or ages, and movements. "A movement," he remarks, "is something that is proclaimed."[4] The Renaissance was therefore a movement. A period can be imposed retrospectively. Nobody ever announced that he or she was living in the Middle Ages, and nobody ever proclaimed "the mannerist movement." It may well be that the proclamation is, at least in some respects, exaggerated or distorted. But so long as its contents are not seen to be false or absurd, the proclamation lends force to the view that it is permissible to speak of *the* Renaissance, though the phenomena will always be difficult to define precisely, and the cut will never again be thought clean.

By the same token it is acceptable to speak of modernism and, perhaps with more reluctance, of postmodernism also, unless it is to be thought of as an epiphenomenon of modernism.[5] Postmodernism has certainly been proclaimed, and to some extent its proclamation itself begets ideas and slogans that testify to the existence of what is proclaimed. There is a sort of program, put together ad hoc; the word presented itself, and it was provided piecemeal with a supporting lexicon and an ideology. It is anti-modernist, opposed to notions of totality; it exhibits an "extreme episte-mological skepticism which reduces everything—philosophy, politics, criticism and 'theory'—to a dead level of suasive or rhetorical effect where consensus-values are the last (indeed the only) court of appeal"; and it is scornful of such metanarrative survivals as reason and truth.[6] Even the distortions and falsities advanced by propagandists and enthusiasts are of historical interest; their proclamations are part of the validating record of the period. They may announce a clean break, they may omit judicious consideration of easily perceptible elements of continuity, but their insis-tence on a *coupure* is still, when cautiously handled, part of the evidence that there has been one. And it is easy enough to give it that larger context—technological, sociological, and philosophical—that is essential to concepts of epistemic break.

The epistemic, epochal break is now a very familiar conceptual instru-ment. Michel Foucault, who put into circulation a modern (and decidedly apocalyptic) form of an idea that has its origins in antiquity, and which has rarely been quite absent from historical thinking, applied a sharp knife: his tomato was permitted no roughnesses. It can be said (against some opposition, admittedly) that according to *Les Mots et les choses* there was no carry-over from one epoch to another; one episteme yielded absolutely to the next. Of course Foucault was speaking of systematic formations at so deep a level that the Renaissance itself could probably be regarded as a superficial manifestation, much like Marx's thought, de-scribed by the same author as a mere storm in a children's paddling pool. It might be argued that the present discontents in the humanities, pro-foundly disturbing though they seem to all who have to deal with them, are fairly trivial according to this Olympian view. And it is true that we need to keep some such deeper perspective, for in the context of enormous change our local malaise can hardly be thought of as more than symptomatic. It may be that by making habitual resort to notions of continuity, and by demonstrating a professional inability to be rid of brainwashed notions of aesthetic value and truth, one is disqualified from profound epochal speculation. All the same there is, even among the rejectors, that habitual backward glance, stare, or glare. The haunting cultural memory has, for good or ill, wanted or not, been part of the discourse of every episteme—obviously of the Renaissance, also of the Enlightenment; it is quite hard to imagine a break so clean that it will not recur. Of course it may take the form of a willed *anti-passéisme*, descended from the variety that in the early years of the century, especially in the form of Dada, was the twin of the revisionist historiographies of modernism.

Anyway, we may suppose that there is something to be learned from the Renaissance. It did happen; it transformed the arts and literature and scholarship. We are right to think it distinctive. But one must also remember the indisputably rough edge of its cut. Johan Huizinga remarked that what we call the Renaissance was only one aspect of sixteenth-century culture; a lot was going on that does not fit into the concept—a lot of rough skin, as it were, ignored by devotees of the clean cut. Much scholarship has been devoted to showing that Renaissance notions of antiquity, *sacrosancta vetustas*, were pretty chaotic, and the "break" from the late Middle Ages was, on inspection, much less complete than some contemporaries, and some nineteenth-century historians, may have thought. The same may turn out to be true of our own *coupure*. We are repeatedly and excitedly assured that our culture has also suffered a pretty clean historical break. This is, with important qualifications, admitted. But a lot else is going on. And we should here as elsewhere make allowances for the rhetoric of proclamation—it is rather thrilling, and it excites audiences, to assert that all continuity has gone, that the *grands récits* no longer have ethical or aesthetic or any other kind of paradigmatic force, that we can do as we please with the past. In a culture so saturated by advertising it is important not to take mere labels and slogans too seriously. They have their importance, but we should treat such proclamations critically.

It may be that the rejection of the past—which happens to some extent, though as I have suggested, nearly always imperfectly, in most ages, and is also a proclaimed feature of many of the art movements we admire—is now made more impatiently or arrogantly. It is less a reaction against something known, studied, and then declared obsolete than an attempt at total rejection of literature and certain ideas because they are past; an attack that is supported not by detailed dismissive study of documents but by grand theoretical efforts to occlude completely any consideration of them, for such consideration would be in danger of falling under the influence of paradigms already rejected in principle.

Here the prefix *post-* is of great value because it crudely situates whatever it adheres to in the admirable present, whereas whatever it cannot be applied to is obsolete and probably malign, like modernism to postmodernists. Respected works of modernism (Mallarmé, Joyce, Pound) can always be coopted as early or premonitory examples of postmodernism. As a way of justifying this historical kidnapping, it is sometimes argued that postmodernism logically precedes modernism, or at any rate that they can exist contemporaneously; so it may be that Dada was not so much a nihilistic form of modernism as an early postmodernism that simply assumed, without having much of a theory about it, the necessary demise of the *grands récits*. But this kind of talk is surely, in the end, unhelpful; it resembles the sort of thing that has been said about *Baroque*, first invented to name a historical period and then used more and more loosely to refer to anything perceived as having comparable stylistic characteristics. *Post-* is too malleable to tell us much.

Complaints about terminology are inevitable but barely scratch the surface of the problem. However one may wish to purge the new terminology and resist some theoretical claims (as I have tried in the past to do[7]), it can hardly be denied that the arts and the humanities generally, all of which depend on systems of communication, will be affected in unpredictable ways by technological changes so enormous that Gutenberg is useful only as a vague analogue. The power of individual communicators is now far greater (in extent and speed) than that afforded by moveable types, not in the measure that print surpassed the range of manuscript copies, but on a scale very much greater; and we are as yet only at the beginning of this revolution. The book is not yet dead and may not even be dying; but the Internet is not yet universal, digital television is still only a glorious promise, and we do not need much millennialist fervor to imagine, with joy or terror, what they may do to us and our children.

Though we cannot honestly make detailed predictions, post-McLuhanite reasoning suggests that the changes will not be simply quantitative. The modern condition of the arts requires them to live in change, to demonstrate that restlessness long ago deplored by Wyndham Lewis, who saw new fashions come and go like new models of washing machines. But postmodern change is no longer the simpler sort of thing he deplored, simply from one manifesto or one fashion to another. The claim is more drastic and of more universal scope, and it implies, among many other consequences, that attitudes toward the study of literature will be radically altered.

This is of course what we fancy we see happening all about us, a matter of common observation within the academy. Even before the times grew as intellectually turbulent as they now are, the academy, perhaps in the premonitory phase of epistemic change, was forced into the position of being virtually the sole site of serious reading and commentary. It has been the blessing and the curse of literary academics that they have been deputed to do the culture's reading for it. At one time there was an expectation that they would report back to their employers. But what Lionel Trilling called keeping the road open—ensuring, by proper provision of high journalism, the continuance of contact between experts and the educated public at large—is no longer thought a plain necessity of intellectual and social health, as it was in the nineteenth and early twentieth centuries. Communication from professors to the otherwise educated laity has almost, if not quite, broken down. Their relationship to their students is also more problematical. This is partly the fault of the professors, the professionals, who notoriously speak to and write only for one another, inventing arcane dialects to keep out the uninitiated. They lament the ignorance of freshmen, but when they get them into graduate school ensure that they protect their careers by learning to talk as the teachers do—so maintaining the fence between academic criticism and the intelligent world outside.

There is a reciprocal decline of interest on the part of that lay audience, which no longer looks to professors for wisdom, nor assumes that the humanities offer a defense against the increasing horrors of modern life, as it was believed they did in the time of the great nineteenth-century periodicals. And there are few inducements of a gentler sort, that simply make the reading of literature seem a task in which the pleasure might conceivably outweigh the labor.

Consequently academic humanists, once so proud, so confident, may feel isolated, or dependent on the professional comfort of a school of thought or of theory. Meanwhile it is generally acknowledged that the students for whom they must care arrive in college having read much less, even in their own language, than their parents had; and if we consider their ignorance of other modern languages (to say nothing of the classical languages that were until quite recently assumed to be valuable instruments of humanistic culture), we see what a fearful task it must be to commence their education, supposing what is meant by that word remains roughly what it did a couple of generations back. For now books are less familiar objects, and nobody has much desire to explain why they were also privileged objects. And there may now be a majority of teachers in the humanities who would regard such explanations as in manifest bad faith, not worth contesting.

Wishing to examine, however cursorily, the conditions of epoch-change, we are obliged to try to connect these troublesome but relatively domestic difficulties with immense and obvious alterations in the world at large. We need to ask whether the cut is a clean one. It may not yet be clear how clean it is. Is it absurdly optimistic to suppose that, as with the Renaissance, it may turn out on mature inspection that the older culture, however impaired or scorned, will find a form in which it can survive? If a major change has been forced on us by technologies inimical to the old print culture, is it not at least possible that there can remain, at any rate for some, modes of useful communication with that culture and indeed with the past and with at least some of the *grands récits* (among which we can include literature)?

We see from the graphs and tables provided in the appendix to this volume that the numbers of students taking humanities courses are falling (the apparently anomalous increase in numbers choosing to study "English" is probably not significant and may simply reflect the larger entry of women students still denied the early training required for the sciences). In this reduced enrollment there may not be many who strike us, vanity apart, as being likely to fill our places in what we might think an adequate manner. Nevertheless one comes across wonderfully well-read young men and women, dedicated in their bright archaic way to canonical works of which they already apprehend the value; so there is at least likely to be what in other contexts might be called a saving remnant, willing to be despised as aesthetes or ideological innocents—as, in a bizarrely anachronistic way, dedicated to *literature*. It may be objected that such freaks could come to our aid merely by chance; but so does a great deal of literature.

Compelled into prediction, into gambling on the future, on the prospect that mere statistical probability may produce a few archaizing poetry-lovers, one cannot avoid pondering the operations of chance. We might well give more thought to the question of survival in art, to the chances that have to be taken when they come along. We have seven plays of Sophocles, selected from the whole corpus of over a hundred by a school-master as texts for a grammar class and sold—in a unique copy—out of Constantinople just before the sack of 1453. Only then could virtuously preservative scholarship do its work. Of the tragedies of Euphorion, who beat Sophocles and Aeschylus in fair Athenian competition, no trace remains. The survival of the venerated objects of a culture has quite often depended on a hair-rising combination of luck and cunning. Improving on luck is part of the game for people who do not despise the past. Devotees of those objects must be valued in much the same way as the objects themselves; arriving by chance, these aliens must be cunningly fostered. They are the students who already have that intuition of value without which the task is nearly hopeless. Dr. Johnson ruled that it "ought to be the first endeavour of a writer to distinguish . . . that which is established because it is right from that which is right only because it is established." Some believe they have seen through this sturdy appearance of common sense; what is said to be right is so only because it is established. In that analysis Johnson's remark ceases to make sense. Our remnant will contest on instinct the opinion that value is never inherent but a fiction imposed by an oppressive institution, and that no other view makes sense.

What is now thought to make sense in literary studies? It is unnecessary at this stage to resume the debate about canons, a debate always in the end without much sense, since the opponents of canons, apart from a few total abolitionists, really just want their own canons, and the defenders, apart from a few extremists, do not in any case hold the reactionary views with which propaganda credits them. There is nothing in the least sacred or magical or, as the fashionable jargon has it, "mystified" about canons. There can be no objection in principle to any attempt to enlarge or alter reading lists and to include, say, the works of neglected women, Afro-American, and other "minority" writers. Canons are reading lists, but of course they are also rather more than that: they are necessarily selective reading lists. Everybody uses them. And it is always to be remembered that canons consist not of static texts alone—texts frozen in time, monuments in a heritage park, objects of a kind of snobbish archaeology—but also of continuing commentary on the texts; that is what preserves canonicity and makes the members of a canon as modern as yesterday's poem. Good commentary may of course cease, and the once canonical work can cease to be so. To ensure the entry of new works or the exclusion of old ones all that is needed is persuasive, perpetuating commentary on the one hand and neglect or informed hostility on the other.

It is, of course, a worry that the proponents of a new posthumanism have no regard for commentary (at its best, convincing exploration of particular texts or works) and concern themselves instead with such questions as canonicity, or what it is to read, or what distinguishes a work from a text, or what is the just relation of texts to their historical and ideological circumstances, and so on. At this stage the intoxicating impetus of literary theory in the last quarter century needs no description. The appeal of "theory" to large numbers of younger teachers may be pessimistically explained as a consequence of the drop in writing and reading skills that should have been acquired much earlier; this is the plausible view of Alvin Kernan. The decay of what used to be called literature is symbolized for him by the physical decay of thousands of books rotting in libraries, but also by the enormous piling up of new books that hardly anybody reads.[8]

The catalogue of Messrs. Routledge & Kegan Paul, publishers once proud of their literary criticism list, is now dominated by works more properly categorized as cultural materialism, feminism, popular culture, and poststructuralism. Bill Germano of Routledge's American office claims, in a recent interview, to be "making things happen in the culture."

His interviewer says it is certain that "by spotting intellectual trends ahead of the curve and responding with a flash flood of suitable titles Germano has changed the face of academic publishing in the humanities." He has supplied "the software" needed for university programs in film studies, gay studies, and so on, courses with reading lists understandably dominated by Routledge books.[9] Of course the job of publishers is to supply— and if they can even create—an audience, but in this instance, if one may borrow terms of abuse that are frequently employed in some of the books that appear in such lists, it might be proper to speak of commodification and colonialism.

Unlike Germano, I do not know where this "curve" is heading; the market glut and the restlessness of young academics, whose tenure can now depend on finding something new to say by way of Theory, guarantee fairly rapid change. It can hardly be otherwise in a community where one is obliged to be skeptical about everybody else's theory save one's own.

One of the books recently published by Routledge is Thomas Docherty's *After Theory*. Docherty, as his blurb expresses it, contends that the Enlightenment project of emancipation through knowledge has ended in failure by allowing the academy to "become a prison-house for the institutionaliztion of critique." The agent of this imprisonment is Theory, so he contends that Theory needs liberating in its turn. After theory there needs to be a postmodernism that "questions every manner of binding or framing," that valorizes transgression and "error," "error" being "'criminal' in the eyes of the white fathers, the acknowledged legislators behind the law of the imperialist enlightenment of the dark tropics of discourse; but the 'criminality' remains fully justified if we wish to reject the parameters of an imperialist mode of politics and an imperialist mode of conversation or social understanding." Finally Docherty wants thought to be liberated from all theory. "It is only in the refusal to be answerable to a governing theory that thought, and above all theoretical thought, becomes possible once more."[10] The dismissal of theoretical thought by means of posttheoretical thought in order to make theoretical thought possible, with the consequence adumbrated in the argument (theory liberated by posttheory, in order to be liberated again, and so on for ever) is a characteristically "oppositional" proposal. The association of older modes of thinking with imperialism simply goes without saying, and what used to be thought of as "primary" text is at no stage involved in the argument. Why should it be, when there simply is no such thing? It is a sign of the times that Docherty is described as a professor of *English*.

And so these new professionals spiral away from anything resembling what one stubbornly continues to describe as the study of literature. Practitioners of that study did of course have theories of criticism; the New Criticism had theories, and it flourished along with several rivals. But now theory is an opponent, and a difficult one, as hard to get around as Peer Gynt found the Boyg. It is many-headed, zealous, deliberately dark, and by no means all foolish. Our remnant will need literary theories, though of another stripe, founded in the literary text; they may find it best to avoid the Boyg's territory altogether.

Five years ago the Modern Language Association of America (MLA) published a collection of essays entitled *Redrawing the Boundaries*, thus endorsing the argument that the area of studies over which it presides had indeed changed. The resulting volume makes the redrawing of boundaries look almost Yugoslavian, but there are hints that, as in the concept of the Renaissance, the tomato has not cut quite cleanly, that the *coupure* may still have interestingly ragged edges. Richard Marius, discussing "composition studies," reflects that Theory has made little difference to them; they are mostly in a terrible state, taught by ill-paid, reluctant, over-worked part-timers using ill-written textbooks to instruct dismally inadequate students, who, far from needing instruction in Theory, need help to understand elementary written English. It is not really their fault; they are trying to learn too late what they should have been taught years before. To some of them reading is a new experience, and they can hardly be expected to begin instantly to meditate on what it means to read, or to expose the duplicity of the texts they are studying by deconstructing them, when the obvious sense, however simple—that Derridean guardrail—is still hard for them to hold on to. Meanwhile their instructors would almost certainly prefer to be doing something else, something expounded in the more exciting chapters of the MLA book. The gap between their students' performances and the rapt theoretical discourse of senior members of the institution is as unbridgeably wide as that between the discourse of those scholars and the interest of the educated laity.

It remains something of a surprise that not every article in the MLA book is curtly dismissive of older criticism. Some are, of course, but William Kerrigan, writing on seventeenth-century studies, is skeptical of some current developments. For example, he agrees with the author of the chapter on Renaissance/early modern studies (Leah Marcus) that Milton has proved a stumbling block to opponents of "anti-author-ity," but they differ about the significance of this. She seems on the whole content to think that as a consequence of this difficulty Milton must drop out of consideration unless and until postmodernism finds its own way of dealing with him—and, with a certain effect of oddity, she cites as hopeful evidence that this is beginning to happen B. Rajan's book on *Paradise Lost*, seemingly unaware that it was unpostmodernly published in 1947, not a date you would expect to find on a book worth reading. For his part Kerrigan takes an intelligent look at some postmodernist struggles with Milton but concludes, with evident but unfashionable satisfaction, that "the tradition lives." It is just the kind of remnant to match our remnant of literary students.

In their introduction to the MLA volume the editors, Stephen Greenblatt and Giles Gunn, ponder the general question of boundaries, alleging that the nature of their volume "obliged them to place a disproportionate emphasis on significant departures rather than important continuities." They modestly support the departures—canon changes, the disappearance of the author, attention to signifiers rather than signifieds, "the interrogation of boundaries." (I have noticed before a tendency for theory enthusiasts to treat dissident persons and ideas as political prisoners.) But they reasonably doubt whether the present degree of theoretical consensus, such as it is, can be maintained indefinitely. In their capacity as moderators they refrain from advocating any change, but they confidently expect it. They speak of "conversations" conducted over the shifting frontiers between literary studies and adjacent interests. Since they allow for the existence of "important continuities," it may be supposed that in principle they do not rule out a dialogue between the present of theory (with its uncertain future, its risk of sterile institutionalization) and the past (with its perhaps not yet totally exploded mythologies of authorship and "works").[11] There may be an interesting, as yet unquantifiable, remnant of skin.

All this may sound as if I am conceding that all who retain a somewhat different attitude, both to the criticism of literature and to the instruction of students, should just hang on and wait for better times, hoping against hope they will come around again before we die. But what would we be hanging on to and why, if unstoppable cultural forces are at work to deprive us (our remnant apart) of suitable students to teach and a suitable audience to address? And why does the very thought of hanging on tend to make us feel guilty, make us duck when we hear the word *elitist*? It has been plain for a long time that the writings humanists value as "literature" (now a contested category) are difficult in themselves, and that they are therefore primarily the preserve of what, in a probably vain attempt to avoid the facile imputation of elitism, we can call a *clerisy*. The word was invented by Coleridge and adopted by Emerson, but the idea existed independently of the word and was associated with a nineteenth-century intellectual and cultural effort to escape from the advances of materialism—to reverse the apparently growing social and cultural decadence, often by a contemplation of literature.[12]

The tradition of a clerisy persisted and in England found a belated but embattled champion in F. R. Leavis. He made a celebrated assault on C. P. Snow for his lecture on the separation of the two cultures, scientific and humanist. In 1959 Snow—by profession a science administrator, by avocation a novelist—had given a lecture in Cambridge called "The Two

Cultures and the Scientific Revolution," in which he compared, unfavorably, the social and political attitudes of literary people with those of scientists. He found the scientists humanly useful and the literary people uselessly frivolous; he pointed to the social advances that had come or were coming about everywhere as a result of technological advance and castigated as snobbery the literary habit of deploring the loss of amenity such an advance entailed. He despised our ignorance, famously asserting that he could ask a literary person to tell him the second law of thermodynamics in complete confidence that the humanist would be baffled.

In my experience Snow was a civil, friendly, though opinionated man. I remember him telling me with great emphasis how deplorable he found Virginia Woolf, and there is little doubt that she in her turn would have thought even less of his novels than she did of Arnold Bennett's. But this looked like a straightforward quarrel between the realist and the poetic or avant-garde novelist rather than a deep cultural divide. In Snow's living room there hung a large painting by the modernist Australian artist Sydney Nolan of the outback outlaw Ned Kelly, and I thought of this as some sort of measure of Snow's rebellion against what he took to be the cultural establishment of the day. Although he is now completely out of fashion, his *roman-fleuve Strangers and Brothers* was welcomed by the educated public of its time; and one novel of the sequence, *The Masters* (1951), about Cambridge college politics, had much success not only in Britain but also in the Soviet Union. He was a public figure respected as serious and could hardly have foreseen that Leavis, with whom he had a polite acquaintance, would react with such vehemence to his lecture.

In his response, a lecture called "The Two Cultures: The Significance of C. P. Snow," Leavis described Snow as "portentously ignorant" and insisted that although he had been right about the advance of science and technology, he was quite wrong about its cost and had failed to see that it brought with it "tests and challenges so unprecedented . . . that mankind—this is surely clear—will need to be in full intelligent possession of its full humanity." He added that he was not talking about "traditional wisdom," which would suggest a conservatism he also regarded as an enemy. What he meant was "intelligence, a power . . . of creative response to the new challenges of time; something that is alien to either of Snow's cultures."

The argument was that Snow entirely neglected something preciously human, that kind of discourse that occupies the human space between men and women who belong to a community of language, a language that is recognized as "opening . . . into the unknown and itself unknowable." Where would one go to study this language if not to great literature? At the time the controversy was recognized as important; it continued for a long time and has recently been revived.[13]

I have been dwelling on what might seem, in the very large context of the present inquiries, a rather parochial dispute—a matter for the English, even a matter for the unrepresentative selection of the English who like to quarrel in Cambridge. But I take it to have a more general importance. Anglophone countries have never quite managed to grant humanistic studies the dignity conferred on them in German usage by the title of *Geisteswissenschaften.* There is a science of what can only be known from within, as Dilthey expressed it, as when one "lives through" a poem;[14] and on some such argument the humanities can defend themselves against the incomprehension of scientists—some scientists, I should say, for there are many who know very well that the human sciences are necessary and complementary, and may even, on occasion, enrich "hard" science.

So there is reason, in the present context, to mention Leavis's conviction that society needs a highly intelligent humanist elite or remnant, sensibilities trained by an intense participation in literature (considered as the site of the most significant uses of language). The emphasis here is on literary study, but the position can be held in various ways. Francis Mulhern has argued that *Scrutiny*'s call for an embattled elite, engaged in a perpetual struggle with a society and a culture degenerating into a mechanical and polluted barbarism,was echoed by certain contemporary European protesters. For some "the critique of historical decline" centered on sociology rather than literature. Though *Scrutiny* did not neglect sociology, it was literary criticism in its Leavisian forms and with its Leavisian intentions— its certainty that deep critical involvement in great texts was essential— that distinguished the Cambridge school from their European cousins; but all parties felt the same need—to save the humanities from historical decline.[15]

It may be objected that these instances lack relevance to our immediate situation. Agreed, they were certain that the humanities were under threat, they proposed remedies for what they saw as their decay; but what has that to do with the situation now? Informed that there were still a great many people at college studying literature, Leavis would ask, knowing in advance the answer, how many were studying it with the requisite, intense kind of attention, the kind of which Snow, though a prolific writer and critic, had shown himself incapable.

We may feel we are overfamiliar with this kind of talk of decadence, but it is reasonable to believe that by a Leavisian or any comparable estimate the situation really has grown worse. Simply to advocate intense reading may, in our circumstances, seem very inadequate. Epochal breaks, epistemic *coupures,* are shadows of apocalyptic thought, and it is easy to feel that the decadence is terminal, that we are closer to what feels like a decisive break rather than a gradual decline. The former vision of disaster lacked the decisiveness of apocalypse. A further sign of the enormous times may be that in the old days the threat seemed to be coming mostly from outside the humanities. Now—more pointed, more clearly abolitionist—it comes from within.

The imminence of the millennium has at least something of the effect observed earlier at the approach of certain dates; it is not that people do not understand their arbitrariness but that they cannot refrain from projecting onto them aspirations and anxieties that strictly have nothing to do with them. The date can be a death-substitute, an end-substitute, a moment beautifully apt for sensational *coupures*, whether for individuals or institutions; and I believe this fact now tends to color our own thinking, as well as the more exultant thinking of the abolitionists, about the shape of our studies: they had a beginning, they are still surviving in a middle, and why should they not have an end?

Or, if not yet quite an end, an immediate future much changed and diminished? Bernard Bergonzi speaks of "exploding English." Taking notice of such remarks as Catherine Belsey's, that "only by closing the doors of the English Department against theoretical challenges from outside can we continue to ignore the 'Copernican' revolution which is currently taking place," he deconstructs it: "revolution" is an ambiguous trope, meaning something decisive, like the Copernican revolution or the French Revolution; or it may mean "a mere turning, continual movement without progress."

The solution Bergonzi proposes in his valuable and patient book is to split off conventional literary study from the activity now known as "cultural studies." He means that people who want to consider literature only as a discipline ancillary to some other disciplines or doctrines, as for instance "cultural materialism," should be educated separately from those who, whether for Leavisian or other reasons, want to read *literature*, and possess, or hope to develop, "literary sensibility."[16] It is a shamefully vague expression, but it corresponds to something that certainly exists; those who have it know it exists and easily recognize its absence in those who do not. In what measure it could be transmitted under the conditions prescribed by Bergonzi—and far more threateningly under an achieved new epistemic dispensation, when all our relations to the world must be drastically altered—is more than I can guess. But, like Bergonzi, I believe in the remnant.

Opponents will contend that notions such as "literary sensibility" are precisely part of the battered luggage of the past—loaded with the broken fragments of the aesthetic ideology, tradition, *grands récits*, canonical works distinguished from all others by centuries of bourgeois propaganda—that must be discarded. The "aesthetic ideology," they are sure, belongs to a superseded *episteme*. The problem of dealing with these dismissive arguments is that there is no common ground. The canonical works are not read by those who despise or mistrust them, tradition is irrelevant ex hypothesi, all is text (which is true if you allow that certain critical operations turn some texts into works, a point not to be conceded).

There may be little use in pretending to see, from where we now stand, the final effect of the change now believed to be under way. If we wanted to be truly apocalyptic we should even have to consider the possibility that nothing of much present concern either to "humanists" or to their opponents will long survive. But it is impossible that we should not be interested and worried about our more local problem. There will be much argument, ultimately about value, and especially about value as attributed to that which, merely by being past, can be held to be without relevance, or certainly not to have relevance merely by virtue of its being past. As we may see from the current debasement of the word *heritage*, there is much popular confusion about what is valuable in the past, and why, and if anybody can sort it out it will be the old guard or what is left of it, not the new.

Comfort may come from the reflection that the great Renaissance, which dumped a long past into an epochal oubliette labeled the Middle Ages and brought about changes that, great as they were, turned out to be rather less total than it proclaimed, so that it even became possible to think of it as continuous with what its propagandists claimed to have dumped. Hercules got back his club and lion's skin but remained in the same place in the star map. The tomato was not, after all, "en vérité sans défaut," and our recalcitrant strand of skin, our remnant, may finally turn out to be more interesting than the sharp regularity demanded by the slicers.

I had already written this essay when I found in the indispensable *Times Literary Supplement* a quotation from Julien Benda's *La Trahison des clercs*, a book published long ago and still famous, though as John Casey, the reviewer, remarks, no longer much read. "Our age is indeed the age of the intellectual organization of hatred."[17] Benda was of course thinking more of politics than of art; but in our present situation his sentence surely loses nothing of its force. For we all have colleagues who hate or despise literature and the study of literature, and institutional change has given them power. Our remnant will not have an easy life.

Notes

1. See, e.g., Stephen Heath, *The Nouveau Roman: Studies in the Practice of Writing* (London: Elek, 1972), 113–14, and John Sturrock, *The French New Novel* (Oxford: Oxford University Press, 1969), 196–97.

2. Jean Seznec, *The Survival of the Pagan Gods: The Mythological Tradition and Its Place in Renaissance Humanism and Art*, tr. Barbara F. Sessions, Bollingen Series 38 (New York: Pantheon, 1953), 185–88 and 211–13.

3. Erwin Panofsky, *Renaissance and Renascences in Western Art*, 2d ed. (New York: Harper Torchbooks, 1969), 1–35.

4. E. H. Gombrich, "The Renaissance: Period or Movement?" in *Background to the English Renaissance*, ed. J. B. Trapp (London: Gray-Mills, 1974), 9–30.

5. The tortuous business of nomenclature is well examined by Hans Bertens, *The Idea of the Postmodern* (London: Routledge & Kegan Paul, 1995).

6. Christopher Norris, introduction to *What's Wrong with Postmodernism* (Hempel Hempstead, U.K.: Harvester, 1990), especially 4.

7. Frank Kermode, *History and Value* (Oxford: Oxford University Press, 1988), 128–46.

8. Alvin Kernan, *The Death of Literature* (New Haven, Conn.: Yale University Press, 1990), 83, 135–36, and 151.

9. Robert S. Boynton, "The Routledge Revolution," *Lingua Franca: The Review of Academic Life* 5, no. 3 (April 1995): 26–32.

10. Thomas Docherty, *After Theory* (London and New York: Routledge & Kegan Paul, 1990), 27, 58, and 219.

11. Stephen Greenblatt and Giles Gunn, eds., *Redrawing the Boundaries: The Transformation of English and American Literary Studies* (New York: Modern Language Association of America, 1992), 1–11.

12. See Ben Knights, *The Idea of the Clerisy in the Nineteenth Century* (Cambridge: Cambridge University Press, 1978).

13. For a fuller account, see Ian MacKillop, *F. R. Leavis: A Life in Criticism* (London: Penguin Press, 1995), 314–25; but MacKillop argues that the disagreement between the two lecturers was, at bottom, about history (notably the Industrial Revolution) and, though I acknowledge the importance of this point, I prefer to understand them otherwise, as the sequel shows.

14. I find, a little to my surprise, that I developed this point at some length in an essay of 1965, "The University and the Literary Public," in Thomas B. Stroup, ed., *The Humanities and the Understanding of Reality* (Lexington: University of Kentucky Press, 1966), 55–74.

15. See Francis Mulhern, *The Moment of "Scrutiny"* (London: New Left, 1978), 305ff.

16. Bernard Bergonzi, *Exploding English: Criticism, Theory, Culture* (Oxford: Clarendon, 1990), 100–101.

17. John Casey, "Canon to the Right of Them," *Times Literary Supplement*, November 10, 1995, 19.

Nine

The Pursuit of Metaphor

CHRISTOPHER RICKS

I

BEING in a quandary, I shall be turning to study the quandary that the study of metaphor continues to be in.

My own quandary is immeasurably less important (except to me) but not less real. When this collection of essays was being bruited, I found myself saying at an explorers' meeting that instead of everybody's talking, yet once more, about "the state of the humanities" and the changes and chances of late, those of us who resist the claims of certain recent developments—as not truly or not sufficiently developments at all—would do better to get on with such work as we believe in.

For to argue that current literary theory's claims are inordinate may be held to be—losingly therefore—engaging in current literary theory. And to argue that literary theory's claims deserve less attention than they have courted or extorted is, losingly again, to lavish yet more attention upon what (some of us believe) has been quite sufficiently garlanded with attentions already. So (I mooted at this meeting), instead of spending time arguing in favor of doing something other than such recencies as the Other, it would be wise for others simply to do otherwise. The alternative, not the Alterity. This, in the hope that one might strengthen the things that remain. End of my contribution to the meeting.

But not the end of the contribution question. For, alert in genial appropriation, the begetter of this book (a.k.a. A.K.) promptly wrote asking me to write along—or between—these very lines. "It is probably ironic, as you more than anyone else will instantly realize, to ask you to participate in a volume that in many ways is doing just exactly what you say we should not do." Well, such ironic contradictories are often an entertaining sideshow in this life, whether with Sideshow Bob in *The Simpsons*, who goes on television to extirpate television, or with R. S. Thomas, who writes from his Welsh fastness poems in English about how systemically and systematically corrupt English is. But there remains the particular contradictory quandary. How can one engage in arguing that one would do better not to engage in such arguments? And how, on the other hand, could it be deemed proper to submit here a piece of work genuinely and entirely other than the present setup—an essay on, say, the young T. S. Eliot's fascination with Jules Laforgue, as evidenced in certain Eliot manuscripts.

I have decided to consider metaphor, or rather the pursuit of metaphor. This because of an instructive intractability such as forever balks pursuit. Balking philosophy, it balks theory—and not just theory's recent manifestations. If this assertion can be made good, if it can be shown how demonstrably not at all far any thinking can reasonably get, the further final question will be this: what might we learn from our being so balked? Sweet are the ruses of adversity.

II

One of the most signal changes in the humanities (more so than in the arts themselves) has been the expanded wholesale trade in philosophizing. Some philosophers have argued that most of what has subsequently been retailed lacks the cogent probity of philosophy, being quasi- and even pseudo-philosophical. It may be ill judged of people in literary studies to jump in to adjudicate between, say, Searle and Derrida (or between Searle and Rorty); we tend to plump. But the large matter is not that of the particular philosophical deficiencies of much recent theorizing (hygienic though the demonstration of these can duly prove), but that of the endemic and valuable resistance, not hostility, that literary studies (no less than literature) have always needed, of their nature, to put up to the fellow-humanities philosophy and history: history, with its claim that the establishing of facts is its province, and (more pressingly of late) philosophy, with its claim that the pursuit of truth is its province.

For those of us to whom Samuel Johnson is the greatest of English critics, his greatness will not be distinct from his sustained and rational opposition to philosophy and to theory. "The task of criticism" was, for Johnson, "to establish principles,"[1] and he everywhere made clear that his refusal to elaborate and concatenate the needed concepts beyond a certain point (a point reached early) was not a refusal to continue to think, but a decision to think thereafter about the application of the principles rather than to elaborate principle into theory.[2]

This particular critical tradition (which is plainly not the only one) continues from Johnson to Leavis, to Empson and Winters and Trilling, and to Davie and Kenner. Philosopher-theorists none. "I do not think," says Leavis, but only en route to "that much profit": "But here it may seem that the question of definition comes up again. What is metaphor? What is imagery? I do not think that much profit is likely to come of trying to answer these questions directly, in general terms."[3] Such staunch criticism is manifestly not of theoretical or philosophical bent. For thinking that much profit is likely to come of trying to answer these questions ("What is metaphor?") directly, in general terms, must constitute a great part of theoretical criticism.

Resistance these days to theory's empire (an empire zealously inquisitorial about every form of empire but its own) may take many forms. Sometimes the resistance may seek to show the intellectual deficiencies of a particular argument, the non sequiturs, the untruths, and especially the straw men (a growth industry, this last—but then you can't as easily make brickbats without straw men). Sometimes the resistance may argue more experientially, more practically—may, for instance, put the case for proportions, priorities, or fair shares. Time, energy, attention: these are limited resources, and if any opportunity at all is to be found for reading some actual narratives, narratology may have to relinquish some of its demands. These are working considerations, competing claims; they will continue to be argued, as they always have been, with some light and much heat, with some good will and much ill will; but they need not constitute, on either side, an immitigable philosophical disagreement. They permit, fortunately, of honorable concessions and compromises.

Many disagreements are of this last kind. Some are more disagreeable, in that they have to do, not with the strength of claims, but with their falsity or falsehood: the claims, say, from publicists of theory that everyone theorizes whether nilly or willy, or that everyone should feel obliged to theorize explicitly and elaboratedly.

There remains, though, an obligation, hard to meet and yet dishonorable to waive, incumbent on those of us who elect principles not theories. The obligation is to set fairly before oneself the least compromising form of the question emanating from the opposition. Why, or when, is it proper to desist from further elaborating of the argument, from further philosophizing? How, in reply to this, would one make the case that pursuit of the theoretical elaborations may be intrinsically misguided, and therefore, though onerous, idle?

Not that such an onus rests only upon those who set store by Horatio's admonition: "'Twere to consider too curiously to consider so." For if it is incumbent on the likes of me to give an instance of, and a succinct argument about, the futility of boundless pursuit, of too curious a considering, it is no less incumbent on the other side, the philosophizers, that they too give arguments, only this time arguments as to why it could never be right to desist from pursuit, or even arguments as to when it just might be right. The philosopher's or theorist's recourse to the accusatory terms "underdescribed" and "underargued" may legitimately be met by an interrogative retort as to whether there is such a thing as overdescription or overargument to which their enterprise must sometimes be damagingly open.

But from my side: on what grounds might one reasonably abstain from
further pursuit and conceptualizing? What would save this from being just
a defection, a laziness or cowardice? I take metaphor as a case study in
such intractabilities as might honorably give us not only pause but remission. And I take up the pursuit of metaphor for several reasons. First, that
it is genuinely, not factitiously, of great philosophical interest. Second, that
it has been increasingly attended to, by both philosophers and theorists,
during the last half century. And third, that it is agreeably free from some
of the dust and heat lately stirred and stoked by other contentions or
contests. The pursuit of metaphor—though like everything else it can be
invaluably or unvaluably considered under the aspect of politics—has not
been party to the harsh political polemics that have been incited by "the
canon." So it may permit of a larger air, of more light than heat.

As summary justice: no one has ever been able to arrive at satisfactory
terms for the constituents, the elements, of a metaphor. If I am right in
saying this (and I shall try to make it good), then the pursuit of metaphor—in the abstract, that is to say theoretically or philosophically—is
immediately blocked. The constitutive terms, the antitheses, with which
we have to make do, will not do. They are indispensable, inadequate,
misleading, and unimprovable. Extraordinary efforts have been made; all
have failed. The rudiments are immediately the impassable impediments.

III

Shelley insisted that "Language is vitally metaphorical; that is, it marks
the before unapprehended relations of things." The definition of *metaphor*
in *The Princeton Encyclopedia of Poetry and Poetics* opens: "A condensed
verbal relation."[4] Whatever else a metaphor may be, it is a relation; on this
the ponderings of metaphor concur, whether giving salience to comparison, to similarity, to substitution, or to interaction. But what then are we
to make of one immediate token of the immitigable oddities: our en-
grained, natural, but misleading and entangling habit of using such
phrases as "a metaphor for the times" or "the metaphor of the rose"?

Since a metaphor is a relation, how can it be right to say, as we all do all
the time, "metaphor *for*"? You would not say, in any such context, "relation for," and, to use a more fitting way of putting it, "relation of" or
"relation between," might immediately press you to ponder the constituents—the relation *of* this *to* that, *between* x *and* y. Plainly we know what
we mean when we say "a metaphor for," but what do we mean by it, and
what might such a usage tell us about those root quandaries that (I
believe) are definitional and more?

On the day on which I type this paragraph (December 12, 1995), the *Boston Globe* describes the appalling killing of two children: "But here you had a metaphor for the times: Two people, a mother and father, walking through a dying city with dead babies in a cloth sack."

The sentence is honorable and telling. What it supposes of society is clear. What—less urgently, less searingly, but in another context crucially —it supposes of metaphor is another matter.

Take the same idiom in the cooler setting of the *Times Literary Supplement* (March 24, 1995), Bernard Crick in defense of Robert Altman's film *Prêt-à-Porter:* "[A hostile reviewer] suggests that 'it has been consumed by its subject.' But what is its subject—surely not fashion? Surely fashion is only a metaphor for a truly Swiftian satire of the world." Anyone who uses "surely" twice in four words ought surely to be resisted, but what matters more is "only a metaphor for." There is the propensity for depreciation in "only" there, with metaphor dwindling into being the member of the entourage who is paid off, dismissed.

Charles Lamb, in 1821, was wary of the Scot: "You must speak upon the square with him. He stops a metaphor like a suspected person in an enemy's country. 'A healthy book!' . . . 'did I catch rightly what you said?'"[5] There is a long history of hostility to metaphor, with Bishop Sprat fiercely blessing the troops in 1667.

One way to underrate and misapprehend metaphor is to slight the literal that goes to the making of it, and the other is to slight that which is not literal. To slight either is to slight the relation itself. Added to which, the concept of the literal is itself stubbornly resistant to clarification, both within and without the relation that is metaphor.

I once asked a friend what would be wrong with my describing the tie I was wearing, one decorated with poisonous frogs, as a metaphor for my enemies within the university "community." Sharing my dislike of those particular people, he gratifyingly answered "Nothing." Gratifyingly, and yet precariously, I pounced—for the *tie* is not the metaphor; the metaphor is the relation between the tie and those people. When we say "metaphor for," we are diverting the word "metaphor" to mean the constituent or the element of the metaphor that is not—not what exactly? . . . And here we fall back upon "literal."

Daily impatience, all busyness, chafes at the dual nature of the transfer that metaphor, this recommender of patience, asks us to appreciate. The same goes for our speaking casually, as we do and will continue to do (for reasons that may prove worth attention), of "the metaphor *of* such-and-such": such as the metaphor of the rose, when what we ought to be identifying as the metaphor is the relation of the rose to, say, human beauty; or the metaphor of the journey, when the metaphor is rather the relation of the journey to, say, aging. Like "metaphor for," "metaphor of" is a phrase designed to veil (and so might help us by directing attention to) inexpugnable difficulties, for the phrase contributes to misimpressions, and works against the realization that what is of the essence is a relation. Metaphor is not only far from simple-minded, it is not single-minded. It is often myriad-minded.

Metaphor asks us not only to balance but to value balancing. There is the danger of imbalance in a notable essay by Fiona Macintosh on the Victorian and Edwardian stage-ban on *Oedipus Rex:*

> It may seem incredible to us that Sophocles' tragedy can be reduced to a play about incest *tout court.* But it is important to remember that our readings of the play are essentially post-Romantic and post-Nietzschean, if not also part-psychological and part-anthropological, whereas Redford [Examiner of Plays, 1909] and his colleagues are subjecting Sophocles' play to a reading where incest in its most literal sense is the stumbling block. For us, the incest of Oedipus and Jocasta has been raised to an image of cosmic disorder, a metaphor of the multilayered self, or a schema of the threat to boundaries on which civilization depends. For the late nineteenth and early twentieth-century reader, however, the indelicacy of the subject matter obtrudes.[6]

Thoroughly aware of the old-time danger of reducing *Oedipus Rex* "to a play about incest *tout court*," this does not beware of the danger attendant upon "our readings of the play": "For us, the incest of Oedipus and Jocasta has been raised to an image of cosmic disorder, a metaphor of the multi-layered self." Here the phrase "a metaphor of" too much sets "the subject matter" aside. It was unbalanced of the previous age, fearful of "incest in its most literal sense," to wince away ("the indelicacy of the subject matter obtrudes"). But is our age any more honorably respectful of "the subject matter" when we exercise our own way of not having the subject matter obtrude: by lowering it (while claiming to have "raised" it) to its *least* literal sense or rather to the not-literal-at-all, "a metaphor of the multilay-ered self"?

"A metaphor of"? "A metaphor for"? Or, another member of the same family, "as metaphor"? This last has been elevated to the modishly titular, thanks to Susan Sontag, *Illness as Metaphor.*[7] The observation, which then constitutes the ineradicable frustration, is obvious: that it is natural to the language to use the word "metaphor" not only for the whole but for one of its parts. This, which is not the same as metonymy, is so effortless as seldom to be attended to, but pressure does not have to be effortful.

Reflect upon the oddity of this ordinary usage by which we speak of one aspect or part of metaphor as the metaphor or as metaphorical. From a recent *Times Literary Supplement* again, a review of Terry Eagleton's *Heathcliff and the Great Hunger:* "[The first chapter] argues that Heathcliff, who is picked up from the streets of Liverpool by Earnshaw senior, is, whether metaphorically or literally, an Irish victim of the famine." Set aside (as a particular case) the convenient airiness of "whether metaphorically or literally," its handsomely relieving the political argument of so many unwelcome responsibilities; what might induce a more generalized concern is this practice of the language itself, in so speaking—unmisgivingly, it must seem—of something within metaphor as the metaphor or as metaphorical.

Yet the practice is neither recent nor perverse,[8] while at the same time it embodies a central thwarting of elaborated understanding, an imperviousness to philosophical elucidation.

The twentieth-century poet who enjoyed the best philosophical training, and who made the best use, not only in his criticism but in his poetry, of imperviousness to philosophical elucidation, wrote in 1918: "The healthy metaphor adds to the strength of the language; it makes available some of that physical source of energy upon which the life of language depends. '. . . [I]n her strong toil of grace' is a complicated metaphor which has this effect; and as in most good metaphor, you can hardly say where the metaphorical and the literal meet."[9] But the complications of metaphor extend even beyond T. S. Eliot's case of "a complicated metaphor" in Shakespeare; not only is there the difficulty of saying where the metaphorical and the literal meet,[10] there is the difficulty—or rather the recognition of an intractability that passes beyond difficulty into impossibility—that is alive in our using the terms "metaphorical" (or "the metaphor") and "literal" for the opposing constituents of a metaphor. Strong toil, strong toils, indeed.

IV

That you can hardly say where the metaphorical and the literal meet—that even a great poet and great critic such as Eliot can hardly say—this is plenty, this is more than enough. But it is not, in itself, enough to make the case of metaphor unusual in perplexity. As John Searle has observed, arguing against deconstruction and about literary theory,

> it is not necessarily an objection to a conceptual analysis, or to a distinction, that there are no rigorous or precise boundaries to the concept analyzed or the distinction being drawn. It is not necessarily an objection even to theoretical concepts that they admit of application *more or less*. This is something of a cliché in analytic philosophy: most concepts and distinctions are rough at the edges and do not have sharp boundaries. The distinctions between fat and thin, rich and poor, democracy and authoritarianism, for example, do not have sharp boundaries. More important for our present discussion, the distinctions between

literal and metaphorical, serious and nonserious, fiction and nonfiction and, yes, even true and false, admit of degrees and all apply *more or less*. It is, in short, generally accepted that many, perhaps most, concepts do not have sharp boundaries, and since 1953 we have begun to develop theories to explain why they *cannot*.[11]

My own allegiances, as is evident, are with Searle, but there remains the oddity, unremarked in his list, of a particular one of those indispensable distinctions such as are not susceptible of strict boundaries. For, offering first of all three wide cases and then four of a kind "more important to our present discussion," Searle sees no need to acknowledge the crucial difference between the first of the latter four and any others of his seven instances: "the distinctions between literal and metaphorical." Yet there is a crucial distinction to be made between this first one and all the others: that it is only in the case of the distinction between literal and metaphorical that there obtains the irksome quirk, with its power to balk, that "metaphorical," like "metaphor," is not only one of the antithetical terms up for distinction but also the term for the whole within which the distinction is to be made. No such thing is true of the distinctions between fat and thin, rich and poor, democracy and authoritarianism, or those between serious and nonserious, fiction and nonfiction, and, yes, even true and false.

Sometimes in such cogitations a warning may be seen to stand in for an authentic wariness. Take Robert J. Fogelin, in *Figuratively Speaking*: "At various places I have fallen in with others by speaking about the metaphorical or figurative meaning of some expression. There is really nothing wrong with speaking in this way except that it might suggest that an expression can have two distinct meanings, a literal meaning and a metaphorical (or figurative) meaning, and that, in turn, might suggest a commitment to a meaning-shift theory of metaphors of the kind I reject."[12] But this makes it sound as though falling in with others is a camaraderie (better than falling out with others, eh?), whereas the fact is that no more than the rest of us can Fogelin conceive of not having to fall back upon speaking of "the metaphorical or figurative" within our understanding of what is within metaphor. "There is really nothing wrong with speaking in this way"—and then, a touch wistfully still—"except that it might suggest. . . ." No, the case is harsher. What is askew is not just the possible suggestion that the "literal" and the "metaphorical (or figurative)" are "two distinct meanings," but the ubiquitous use of the terms "literal" and "metaphorical" at all. Fogelin placates: "There is really nothing wrong with speaking in this way except. . . ." (The theorists of metaphor have frequent recourse to "really," sometimes deepened to *"really"*; they ought to be so good as to pay the word a handsome bonus, given how much work they ask of it.) I should not want to retort to Fogelin that there is really something wrong. Rather, that there is really something recalcitrant at the core, such as "might suggest" that the enterprising pursuit is doomed.

Fogelin has his admonitions: "Now that does not mean that satires are metaphors, although speaking that way can have a specious ring of profundity. It is easy to understand the temptation to let one member of a family of concepts become the representative of all the rest."[13] But he does not confront the trickier case, which is not a temptation but a tradition, and which is not that of letting one member of a family of concepts become the representative of all the rest ("metaphor" too lavishly invoked), but that of unrepiningly letting one of the opposing terms within an antithesis also be the term for that which the antithesis comprises.

I. A. Richards asks, in all but innocence, "when a man has a wooden leg, is it a metaphoric or a literal leg?"[14] It is not the least of the stumbling blocks that the concept of the literal is itself so perplexing, such a knotting of the handily indispensable and the hand-wringingly unclarifiable. Despite all the wrestling that there has been with the word and the concept of the literal, there has been nothing of an outcome. True, there is many a word or concept by which philosophy continues to be thwarted, but it certainly contributes to the misty mystery of metaphor that what might have been thought to be the more sturdy of the two terms within it, the "literal," when approached dissolves into the air.[15]

The Cambridge Dictionary of Philosophy (1995) enters with a definition of *metaphor* as "a figure of speech (or a trope) in which a word or phrase that literally denotes one thing is used to denote another, thereby implicitly comparing the two things." The dictionary duly exits with a paragraph about the rejection for the past two centuries of both of the "traditional themes" in the understanding of metaphor (decorations? elliptical similes?), only, in closing, to fade away into the forest dim: "And though no consensus has yet emerged on how and what metaphors contribute to meaning, nor how we recognize what they contribute, near-consensus has emerged on the thesis that they do not work as elliptical similes." Adieu. Either that or a submission to the *Journal of Negative Results.*

Other theorists "simply assume a commonsense recognition," in a manner that may be creditable but does lessen the layman's awe at philosophical credentials: "We should be cautious about using the term *literal.* Not only is it difficult in many instances to determine what is and what is not literal, but there are theorists who deny the distinction between literal and metaphorical language. At this stage of the study, I shall simply assume a commonsense recognition that there are times when we speak literally and at other times figuratively and that many of us recognise a figurative expression. I shall return to this issue later."[16] But what does it mean to say that we should be cautious about using the term "literal" and then feel so free to use it? The warning seems nothing more than small-print against the literally litigious. For, returning to this issue later, we enter a section boldly entitled "**Interaction in Metaphorical and Literal Expression:** Literal and Metaphorical Interaction," and are then assured that "The problem of distinguishing literal from figurative expressions was broached in the Introduction." Broaching is acknowledged to be philosophically insufficient, but the next page arrives at no more of an advance than this: "Let it be conceded that although a hard and fast distinction between literal and metaphorical expressions is not always obvious, there are contrasts evident when a fresh metaphor stands out from the midst of otherwise conventionally used literal discourse."[17] In any case, there remains, undisentangled by Hausman, the even more snagged matter of "metaphorical" and "figurative" there *within* metaphors and figures of speech.

These tangles do much to explain, though little to justify, another turn within what Monroe C. Beardsley once dubbed "The Metaphorical Twist," namely the use of "literally" to mean "metaphorically." *Private Eye* has long had its eyes and ears open for what, in a metaphor of which one member is the sports commentator David Coleman, it calls "Colemanballs." "And Greg Lemond has literally come back from the dead to lead the Tour de France." "When those stalls open, the horses are literally going to explode." The grammarians sort it out: "It would seem that the speaker wishes to emphasize the extraordinary nature of what he is describing— 'Believe it or not!'—, as well as to draw attention to the hyperbolic language used to describe it. The insertion of *literally* seems often to acknowledge that people tend to use the expression concerned (*somersault, earth shaking*) as merely figurative or exaggeratedly colourful whereas in the present instance the word is to be taken in its literal meaning."[18] Perhaps. But notice the revenge taken by "literally," back from the dead: "merely figurative." And if "the figure" and "the metaphor" can elsewhere be allowed to usurp not only the *galère* but one of the two elements comprising it, why shouldn't the other element "literally" put in its usurpatious counterclaim?

In defining "metaphorical," Dr. Johnson could not escape "literal": "not literal," following this at once with "not according to the primitive meaning of the word." But in defining "metaphor," he tried to do without "literally": "The application of a word to an use to which, in its original import, it cannot be put: as, he *bridles* his anger." But "original," like "primitive," is no less dubious, albeit differently so, than "literal." For the origins of words, as to the "literal" and its other (or the "metaphorical" and its other), are chicken and egg. (Which came first? In the beginning was the word.)

It is all such a mire that a will-o'-the-wisp is only to be expected: how about just calling one of the terms the "nonmetaphorical" and the other the "nonliteral"? This is easily effected. But ineffectual. For although such a presto may relieve the prestidigitators, this feint does not bring to lucid order the complication by which there is within the "nonliteral" something that is then to be differentiated as "nonliteral."

V

This century's most inaugurative contribution to the understanding of metaphor was made by I. A. Richards in *The Philosophy of Rhetoric* (1936), and it is high time that I acknowledged it; and then, as a contribution to the higher ingratitude, I'll set a bourne how far it's to be believed.

It is greatly to Richards's credit that, introducing his "two technical terms" ("tenor" and "vehicle"), he so lucidly identified the crux:

> One of the oddest of the many odd things about the whole topic is that we have no agreed distinguishing terms for these two halves of a metaphor—in spite of the immense convenience, almost the necessity, of such terms if we are to make any analyses without confusion. For the whole task is to compare the different relations which, in different cases, these two members of a metaphor hold to one another, and we are confused at the start if we do not know which of the two we are talking about. At present we have only some clumsy descriptive phrases with which to separate them. "The original idea" and "the borrowed one"; "what is really being said or thought of" and "what it is compared to"; "the underlying idea" and "the imagined nature"; "the principal subject" and "what it resembles" or, still more confusing, simply "the meaning" and "the metaphor" or "the idea" and "its image."
>
> How confusing these ideas must be is easily seen, and experience with the analysis of metaphors fully confirms the worst expectations. We need the word "metaphor" for the whole double unit, and to use it sometimes for one of the two components in separation from the other is as injudicious as that other trick by which we use "the meaning" here sometimes for the work that the whole double unit does and sometimes for the other component—the tenor, as I am calling it—the underlying idea or principal subject which the vehicle or figure means.[19]

This stands in need of being quizzed: "almost the necessity"—why only "almost"? And what about the use of "figure" at the end there, to mean one constituent of the figure, in just the way that Richards reprehends with "metaphor"—and, on the next page, reprehends with "figure" itself and with "image"? But Richards's page does stand, and with an unmistakable centrality.

The most successful attempt to identify the constituents of a metaphor has undoubtedly been this of Richards's, with his "tenor" and "vehicle." But the success is that of having become adopted, not that of having escaped the fire as well as the frying pan.[20] For just as the trouble with the analogous subdivision of "sign" into "signifier" and "signified" is that what is signified by the sign is rather the relation of the "signifier" to the "signified," and just as the trouble with McLuhan's analogous subdivision into "medium" and "message" is that the message is rather the relation of the "medium" to the "message," so, upon reflection, the tenor of a metaphor has to be understood as the relation of the "tenor" to the "vehicle." In escaping one particular form taken by the problem of the head term's also being one of the constituents ("metaphor" and "metaphorical" within metaphor), Richards did not escape the encompassing problem itself.

Nor did he escape putting his thumb on the scale. For even as it becomes too easy to speak of the *merely* metaphorical or the *merely* literal, so it becomes too easy to think less well of a "vehicle." All a vehicle does, after all, is deliver, not affect or effect. There is not a due evenhandedness about Richards's very handy terms. "Tenor" claims too much, since, fully grasped, the tenor of a metaphor is not its "tenor" but the relation of that to its "vehicle"; and "vehicle" is granted too little, has arrived to be dismissed. Which is not at all what Richards's "interaction" theory of metaphor believes or wants. But then, as often happens, one's terms defy one's arguments.

Richards—this was his most engaging and endearing quality—never lacked hope. His hopes for the clarification of metaphor keep returning to what he trusts will prove to have been the needless confusions of "traditional" thinking about metaphor. The salvific insights "have not yet been taken account of"; we need a better theory "than is yet available"; "the time was not ripe," and "I am not sure that it is yet ripe." Yet me no yets.

T. S. Eliot was right to praise Richards, with circumspection and circumscription: "Mr. Richards' importance—and I have suggested that he is indeed important—is not in his solutions but in his perception of problems. There is a certain discrepancy between the size of his problems and the size of his solutions. That is natural: when one perceives a great problem, one is the size of one's vision; but when one supplies a solution, one is the size of one's training.[21]

Richards saw clearly the oddity by which the crucial terms are used both for the whole and for a part: "All these words, *meaning, expression, metaphor, comparison, subject, figure, image*, behave so, and when we recognize this we need look no further for a part, at least, of the explanation of the backward state of the study."[22] But his next sentences falter somewhat: "Why rhetoricians have not long ago remedied this defect of language for their purpose, would perhaps be a profitable matter for reflection. I do not know a satisfactory answer." One satisfactory answer to this question, and to Richards's musing, might be that the defect is irremediable, and is one that salutarily sets a limit to the philosophizing drive.

Is philosophizing the proper way of thinking about "the metaphor proper"? The term is used by *The Oxford Companion to the English Language* (1992): "Commentators, however, are not usually precise about where the metaphor proper resides: it is sometimes defined as the vehicle alone, sometimes as the combination of tenor and vehicle, and sometimes as tenor, vehicle, and ground together."[23] Richards's "ground" never took off. The "tenor" succeeded in ringing out, and the "vehicle" in getting moving. But.[24]

It is not that I think I can do any better; rather, that no one can do any better, for reasons that might excite a healthy respect for metaphor's supple obduracy and might discourage philosophy's unsupple such.

And similar objections can immediately be made to the other terminological candidates.

For instance, Max Black asks that a metaphor be understood as having two distinct "subjects," the "primary" subject and the "secondary" one (formerly in Black's account they had been the "principal" and "subsidiary" "subjects"); he asks too that "the word used nonliterally" be the "focus," and the literal be the "frame."[25] The terminology may have its uses, but it raises more questions than it settles, not least the tendency of its own metaphors ("focus" and "frame") and the way in which Black's well-motivated change from "principal" and "subsidiary" into "primary" and "secondary" fails to abolish the inappropriate intrusion of a set order of importance.

Carl Hausman says, "I shall call the primary unit the *nucleus*"; he speaks proliferatingly of the "subjects or anchoring terms of metaphors," of "what is spoken about, the anchoring nucleus," of "the subject term" and "the anchoring subject." These are not terms that will ever adhere, let alone anchor. As an effort at "the differentiation of the elements that comprise a metaphor," this too may be valiant, but it lacks the better part of valour.[26]

Monroe C. Beardsley's "subject" and "modifier"; Allan Paivio's and Andrew Ortony's "topic" and "vehicle" (for "the similarity metaphor"); George A. Miller's "referent" and "relatum" (with its needed note, then, that Tversky [1977] "calls the referent the 'subject' and the relatum the 'referent'"); J. D. Sapir's "continuous term" and "discontinuous term": *ubi sunt*? Well, all are in *Metaphor and Thought*, edited by Andrew Ortony (1979); but none thrives, or ought to.

VI

What then remains? The imaginative skill by which metaphors are created, especially within great literature. The imaginative skill by which metaphors are apprehended, especially within great criticism. The imaginative skill by which metaphors are made to generalize themselves, especially within great formulations of principle. ("Make the facts generalize themselves": T. S. Eliot's great navigation, working its way between the rock of "Make the facts into a generalization" and the whirlpool of "Let the facts generalize themselves.") This last way of thinking, by courtesy not of theories but of principles, is an indispensable alternative to the elaborated and concatenated thinking, and one of its great exponents is Lichtenberg. "Most of the expressions we use are metaphorical: they contain the philosophy of our ancestors." "We do not think metaphors are anything very important, but I think a good metaphor is something even the police should keep an eye on." "The metaphor is much more subtle than its inventor, and so are many things."[27]

But the phenomenon of metaphor's intractability can itself be drawn upon. We might compare its not being possible to come up with satisfactory terms for the components or constitution of metaphor with other cases, such as the enduring and valuable unsatisfactoriness of our terms for the numinous or for the sexual, or our inability even to say satisfactorily what *kind* of distinction is the prose/poetry distinction, and our inability to find a satisfactory term for what, within a long poem, may unsatisfactorily have to be called a stanza, when it is no such thing, or a verse paragraph, likewise. In all these cases it may be reasonable to wonder whether the matter itself, in refusing to abide our question let alone answer it, is not telling us something. Issuing perhaps a courteous refusal, a chastening answer to our craving for answers and for labels. Knowing to know no more. Bearing witness, yet once more, to the positive truth of Keats's Negative Capability, where it was because several things dovetailed in his mind that he was able to see reason's dovetailing, in imaginative matters, as a lesser capability: "I had not a dispute but a disquisition with Dilke, on various subjects; several things dovetailed in my mind, & at once it struck me, what quality went to form a Man of Achievement especially in Literature & which Shakespeare posessed so enormously—I mean *Negative Capability*; that is when man is capable of being in uncertainties, Mysteries, doubts, without any irritable reaching after fact & reason."[28]

To my mind, therefore, Carl Hausman's honorable words in *Metaphor and Art* are inadvertently misleading in that they narrow the forms an honorable dissent from any such enterprise as his might take:

What is the point of trying to understand a phenomenon that has long been so elusive? Why should writers devote so much effort to the topic? The answer may seem obvious to those who already have been drawn into a study of it. And the need to raise the question may seem pointless to those who have simply appreciated the power of metaphor or who have only wanted to create and use metaphors for poetic or other purposes. But to all who reflect on what fascinates them, the question is important to consider because even if in its general outlines the answer is obvious, what may not be so obvious is the extent to which both the question and its answers differ depending on the professional perspective.[29]

But someone might decline to pursue "a phenomenon that has long been so elusive" not just because of being one of "those who have simply appreciated the power of metaphor or who have only wanted to create and use metaphors for poetic or other purposes." (*"Only* wanted to create"?) Neither of Hausman's categories would have room for a profoundly imaginative literary critic (*"simply* appreciated"?) or for a thinker whose thought chose to exercise itself not in theory but in principle—or would have room, *a fortiori*, for a great poet such as Wallace Stevens. "But to all who reflect on what fascinates them": on reflection, this excludes from the reflective everyone other than philosophers, pursuers who are tempted to set no limits to elaborated pursuit, as against a fully realized local attention, not extending but rather in its wholeness wholly attending to the particulars of rapture.

A substantial change of scale is a change of enterprise. The best book on metaphor is the brisk one by Terence Hawkes, *Metaphor* (London: Methuen, 1972), the 102 pages of which necessarily mount to no more—but no less—than a canter round the field, not a pursuit of the blatant beast of metaphor. Added to which, Hawkes had the wit to furnish for each chapter an epigraph from the most deeply apt of modern poets, Wallace Stevens.

For it is Stevens whose art most comprehends the demarcations of philosophical pursuit. The poem "The Motive for Metaphor" depends upon its giving a turn to the locution "a metaphor for." "Metaphors of a Magnifico" are not metaphors for a magnifico. "Thinking of a Relation between the Images of Metaphors" begins its realization of relation by putting before us a simple dual impossibility, that of either including the musical sense of "bass" (the sound of the word, so sounded, being so different from the silent fish for whom it angles) or of excluding it: "The wood-doves are singing along the Perkiomen. / The bass lie deep, still afraid of the Indians." Nothing will permit of our hearing a bass voice; nothing will permit, given "singing" and "deep," of our not straining our ear for that sound too. For the next couplet is this: "In the one ear of the fisherman, who is all / One ear, the wood-doves are singing a single song."

It is Stevens who sees from many angles the configuration of these intractables, the opposite and the conceptual oppositions:

> Two things of opposite natures seem to depend
> On one another, as a man depends
> On a woman, day on night, the imagined
>
> On the real. This is the origin of change.
> Winter and spring, cold copulars, embrace
> And forth the particulars of rapture come.
>
>   ("Notes towards a Supreme Fiction: It Must Change" IV)

The word "man" may include woman; the word "day" may include night; as with the word "metaphor," the term for the whole is also a term for a part. What then, after "man/woman" and "day/night," of Stevens's "imagined/real"? A calmly colossal two-legged enjambment, which "depends" not only *on* but from, from a line-ending that then proves to be a triplet-ending:

>   as a man depends
> On a woman, day on night, the imagined
>
> On the real.

Does imagination "embrace" reality, or is there a turn, with reality embracing imagination? Why is not the imagined, like the imagination, as much a part of reality, albeit differently so, as anything else? Independence of mind imagines interdependences.

We cannot imagine doing without the opposition of the imagined and the real, and yet we cannot imagine finding it altogether fitting either. We cannot imagine doing without the opposition of literature and life, even while we fully grant not just the legitimacy but the necessity of T. S. Eliot's objection to the opposition or antinomy: "It is the function of a literary review to maintain the autonomy and disinterestedness of literature, and at the same time to exhibit the relations of literature—not to 'life,' as something contrasted to literature, but to all the other activities which, together with literature, are the components of life."[30]

All such intractabilities preclude pursuit. A burden, they yet are so good as to rid us of other burdens. A warning against any hubris of the antiphilosophical (different from the right not to accede to philosophy's sway), they also constitute a warning against philosophical hubris, even of the kind that chooses to speak modestly. "What is your aim in philosophy? —To show the fly the way out of the fly-bottle."[31] But it is not possible to show the fly the way off the flypaper.

The pursuit of metaphor, then, is offered here as a case (forming part of the case for the committing of energies elsewhere) in which declining the pursuit is not abdication. A reasonable conclusion here might be the words with which Jonathan Culler once concluded the issue of metaphor and the issue of *New Literary History* "On Metaphor," a gathering that had included Derrida, Ricoeur, and Todorov. Culler's position is not mine (since I continue to believe in "the notion of metaphor" and to judge it fruitful—it is only the theorizing of metaphor about which I am happily despondent), but he does lend his authority to skepticism about the pursuit of metaphor: "To say that the notion of metaphor should be scrapped, that it is a positive hindrance to our understanding of reading because it conceals the complexities of interpretation, is an ungenerous conclusion to an issue on metaphor; but the best essays here presented point this way. They explore the paradoxes and impossibilities of the notion (sometimes by illustrating its triviality), or else escape from it to the general problems of interpretation."[32] Escape? "What mad pursuit? What struggle to escape?" In concurring, and with a conspicuous theorist to boot, that someone may reasonably refuse to join the pursuit, that the pursuit might even be called off, I should not have to maintain that the pursuit is mad, only that any such refusal is imperfectly sane.

Notes

1. Samuel Johnson, *Rambler* no. 92, February 2, 1751.

2. I have written about this in "Literary Principles as against Theory" (1985), collected in *Essays in Appreciation* (Oxford: Clarendon Press, 1996).

3. F. R. Leavis, *Education and the University* (London: Chatto & Windus, 1943), 78.

4. *The Princeton Encyclopedia of Poetry and Poetics*, ed. Alex Preminger et al. (Princeton, N.J.: Princeton University Press, 1965), entry by George Whalley. See also *The New Princeton Encyclopedia of Poetry and Poetics*, ed. Alex Preminger et al. (Princeton, N.J.: Princeton University Press, 1993), in which the new entry for *metaphor*, by Wallace Martin, is no less admirably thorough, lucid, and fair-minded.

5. Charles Lamb, "Imperfect Sympathies," *The London Magazine* (August 1821). There is the life of metaphor in the move from "healthy" to "catch."

6. Fiona Macintosh, "Under the Blue Pencil: Greek Tragedy and the British Censor," *Dialogos* 2 (1995): 61–62.

7. Susan Sontag, *Illness as Metaphor* (New York: Farrar, Straus & Giroux, 1978). Recent goings with this flow: Hermann Haken et al., *The Machine as Metaphor and Tool* (New York: Springer-Verlag, 1993); A. J. Soyland, *Psychology as Metaphor* (London: Sage, 1994); Leonardo Sciascia, *Sicily as Metaphor* (Marl-

boro, Vt.: Marlboro Press, 1994); Martin Friedman et al., *Visions of America: Landscape as Metaphor in the Late Twentieth Century* (New York: Harry N. Abrams, 1994); Kojin Karatani, *Architecture as Metaphor* (Cambridge, Mass.: MIT Press, 1995); and Elaine Marks, *Marrano as Metaphor* (New York: Columbia University Press, 1996).

8. See Johnson's *Dictionary:* "metaphorical: Not literal; not according to the primitive meaning of the word; figurative. 'The words which were do continue; the only difference is, that whereas before they had a literal, they now have a metaphorical use.' Hooker."

9. T. S. Eliot, *The Egoist* 5 (October 1918): 114. Quoting *Antony and Cleopatra* Act 5, scene ii.

10. Simon Blackburn gives pride of place to this problem, in the entry for *metaphor* in his *Oxford Dictionary of Philosophy* (Oxford: Oxford University Press, 1994): "Philosophical problems include deciding how the border between literal and metaphorical meaning is to be drawn."

11. John R. Searle, "Literary Theory and Its Discontents," *New Literary History* 25 (1994): 638.

12. Robert J. Fogelin, *Figuratively Speaking* (New Haven, Conn.: Yale University Press, 1988), 95.

13. Ibid., 98.

14. I. A. Richards, *The Philosophy of Rhetoric* (New York: Oxford University Press, 1936), 118.

15. See Owen Barfield, "The Meaning of the Word 'Literal,'" in *Metaphor and Symbol*, ed. L. C. Knights and Basil Cottle (London: Butterworths, 1960). Barfield, most courteous of turners of tables, argues that words sometimes held to be based on a transfer from the literal to the metaphorical can be interpreted rather as extended from the metaphorical to the literal. It should be added that the two terms are not equipollent anyway, in that "literal" does not have a noun to which it stands as "metaphorical" does to "metaphor," *literalness* and *literality* being out of the way, and the noun "a literal" being something other.

16. Carl R. Hausman, *Metaphor and Art: Interactionism and Reference in the Verbal and Nonverbal Arts* (Cambridge: Cambridge University Press, 1989), 3.

17. *Metaphor and Art*, 52–53.

18. *A Comprehensive Grammar of the English Language*, ed. Randolph Quirk, Sidney Greenbaum, Geoffrey Leech, and Jan Svartvik (Harlow, U.K.: Longman, 1985), 619.

19. Richards, *The Philosophy of Rhetoric*, 96–97.

20. Fogelin, *Figuratively Speaking*, 107, on Bessie Smith, "He was the first to boil my cabbage": "Here the subject of the sustained metaphor (what I. A. Richards called the *tenor*) is sexual intercourse, and the object of comparison (Richards's *vehicle*) is cooking." By great good fortune (onomastication), Fogelin was in a position to add a footnote: "I owe this example to my colleague, W. W. Cook."

21. T. S. Eliot, "Literature, Science, and Dogma," a review of Richards's *Science and Poetry*, *The Dial* 82 (1927): 239–43.

22. Richards, *The Philosophy of Rhetoric*, 97.

23. *The Oxford Companion to the English Language*, ed. Tom McArthur (Oxford: Oxford University Press, 1992), 653.

24. A further but: when Derrida, or his translator F. C. T. Moore, writes respectfully of "the distinction proposed by I. A. Richards between the metaphorical vehicle and metaphorical tenor," it should be remarked that Richards did not append "metaphorical" to either term, and with good reason since "metaphorical" is so often invoked to distinguish the vehicle from the tenor. Jacques Derrida, "White Mythology," *New Literary History* 6 (1974): 27n.

25. Max Black, "More about Metaphor," in *Metaphor and Thought*, ed. Andrew Ortony (Cambridge: Cambridge University Press, 1979), 28.

26. Hausman, *Metaphor and Art*, 67, 70–71, and 78.

27. Notebook D: 87, Notebook E: 91, Notebook F: 41. Georg Lichtenberg, *Aphorisms*, tr. R. J. Hollingdale (Harmondsworth, U.K.: Penguin, 1990), 63, 79, and 87.

28. To George and Tom Keats, 21, 27(?) December 1817, in *The Letters of John Keats*, ed. Hyder Edward Rollins (Cambridge, Mass.: Harvard University Press, 1958), 1:193.

29. Hausman, *Metaphor and Art*, 6.

30. T. S. Eliot, *The Criterion* 1 (July 1923): 421.

31. Ludwig Wittgenstein, *Philosophical Investigations*, tr. G. E. M. Anscombe (Oxford: Basil Blackwell, 1958), 1:309.

32. Jonathan Culler, *New Literary History* 6 (Autumn 1974): 229.

INSTITUTIONS

Ten

The Demise of Disciplinary Authority

LOUIS MENAND

AN ACADEMIC field of inquiry is a paradigm inhabiting a structure. Thirty years ago, the paradigm for academic literary studies became detached from the institutional structure it inhabited. This phenomenon was masked by the circumstance that the American university was enjoying a period of rapid expansion, which made the discrepancy between scholarly assumptions and institutional determinants easily finessed. Challenges to the received structure of academic inquiry did not have to be faced; they could simply be tacked onto the existing system. Today the effects of that detachment have become apparent. They are reflected in almost every aspect of the profession, from the economic to the philosophical. They can be summed up by saying that the disciplinary structure of literary studies has lost its authority. It is possible that this authority will be recuperated, but not without changes in either the existing system of inquiry or the rationale for academic literary study.

The university system in the United States is one hundred years old. It arose out of the massive transformation of American colleges into research universities that began in the decades immediately following the Civil War. That transformation was led by Cornell, Harvard, Johns Hopkins, and Clark, and by the end of the nineteenth century it had converted most of the leading institutions of higher education in America to the system we know today, the system in which a program of undergraduate instruction is joined to a graduate and professorial operation designed to produce specialized research.

Virtually all the essential elements of this system were introduced between 1870 and 1915; developments since 1915 have served chiefly to reinforce the design of the original model—even when they were intended as correctives to some of its tendencies.[1] These essential elements include an elective system for undergraduates, making it possible to pursue a specialized course of study at the undergraduate level; a graduate school, which produces the specialists needed to train future specialists; the expectation that faculty will have doctorates and produce scholarly publications; the establishment of the principle of academic freedom, signaled by the founding of the American Association of University Professors in 1915;

and the reorganization of knowledge into intellectually autonomous disciplines organized along professional lines, a process essentially completed by 1900.[2]

"Between 1870 and 1900," says Walter Metzger, "nearly every subject in the academic curriculum was fitted out with a new or refurbished external organization—a learned or disciplinary association, national in membership and specialized in scope—and with a new and modified internal organization—a department of instruction made the building block of most academic administrations. These were more than formal arrangements of the campus workforce; they testified to and tightened the hold of specialization in academic life."[3] Thus the American Association for the Advancement of Science, founded in 1848, and the American Social Science Association, founded in 1865, quickly gave way to a dozen more specialized membership organizations, including the Modern Language Association (founded in 1883), the American Historical Association (1884), the American Mathematical Society (1888), the American Physical Society (1889), the American Political Science Association (1903), and the American Sociological Society (1905).[4] At the same time that these national scholarly organizations were establishing themselves, universities were undergoing a period of rapid internal "department formation," and by 1900 a departmental system of administrative organization was in place at most of the leading schools.[5] In short, the system of academic work was completely restructured within the span of a single generation.

This transformation was a response to several developments in the last third of the nineteenth century, the most significant of which, for the academic world, was the professionalization of occupation. Occupations professionalize when they set up ways of controlling membership in a particular line of work, thereby distinguishing licensed practitioners—engineers, lawyers, architects, brain surgeons, anesthesiologists, philosophy professors, rocket scientists, and so on—from lay persons. There are many methods by which this distinction can be made and enforced: by the awarding of an academic degree; by the assignment of a license to practice by some public or quasi-public agency; by the administration of an examination, like the bar exam; by admission to "qualifying associations"; and by various combinations of these things. From the middle of the nineteenth century into the early years of the twentieth century, in England and America, there was a rapid proliferation of these credentialing systems for a wide variety of occupations.[6]

The emergence of the modern university in America was a response to professionalization in two ways. First, it accommodated the need for new professionals by providing a system for training and credentialing them. Thus the significance of the undergraduate elective system: Charles William Eliot, who, as president of Harvard, was the great champion of electives, argued repeatedly for vocational utility, and against the liberal arts—or "culture," as it was referred to at the time—as the underlying rationale for undergraduate instruction. The success of the general reorganization of higher education (in which "culture" was eventually recognized as an important component) in meeting the demand for the training of a new professional middle class is readily measured: in 1870 there were 563 institutions of higher learning in the United States with 52,000 students; in 1890 there were 977 institutions with 238,000 students; by 1930, there were 1,409 schools and 1,101,000 students.[7]

The research university was a response to professionalization in a second way as well. It professionalized the knowledge business. This is one function of the graduate school: it ensures that future scholars will be trained only by established scholars, and it operates as a credentialing system to prevent unqualified persons from entering into practice. By controlling the market for employment, by restricting access to students, and by regulating the publication of new work by the process of peer review, academic professionals make it almost impossible for uncredentialed scholars to participate in the creation and dissemination of specialized knowledge. And as the university expanded, so did the number of professional scholars: there were 5,553 professors in America in 1870; in 1890, there were 15,809; in 1900, there were 23,868—an increase of over 300 percent in thirty years.[8]

From one point of view, professionalization is simply an extension of Adam Smith's theory of the division of labor into higher-status occupations, an extension made necessary by the increasing complexity of modern economies. Advanced economies generate tasks that call for more specialized knowledge than one person can possibly acquire, and professionalization is a mechanism for producing the range of experts needed to perform them. At the same time, though, the monopolistic tendency of professionalism is clearly a reaction against the principles of laissez-faire, and this avoidance of the market is the feature defended in every rationale offered for professionalization in the early decades of this century—in works such as Emile Durkheim's *The Division of Social Labor* (1902) and *Professional Ethics and Civic Morals* (a collection of lectures first delivered in the 1890s and published posthumously in 1937), Herbert Croly's *The Promise of American Life* (1909), and R. H. Tawney's *The Acquisitive Society* (1920). All these writers argued that the protection professions afford against market forces is the only way of elevating excellence over profits in a capitalist economy. In a system designed to be driven by efficiency and self-interest, professions set standards for performance that value quality over dollars.[9]

Professionals, according to this view, are people who, unlike other actors in a capitalist economy, function not self-interestedly, but disinterestedly.

Doctors sacrifice potential short-term profits—by, for example, not performing unnecessary operations—in the interests of "good medicine." Their reward for this unselfishness is permission to work in a protected market; and since entrance into that market is controlled, professionals usually command superior wages and a high degree of job security. By agreeing to forego the windfalls they could enjoy if they exploited their privileged status, professionals take their gains over the long term.

Two features of the professionalized occupation are supposed to make this disinterestedness possible. One is the autonomy of the professional organization. Professions are largely self-regulating: they set the standards for entrance and performance in their specialized areas of work, and they do so by the light of what is proper for the profession rather than what market conditions demand. The American Medical Association exists, among other reasons, to insist that the standard of care not be compromised in response to economic considerations, just as the American Association of University Professors exists to insist that the principle of academic freedom not be compromised in response to political considerations. Since professionals are rewarded (or disciplined) according to standards internal to the profession, they have to adhere only to professional standards.

The second feature of professionalization intended to guarantee disinterestedness is the very act of specialization itself. "The good work which for his own benefit the individual is required to do," Herbert Croly explained, "means primarily technically competent work. . . . Little by little there has been developed in relation to all the liberal arts and occupations certain tested and approved methods. The individual who proposes to occupy himself with any of these arts must first master the foundation of knowledge, of formal traditions, and of manual practice upon which the superstructure is based."[10] Jack of all trades is master of none.

Specialization makes work more productive because it narrows the field and therefore allows it to be more expertly mastered. The worker who pulls the wire for Adam Smith's famous pins pulls it more efficiently for not having spread himself thin by mastering the very different art of affixing the heads. But specialization performs a profoundly important social function as well. For the idea behind it is that the knowledge and skills needed in a particular endeavor are not transferable. Competence in one profession is never translatable into competence in another. Lawyers have no medical authority; physicians have no standing (except as "expert witnesses") in a courtroom. People with doctorates in English cannot decide who deserves a doctorate in sociology. This nontransferability of expertise is the balance wheel of professionalized economies: it prevents overweening claims to authority being made by well-educated people. It provides a check to the elitism inherent in any market-circumventing system. Professionalism is a way of using smart people productively without giving them too much social power.

It is easy enough to see how the modern academic discipline reproduces all the salient features of a professionalized occupation. It is a self-governing and largely closed community of practitioners, which determines the standards for entry, promotion, and dismissal; it relies on a principle of disinterestedness, according to which the production of new scholarship is regulated by measuring it against existing scholarship in the field, rather than by the extent to which it meets the needs of interests external to the field; its credential (as every doctoral candidate looking for work outside the academy quickly learns) is nontransferable; and it encourages—in fact, it mandates—a high degree of specialization. The return for this method of organizing itself is social authority: the product is guaranteed, in effect, by the expertise the system is designed to create. Incompetent practitioners are not admitted to practice; incompetent scholarship is not disseminated.

The spirit in which the business of scholarship and education professionalized itself was deeply influenced by the obsession with pure science that swept the academic world in the late nineteenth century. Croly himself—who was neither a scientist nor an academic but, of all dubiously professional things, a journalist—cited science as the paradigmatic example of disinterested activity: "The perfect type of authoritative technical methods," he wrote, "are those which prevail among scientific men in respect to scientific work. . . . The same standard is applied to everybody, and the jury is incorruptible. The exhibit is nothing if not true, or by way of becoming or being recognized as true."[11] The scientist was the ideal type of the professional worker, so that "during the nineteenth century," as Stephen Brint says, "the appeal to science became a keynote and not just an accompaniment of professionalized activity. A 'scientific' base served as a prima facie argument for incorporation."[12]

The emphasis on pure science had several consequences for the self-conception of American academics. First, it conflicted with two other recognized missions for universities: vocational training and the infusion of liberal culture. The champions of pure science—most famously perhaps Thorstein Veblen, in *The Higher Learning in America* (1916)—objected to the utilitarian attitude toward research adopted by many of the first generation of university presidents in America. The advocates of science insisted on the absolute value of inquiry for its own sake, and their insistence was, on the whole, triumphant. It succeeded in isolating academic intellectual work not only from economic and political forces external to the university, but, to a considerable extent, from intellectual developments external to the university as well—and even from intellectual developments within the university but external to the discipline.

Pure science also provided an epistemological justification for the professionalization of academic work. It meant that the purpose of self-
governance, peer review, disinterestedness, nontransferability, and so forth
was not only to ensure the integrity of the profession but also to advance
the progress of knowledge. The academic discipline became a professional
"community of inquiry": its procedures conduced to the gradual elimina-
tion of error and the increasing fixity of belief.[13] This is the traditional
assumption behind the principle of academic freedom—that unfettered
inquiry is the best path to truth. And, finally, the model of pure science led
to the isolation of the methods and subject matter appropriate to various
fields of knowledge whose claims to a scientific status were still contested
in the nineteenth century—led, that is, to the manufacture of disciplinarity. This shift in emphasis in American higher education from a pedagogical to a research mission, once begun in the latter third of the nineteenth
century, continued throughout the first half of the twentieth century: from
1920 to 1950, undergraduate enrollment increased tenfold, but graduate
enrollment increased fiftyfold.[14]

This is the context for the creation of the modern English department,
an entity that could only come into existence after a radical adjustment of
the status first of the classical and then of the modern languages within the
university system. For "the movement toward specialization," as Laurence
Veysey says, "proceeded no less within the humanities than within the
sciences, despite great resistance to it in some humanistic circles."[15] The
first university English departments were therefore composed of professional scholars who tended to emphasize the utilitarian and scientific value
of their research and pedagogy.[16] And the history of the English department is the history of efforts to fit a series of new paradigms into this
self-consciously science-based structure.

In the beginning, the discipline was dominated by philologists, and so
long as that was the case, the claim that English is a discipline was easily
supported. When philological inquiry became supplemented, and eventually superseded, by literary history as the dominant paradigm, a scientific
claim was still sustainable. The difficulty arose when English professors
proposed to produce literary criticism. The obstacles seem, from an intellectual point of view, slightly absurd, for they were obstacles thrown up
not by problems anyone would otherwise have had with the nature of
literature, but by the bureaucratic design of the academic institution. It
needed to be established that literature is indeed an object which can be
isolated for academic inquiry; that it is a field whose study requires a
special and untranslatable body of knowledge and skills; that literary
criticism, or a particular tradition of literary criticism, constitutes such a
body of knowledge and skills; and that proto-specialists in literary studies
can be vetted and credentialed by the sort of internal review process that

is obviously appropriate for a field such as chemistry or physics, but less obviously so for a "soft" discipline such as literature—that is, by the writing of an original contribution to knowledge, by the submission of research to peer-reviewed journals and presses, by tenure review, and by all the other machinery of the academic profession.

It is clear that to the degree that literary criticism is thought of as the possibly idiosyncratic interpretation and appreciation of works of literature, and the drawing of moral and political reflections from those activities, the university literature department is not especially well suited to the business of producing either good literary criticism or good literary critics. But to the degree that literary criticism is thought of as a discovery about the nature of literature by the application of philosophically grounded methods of inquiry, the modern academy is a congenial place in which to do business. The challenge as it presented itself to literary critics in the first half of the century is summed up by Wallace Martin: "So long as they doggedly insisted on the importance of values and taste, in opposition to the positivistic conception of knowledge defended by the scholars, critics had little to contribute to the institutionalized study of literature. What they opposed, ultimately, was not simply the scholars, but the conception of knowledge on which the modern university is based. In their turn toward principles and theory, they found a means of legitimating criticism as a form of knowledge."[17]

The task of replacing one conception of the function of literary criticism—the appreciatory and moral conception—with another conception —the theoretical and knowledge-producing conception—took a long time to perform. The word *criticism* was not added to the Modern Language Association's constitutional statement of purpose until 1950. The MLA was persuaded to add the term because by 1950 the New Criticism had developed to a point at which it was able to present itself as a method for understanding literary texts based on a theory about the nature of literature as a distinctive genre of writing. For it was the essential claim of the New Criticism that there was something called literature (or, often, "poetry") which could be discussed in abstract or theoretical terms and which there were more and less useful methods for understanding.

One of the capstones in the institutionalization of literary criticism was William K. Wimsatt and Cleanth Brooks's *Literary Criticism: A Short History*, which was published in 1957. What the history of criticism proves, Wimsatt and Brooks argued in that work, is not just that literary criticism is an autonomous discipline (something that had not been evident, for example, to George Saintsbury when he published his *History of Literary Criticism and Taste in Europe* in 1904), but that literature is indeed a distinctive object of study—that literature can be talked about "as literature," and not as a branch of moral philosophy, or of the history

of ideas, or of social history. "Literary problems occur," Wimsatt and
Brooks wrote, "not just because history produces them, but because literature is a thing of such and such a sort, showing such and such a relation
to the history of human experience." The study of literary criticism
therefore opens up "not so many diverse views into multiplicity and chaos
but so many complementary insights into the one deeply rooted and
perennial human truth which is the poetic principle."[18]

There is a temptation to conclude that the New Critics reinvented
literature in order to adapt it to the institutional requirements of the
research university; but this is not quite what happened. The New Critics
did not need to reinvent literature. Literature (or a certain tradition of
literature) had already reinvented itself—and had done so in response to
the same reconception of work that had led to the creation of the disciplinary structure of the modern academy. For the history of modern artistic
formalism, from the aestheticism of the 1880s to the color-field abstrac-
tionism of the 1950s, runs exactly parallel to the emergence and social
dominance of the modern professions, to the emergence of the modern
research university, and, ultimately, to the emergence of departments of
literature and art history within the university. The notion that painting is
essentially a matter of composition, that architecture is essentially a
matter of space and light, that poetry is essentially a matter of the
organization of language—the notions associated with the art and architecture and literature usually called modernist—are notions precisely
compatible with the belief that every higher-status occupational activity
has a unique and isolable element, mastery of which is integral to its
proper performance.[19]

In the case of poetry, for example, the modernist case was stated
succinctly by T. S. Eliot in "Tradition and the Individual Talent" (1919),
an essay whose significance for academic literary criticism was, up to the
1960s, virtually iconic. The question that essay essentially asks is: what
does the poet need to know? The answer it gives is: poetry. The best way
to understand poems is by their relation to other poems: without this
premise, academic literary criticism would be unable to function. For
disciplinary specialization is itself a kind of formalism. It isolates one
aspect of experience and makes that aspect the basis for a discrete field of
inquiry that can be fruitfully pursued without knowledge of any other
field. English professors need not be historians, sociologists, psychologists,
or philosophers to be regarded as full-fledged contributing professionals.
They can be historians, critics, and theorists of literature knowing, in their
professional capacity, only literature.

There are, then, two general background conditions for the existence of
academic literary studies. One is the scientistic idea, implicit in the structure of university departments, that knowledge accumulates brick by

brick. Experts train their epigoni to go out and dig up material that gets molded first into a dissertation, then into a monograph; and eventually these epigoni become experts themselves and take on the job of training the next generation of brickmakers. At the end of inquiry, the bricks have all been carefully piled one on another, the defective ones have been tossed aside, and the arch of knowledge about a field stands clearly defined against the background of mere undisciplined information. The rules of peer review, tenure, and academic freedom ensure that the bricks will be accumulated disinterestedly, and that the knowledge that is produced will be uncontaminated by political, commercial, or any other sort of nonintellectual interest—including, of course, aesthetic interest, or "taste."

The second background condition for the discipline of literary studies is the idea that literature is a distinctive genre of writing defined by its particular engagement with language and with systems of representation generally—metaphor, genre, structure, semiosis, and so forth. Since literature is such a thing, it can therefore profitably be talked about "as literature." This does not preclude talking about it historically, sociologically, psychologically, or in any other plausible interdisciplinary context. But it means that literature is itself to be understood as the subject matter of an independent discipline.

The next point is obvious enough. It is that almost no one in academic literary studies holds those two background assumptions any longer, and the same situation obtains in most of the rest of the humanistic disciplines (the notable exception is philosophy, which, since it suffers from the opposite affliction, only proves the rule) and in the social sciences as well. Why has this happened? The story of the unraveling of the conditions needed for disciplinarity is a little more complicated than the story of the original raveling, since the undoing of disciplinary paradigms took place at the same time that the institutional structure those paradigms inhabited was being functionally reinforced. Universities were expanding and the social demand for everything universities had traditionally represented—knowledge, specialized training, and credentials—was increasing while the paradigms for inquiry were quietly detaching themselves from their institutional structures.

The beliefs that literature is a delimited subject matter and that literary criticism is the proper method for investigating it do not require agreement on how the subject matter is defined and what the proper methods are. There is room within that framework for new paradigms, and even for several paradigms to flourish simultaneously. The brick theory of knowledge is not a mandate for conformity. The story of English departments after the New Criticism brought literary criticism into the academy in the 1940s and 1950s is therefore a series of attempts to introduce new theoretical paradigms using the same old argument—the argument that the new paradigm is more rigorous, truer to the nature of literature, more productive of knowledge, than the one it seeks to supplant.

When Northrop Frye's *Anatomy of Criticism* came out in 1957, for example, Frye accused the New Critics of merely claiming to practice a disinterested method of inquiry, and of using their method of reading to facilitate the covert imposition of a particular aesthetic taste. He proposed an alternative theoretical model, essentially structuralist, which he claimed, quite explicitly, to be genuinely scientific. The shift in literature departments from New Critical to archetypal and structuralist criticism thus did not require any alteration of the background picture. It merely required discrediting the disinterestedness of the earlier paradigm. And this pattern has been repeated ever since.[20]

So that in the early 1970s, when structuralist paradigms came under assault, the so-called Yale critics—Paul de Man, J. Hillis Miller, and Geoffrey Hartman—adapted deconstruction to literary studies by arguing (following Derrida) that structuralism was theoretically flawed, that deconstruction was founded on a better understanding of the nature of language, and that literature was the kind of writing most attuned to what deconstruction knew. "A literary text," de Man wrote in "Semiology and Rhetoric," "simultaneously asserts and denies the authority of its own rhetorical mode. . . . Poetic writing is the most advanced and refined mode of deconstruction."[21] And this notion that literature is essentially "about" what de Man called "vertiginous possibilities of referential aberration"[22] replaced, for many academic critics, the New Critical, structuralist, and phenomenological notions of what literature is "about" without seeming to require any adjustment to the institutional structure in which they pursued their work.

But those critics were wrong. For deconstruction was, it turned out, the end of the line. Once its implications were accepted, no grounds for disciplinarity remained. The point was made emphatically by Richard Rorty in "Philosophy as a Kind of Writing: An Essay on Derrida" (1979): you cannot embrace the principle of "free play" and be "rigorous" at the same time.[23] Looking back, it is striking to see how concentrated the rejection of the assumptions of aesthetic and disciplinary formalism was. Thomas Kuhn's *The Structure of Scientific Revolutions* was published in 1962. Derrida's famous attack on structuralism, "Structure, Sign, and Play in the Discourse of the Human Sciences," was delivered at Johns Hopkins in 1966. Kuhn suggested that "science" is essentially interpretation, and Derrida argued that interpretation is essentially play. Kuhn's book did not have much influence among scientists, and Derrida's writings did not have any influence in philosophy departments; but both were an enormous influence on English professors, because they provided theoretical and historical arguments for something that should have been intuitively obvious, which is that literature does not have an essence and literary criticism is not a science.

But it would be a mistake to blame the transformation of the way literature and criticism were conceived on academic theorists. For modernist assumptions about art and architecture and literature were being abandoned at the same time by artists and critics outside the academy. Pauline Kael's *I Lost It at the Movies* (1965), Susan Sontag's *Against Interpretation* (1966), Robert Venturi and Denise Scott Brown's *Learning from Las Vegas* (1972), the emergence of "metafiction," the new journalism, pop art and conceptual art—these were all reactions against modernist formalism and essentialism.[24] Modernist art and literature, with their emphasis on form and technique, had been a reaction against nineteenth-century didacticism and ornamentalism; but art and literature since the 1960s have tended to be highly didactic and ornamental. Discursive and aesthetic forms have become mixed in precisely the way the moderns despised. And when generic boundaries become blurred, or become objects of parody and reinscription, disciplinary boundaries become harder to defend. As deliberately sealed off from the rest of the culture as it was, academic criticism could hardly ignore these developments.

The reputation of professionalism has followed the same curve. Thomas Haskell has said that he can find in the sociological literature almost nothing negative written about professionalism before 1939 and almost nothing positive written about it after 1960.[25] Scholarly skepticism about the claims of professionals to disinterestedness and altruism have become so thoroughgoing that the whole field of the sociology of the professions has been accused of "demonology."[26] And this academic skepticism is only a little in advance of a popular skepticism that has by now pervaded almost every area of American life. "Professional" has become a synonym for self-aggrandizement.

The social change behind the skepticism about professionalism is the skewing of the American socioeconomic scale, which began in 1973 and which has created an unprecedented gap between the upper and the lower quintiles of income earners, and in particular between the professional two-career family and everybody below it.[27] Professionalism means relative job security for individuals at the social cost of keeping nonprofessionals out of the marketplace. And this generates resentment on the part of those workers whose employment feels relatively insecure and whose incomes are stagnant or in decline. Professionalism has begun to seem like a racket.

The wrinkle in this reaction against professionals is that professional jobs have never been in greater demand. Since 1980, there has been a boom in the professions themselves, with the numbers of undergraduates entering law, medical, business, and other professional schools growing steadily and rapidly. Between 1970 and 1990, the number of B.A.s awarded increased by 28 percent, but the number of M.D.s increased by 88 percent, the number of law degrees by 143 percent, and the number of M.B.A.s by 239 percent.[28] This demand for professional training and credentialing has naturally contributed to the continued expansion of the American system of higher education throughout the Cold War period. The reason for the heightened demand is, of course, the same as the reason for the heightened resentment: it is that a professional career has started to look like the only hope for financial security in the American economy.

This rise in the value of professionalism outside the academy was paralleled by a rise inside the academy, so that even as the institutional logic for academic literary studies was eroding in the 1970s and 1980s, academic professionalism was never more pronounced. As late as 1969, David Damrosch points out, 33 percent of full-time faculty did not hold the Ph.D.; but during the 1970s, doctorates became mandatory for academic employment.[29] The percentage of faculty who said their interests lay in teaching as opposed to research declined from 70 percent in 1975 to 63 percent in 1984; the percentage agreeing with the statement "In my department it is very difficult to achieve tenure without publishing" rose in the same period from 54 percent to 69 percent. In the humanities, these professional pressures were exacerbated by a sharp decline in undergraduate interest and a correlated decline in employment opportunities for new holders of the doctorate. In 1970, 21 percent of college freshmen said they intended to major in the arts and humanities; in 1985, only 8 percent said so.[30]

As David Bromwich has suggested, the discipline of literary studies adjusted to these mixed influences—a higher value placed on professionalism combined with the loss of an institutionally appropriate paradigm for professionalized inquiry—in a peculiar way.[31] It became "hard" and ironic at the same time: it emphasized theoretical rigor and simultaneously debunked all claims to objective knowledge. This mix has proved, as virtually everyone outside the academy has felt for years, an intellectual dead end. The chicken is still running around the yard (though the yard has gotten a lot smaller), but its head is no longer attached.

"The humanities and related disciplines have been in a period of deep transformation and division, born of profound intellectual self-scrutiny and philosophical questioning," write William Bowen and Neil Rudenstine, who argue that the increased length of time needed to get an advanced degree in literature is a function of the lack of clarity in the paradigm of the discipline.[32] A similar skepticism about the philosophical foundations of the disciplines obtains among social scientists. Christopher Jencks and David Riesman, in their classic study, *The Academic Revolution*, had argued in 1968 that "[a] discipline is at bottom nothing more than an administrative category," and that its authority is merely "traditional" and "ad hoc."[33] Clifford Geertz, in a well-known essay of 1980, noted the rise of "genre mixing"[34] in intellectual life; he seemed to feel some promise in the possibilities of interdisciplinarity, as did Hayden White in another landmark essay of the same period, "The Politics of Historical Interpretation: Discipline and De-Sublimation" (1982).[35] But Donald Levine, in a survey of the history and present condition of the social sciences in 1995, concludes that although disciplinarity can now be declared dead, it has not yet been successfully transcended. The social science disciplines, he says, "no longer possess narratives about their historic development with sufficient credibility to anchor a charter for their future. These considerations imply that the social sciences face a genuine crisis. . . . *Their established forms no longer fulfill the function of providing orienting frameworks for intellectual communities.*"[36]

Levine argues that the future does lie in interdisciplinary work, and a number of developments, many dating back to the time of Jencks and Riesman's book, suggest that this is the direction in which academic research is headed. There is, to begin with, the emergence of critical theory as a transdisciplinary vocabulary. Professors in anthropology departments now read the same theoretical texts, and invoke their authority, as professors in French departments. This period has also seen the rise of the "center": it is in areas like women's studies, African American studies, cultural studies, science and technology studies, and so on, and not in the traditional disciplines that most of the scholarly busy-ness is going on in the humanities today. These emerging areas are interdisciplinary by definition; to the extent that they define themselves against the traditional disciplines, they are even antidisciplinary. But there are problems, both intellectual and structural, with postdisciplinarity.

For the erosion of disciplinary authority coincides, unluckily, with a period of contraction in American higher education. The Cold War was very good for universities. From 1940 to 1990, government funding to research universities increased by a factor of twenty-five, and college and university enrollments increased by a factor of ten. Between 1960 and 1970 alone, enrollment grew by 120 percent, and more faculty positions were created than had been created in the entire 325-year history of American higher education to that point. To give a more pointed measure of the change: over the course of the Cold War period, the amount of time professors at research universities spent in the classroom shrank from an average of nine hours a week to an average of four and a half hours a week. In the same period, the percentage of college-age Americans enrolled in college rose from 16 percent to 40 percent, with 50 percent of all Americans having some exposure to higher education at some point in their lives.[37]

This expansion helped make the collapse of traditional disciplinary authority institutionally invisible. For it meant that departments could simply add on new interdisciplinary, postdisciplinary, or essentially non-disciplinary activities (like creative writing) without sacrificing staffing in the traditional fields of inquiry. The academy swallowed up almost everything in American intellectual and cultural life between 1940 and 1980, and spit out very little. It is the general consensus that this expansive period is now over.[38] And if this is so, it is unlikely that English departments can continue to offer plausible raisons-d'être without a reconception of their functions.

Merely imposing interdisciplinarity on the present system will not work in a way satisfactory to most professors (though it may satisfy many provosts). For although "the traditional disciplines," as Stanley Katz has argued, "no longer constitute the organizing principles for much cutting-edge research . . . [universities] have responded to this problem with the creation of off-budget units ('centers' and 'programs'), [and] these are precisely the parts of the university most likely to fall to the budgetary axe in this period of financial stringency and 'downsizing.'"[39] The problem, in a word, is that interdisciplinary work is not professionalized, and its integrity is therefore not protected. Colleges and universities are local, but the disciplines are national. Forty percent of American professors say their campus is "very important" to them; but 77 percent say their discipline is "very important" to them.[40] This is what professional identity consists in—just as a lawyer's loyalty to the law is understood to supersede her loyalty to the particular firm in which she happens to practice. But where there are no departments, there is no autonomy. The market for professors is a national market run by the disciplines, not a local market run by provosts or trustees. Departments decide whom to hire and whom to fire, and they do so according to standards globally interpreted. Academic freedom is a way of saying, "Better the spitefulness and warped judgment of one's peers than the uninformed decision of an administrator." The problem the proliferation of studies centers presents is that it creates a kind of administrative limbo, in which personnel can be shuffled around by manipulating lines in a budget, without any global standards to which to appeal. The disciplines are the linchpins of academic freedom. There may be excellent intellectual reasons for wishing to see them wither away, but they continue to serve institutional functions most professors would not like to abandon.

There are, in fact, intellectual difficulties attending the collapse of disciplinary authority as well. It has become popular, thanks to the impressive efforts of Gerald Graff, to adopt the position that since English professors can no longer all claim to adhere to a single paradigm, they should teach students about the conflicts among paradigms.[41] But this represents a kind of perverse consummation of professionalism, the last refinement on the isolation and self-referentiality of academic studies: it makes what professors do the subject of what professors do. And it is hard to see, in a period of aggravated cost-consciousness, how it will be possible to sell the notion that what students and taxpayers are paying for is not knowledge but rather debates among people who adhere to differing interpretations but who cannot even agree on what would count as a ground for deciding among those interpretations. If opinion is always contingent, why should we subsidize professionals to produce it?

Beyond all these questions, there is the question of what purpose continues to be served by the institutionalization of literary study. It may be that what has happened to the profession is not the consequence of social or philosophical changes, but simply the consequence of a tank now empty. In treating the history of the discipline of literary studies as a conflict between a scientific paradigm, represented by philology, and an interpretive paradigm, represented most successfully by the New Criticism, I have mentioned only briefly the massive body of work that constitutes the real achievement of English departments in the twentieth century. This is literary history.

Literary history is one thing that the academic structure is good for enabling. There was a job of periodizing, of establishing texts, of exhuming neglected or forgotten work, of producing critical biographies, and so on that could only be undertaken on a massive scale, and with due quality control, in a university setting. This work has now, possibly, largely been done. The only interesting new work being undertaken today is an extension of that old work: the business of exploring canonically "marginal" writing. The interest of this activity is largely historical, and it will eventually run out. There will always be scholarly problems to solve, of course, and there will always be room for critical revisionism. But the notion that work that seemed done a mere twenty or thirty years ago now needs to be entirely redone is a notion suggesting that the larder is pretty bare. Academic literary criticism is now largely in the business of consuming itself.

Few people are likely to bet that the institutional structure of academic literary study will change, but this is because in a world of educational expansion, it was always easier, when challenges arose, to change the paradigm instead. In a world of contraction, though, it may be simpler and more sensible to alter the structure. Literary studies has existed since the 1960s in a heavily professionalized system in which the positions are subsidized, the research is subsidized, the journals and presses that publish the research are subsidized, the libraries that buy the journals and monographs are subsidized, and the audience is increasingly limited to peer specialists. There is no "reality check" on this work because the only reality is the rapidly shrinking profession itself, buoyed up by dollars that will now be disappearing. Almost no one outside the profession cares even to understand what goes on inside it; they will, given a choice, certainly not care to pay for it. The best course for humanities departments to take may be to curtail the system of credentialism and specialization, to end the grip of the professionalist mentality, and to open their doors to the art and ideas, and the people who create them, that have always existed beyond their narrow walls.

Notes

1. For example, the institution of the undergraduate major by A. Lawrence Lowell, who succeeded Charles William Eliot as president of Harvard in 1909, was intended to relieve the tendency toward unfocused programs of study endemic in Eliot's free elective system. But it had the effect of placing control over the undergraduate curriculum even more firmly in the hands of the disciplines, thus reinforcing both professionalization (since the disciplines are national and their development is determined by research, rather than pedagogical, interests) and specialization. See Samuel Eliot Morison, *Three Centuries of Harvard, 1636–1936* (Cambridge, Mass.: Harvard University Press, 1936), 446–47.

2. On the elective system, see Henry James, *Charles William Eliot: President of Harvard University, 1869–1909*, 2 vols. (Boston: Houghton Mifflin, 1930), 1:300; and Laurence R. Veysey, *The Emergence of the American University* (Chicago: University of Chicago Press, 1965), 66–68 and 118–19. On the establishment of graduate schools, see Veysey, 121–79. On the requirement of the doctorate and the expectation of publication, see Veysey, 176–77. On the American Association of University Professors, see Richard Hofstadter and Walter P. Metzger, *The Development of Academic Freedom in the United States* (New York: Columbia University Press, 1955), 468–506.

3. Walter P. Metzger, "The Academic Profession in the United States," in *The Academic Profession: National, Disciplinary, and Institutional Settings*, ed. Burton R. Clark (Berkeley and Los Angeles: University of California Press, 1987), 136.

4. See Burton J. Bledstein, *The Culture of Professionalism: The Middle Class and the Development of Higher Education in America* (New York: W. W. Norton, 1976), 86; and Thomas L. Haskell, *The Emergence of Professional Social Science: The American Social Science Association and the Nineteenth-Century Crisis of Authority* (Urbana: University of Illinois Press, 1977).

5. See Veysey, *The Emergence of the American University*, 320–21.

6. See Bledstein *The Culture of Professionalism;* Bruce A. Kimball, *The "True Professional Idea" in America: A History* (Cambridge, Mass.: Blackwell, 1992); Magali Sarfatti Larson, *The Rise of Professionalism: A Sociological Analysis* (Berkeley and Los Angeles: University of California Press, 1977); and Robert H. Wiebe, *The Search for Order, 1877–1920* (New York: Hill & Wang, 1967). On British professionalization, see Geoffrey Millerson, *The Qualifying Associations: A Study in Professionalization* (London: Routledge & Kegan Paul, 1964).

7. See Bledstein, *The Culture of Professionalism*, 297.

8. Ibid., 271.

9. See Thomas L. Haskell, "Professionalism *versus* Capitalism: R. H. Tawney, Emile Durkheim, and C. S. Peirce on the Disinterestedness of Professional Communities," in *The Authority of Experts: Studies in History and Theory*, ed. Thomas L. Haskell (Bloomington: Indiana University Press, 1984), 180–225.

10. Herbert Croly, *The Promise of American Life* (1909; rpt. Boston: Northeastern University Press, 1989), 433.

11. Ibid., 434.

12. Steven Brint, *In an Age of Experts: The Changing Role of Professionals in Politics and Public Life* (Princeton, N.J.: Princeton University Press, 1994), 35. On the importance of the ideal of pure science in the development of higher education, see also Kimball, *The "True Professional Ideal" in America*, 200–230, and Veysey, *The Emergence of the American University*, 124–25.

13. The language of these sentences echoes Charles Sanders Peirce. On Peirce's theory of inquiry as a basis for the principle of academic freedom, see Thomas L. Haskell, "Justifying the Rights of Academic Freedom in the Era of 'Power/Knowledge,'" in *The Future of Academic Freedom*, ed. Louis Menand (Chicago: University of Chicago Press, 1996), 143–90.

14. See Peter M. Blau, *The Organization of Academic Work* (New York: John Wiley, 1973), 5.

15. Laurence R. Veysey, "The Plural Organized World of the Humanities," in *The Organization of Knowledge in Modern America, 1860–1920*, ed. Alexandra Oleson and John Voss (Baltimore, Md.: Johns Hopkins University Press, 1976), 51.

16. On the makeup of the newly professionalized English department, see Wallace Douglas, "Accidental Institution: On the Origin of Modern Language Study," in *Criticism in the University*, ed. Gerald Graff and Reginald Gibbons (Evanston, Ill.: Northwestern University Press, 1985), 35–61; Gerald Graff, *Professing Literature: An Institutional History* (Chicago: University of Chicago Press, 1987), 55–118; Wallace Martin, "Criticism and the Academy," in *The Cambridge History of Literary Criticism*, vol. 7, *Modernism and the New Criticism*, ed. A. Walton Litz, Louis Menand, and Lawrence Rainey (Cambridge: Cambridge University Press, forthcoming); and Michael Warner, "Professionalization and the Rewards of Literature, 1875–1900," *Criticism* 27 (Winter 1985): 1–28. Representative documents from this period are reprinted in *The Origins of Literary Studies in America: A Documentary Anthology*, ed. Gerald Graff and Michael Warner (New York: Routledge, 1989), 17–74.

17. Martin, "Criticism and the Academy," forthcoming.

18. William K. Wimsatt and Cleanth Brooks, *Literary Criticism: A Short History*, 2 vols. (Chicago: University of Chicago Press, 1957), 1:vii and ix–x.

19. I have tried to spell out the isomorphism of modernism and professionalism in *Discovering Modernism: T. S. Eliot and His Context* (New York: Oxford University Press, 1987), 97–132. See also Thomas F. Strychacz, *Modernism, Mass Culture, and Professionalism* (Cambridge: Cambridge University Press, 1993).

20. On the sequence of paradigms for literary study from the New Criticism to deconstruction, see Frank Lentricchia, *After the New Criticism* (Chicago: University of Chicago Press, 1980). On the use of this justificatory argument, and on

institutionalization generally, see Graff, *Professing Literature*, 226–43; John Harwood, *Eliot to Derrida: The Poverty of Interpretation* (Basingstoke, U.K.: Macmillan, 1995); and Alvin Kernan, *The Death of Literature* (New Haven, Conn.: Yale University Press, 1990), 32–59 and 166–67.

21. Paul de Man, *Allegories of Reading: Figural Language in Rousseau, Nietzsche, Rilke, and Proust* (New Haven, Conn.: Yale University Press, 1979), 17. On the institutionalization of deconstruction, see Wallace Martin, Introduction to *The Yale Critics: Deconstruction in America*, ed. Jonathan Arac, Wlad Godzich, and Wallace Martin (Minneapolis: University of Minnesota Press, 1983), xv–xxxvii.

22. De Man, *Allegories of Reading*, 10.

23. Richard Rorty, "Philosophy as a Kind of Writing: An Essay on Derrida," in *Consequences of Pragmatism (Essays: 1972–1980)* (Minneapolis: University of Minnesota Press, 1982), 90–109.

24. On the break with modernism, see Andreas Huyssen, *After the Great Divide: Modernism, Mass Culture, Postmodernism* (Bloomington: Indiana University Press, 1986), 141–221; on the significance of pop art, see Arthur C. Danto, *The State of the Art* (New York: Prentice Hall, 1987), 8–12 and 202–18; on Kael in this context, see Louis Menand, "Finding It at the Movies," *New York Review of Books*, March 23, 1995, 10–17.

25. See Haskell, "Professionalism *versus* Capitalism," 182 and 220n1.

26. Walter P. Metzger, "A Spectre Is Haunting American Scholars: The Spectre of 'Professionism,'" *Educational Researcher* 16 (August-September 1987): 16.

27. On the income gap and its social consequences, see Thomas Byrne Edsall, *The New Politics of Inequality* (New York: W. W. Norton, 1984); Mickey Kaus, *The End of Equality* (New York: Basic Books, 1992); Robert Kuttner, *Economic Illusion* (Boston: Houghton Mifflin, 1984); Frank Levy, *Dollars and Dreams* (New York: Russell Sage, 1987); and William Ryan, *Equality* (New York: Pantheon, 1981).

28. U.S. Bureau of the Census, *Statistical Abstracts of the United States, 1993*, 113th ed. (Washington, D.C., 1993), 184–85.

29. See David Damrosch, *We Scholars: Changing the Culture of the University* (Cambridge, Mass.: Harvard University Press, 1994), 40.

30. See Ernest L. Boyer, *College: The Undergraduate Experience in America* (New York: Harper & Row, 1987), 130 and 105.

31. See David Bromwich, "The Cost of Professionalism in the Humanities," in *Learned Societies and the Evolution of the Disciplines*, ACLS Occasional Paper no. 5 (New York: American Council of Learned Societies, 1988), 9–16.

32. William G. Bowen and Neil L. Rudenstine, *In Pursuit of the Ph.D.* (Princeton, N.J.: Princeton University Press, 1992), 368.

33. Christopher Jencks and David Riesman, *The Academic Revolution* (Garden City, N.Y.: Doubleday, 1968), 523–24.

34. Clifford Geertz, "Blurred Genres: The Refiguration of Social Thought," in *Local Knowledge: Further Essays in Interpretive Anthropology* (New York: Basic Books, 1983), 19.

35. Hayden White, "The Politics of Historical Interpretation: Discipline and De-Sublimation," in *The Politics of Interpretation*, ed. W. J. T. Mitchell (Chicago: University of Chicago Press, 1983), 119–43.

36. Donald N. Levine, *Visions of the Sociological Tradition* (Chicago: University of Chicago Press, 1995), 290.

37. On Cold War spending and enrollment, see Clark Kerr, *The Uses of the University*, 4th ed. (Cambridge, Mass.: Harvard University Press, 1995), 141 (the figure of 4.5 hours is not typical for all higher education); on enrollments in the 1960s, see Kerr, 142; on the creation of faculty positions, see Metzger, "The Academic Profession in the United States," 124; on the decrease in teaching loads, see Kerr, 141; on overall enrollments, see Clark Kerr, *Troubled Times in American Higher Education: The 1990s and Beyond* (Albany: SUNY Press, 1994), 5–6.

38. See, for example, Kerr, *Troubled Times*.

39. Stanley Katz, "Possibilities for Remaking Liberal Education at Century's End," in Bruce A. Kimball, *The Condition of American Liberal Education: Pragmatism and a Changing Tradition*, exec. ed. Robert Orrill (New York: College Board, 1995), 132. I leave aside the question of whether current "studies centers" in fact fulfill the claims that are sometimes made for them; I only want to note the appeal that the idea of dispensing with disciplinary structures obviously has for many professors, whether they are at such a center or not.

40. See Damrosch, *We Scholars*, 202.

41. See Gerald Graff, *Beyond the Culture Wars: How Teaching the Conflicts Can Revitalize American Education* (New York: W. W. Norton, 1992).

Eleven

Scholarship as Social Action

DAVID BROMWICH

THERE have long been university scholars in America dedicated to particular causes or general programs of reform, and often their interests as
scholars have seemed inseparable from their commitments outside scholarship. John Dewey in philosophy is the most celebrated example. Others,
like Helen and Robert Lynd in sociology and F. O. Matthiessen in literature, suggest the range of work that came under this description earlier in
the century: it is hard to think of books like *Middletown* or *The Public and
Its Problems* or *American Renaissance* as separable from the hopes these
scholars cherished for their society and the ambition they harbored for
their scholarly work as a possible influence. But an impression now widely
shared is that since the 1960s the place of advocacy in teaching and
research has become so prominent as almost to constitute in itself a
separate description of what scholarship in the humanities is.

The impression seems to me accurate. It registers, in part, the increasing
penetration of higher education by an ideology of "reflection" that goes as
far back as the early twentieth century:[1] institutions of learning, according
to this view, must reflect the varied elements of the society they serve. The
picture has been further complicated in the past twenty years by a newer
ideology of "representation." If a scholar is asked to stand for a minority
or marginalized group in the society at large, the work of representation is
taken to include not just being a member of the relevant group, but talking
in the classroom about it and publishing books about it, so that the talk
and books become part of one's scholarly profile. The advance of reflection theory and the advent of representational practice are large factors in
the change of climate in the arts and letters that I will be discussing only
implicitly. For the past generation has seen a partial shift of feeling about
the vocation of scholarship and the purpose of teaching that makes a
substantial cause of change in its own right.

In the careers of reformers like Dewey and the Lynds and even in that
of a fellow-traveling socialist like Matthiessen, one does not find a pronounced desire to connect the worth of scholarship with the morality of
social commitments. The two went together (they thought); intellectual
work anyway had its distinct field of exercise, its choice of emphasis

decided by elective affinity. By no member of the generation of the 1920s, 1930s, 1940s, or 1950s would it have been pretended that the orthodox Christian views of a scholar like E. M. W. Tillyard, which led him to write faithful and interested descriptions of the Elizabethan world picture, were either a more or a less appropriate adaptation of personal interest to subject matter than the beliefs in equality and solidarity that led Kenneth Burke to assist the suasive efforts of the New Deal by writing *Permanence and Change* and *Attitudes Toward History*. To make the most of the habitual perceptions of an ideology, a scholar will often want to inhabit that ideology, and the point at which unconscious sympathy passes into identification is not always easy to mark. To judge by the tenor of their writings, from the generation of the 1920s to that of the 1950s the practice of activist scholars was touched by Max Weber's advice that "the primary task of a useful teacher is to teach his students to recognize 'inconvenient' facts—I mean facts that are inconvenient for their party opinions."[2] This element of highmindedness in the declared morality of educators was still going strong in the McCarthy period; it was a source of resistance to the loyalty oaths and less openly coercive avowals of "Americanism." An objection not to the content of the politics extrinsically imposed, but to the fact that political expectations were introduced at all, formed the basis of the scholar's agreement to work in society on terms shaped in detail by the vocation of scholarship.

What drove out this morality? The turning point was the Vietnam War. It was in the late 1960s that scholars in the humanities and social sciences first began to hear, broadly diffused, the charge that all choices are political choices, that every intellectual interest serves some social end. The suggestion of these axioms was that the dissident scholar who declared his or her serviceability always stood on higher ground than the "disinterested" scholar who held affiliations in reserve. Among the early dissenters from the war policy were distinguished liberal anticommunists like Hans Morgenthau and George Kennan; but the war itself, as prosecuted by President Johnson, was viewed as a product of the liberal establishment: from this it was a short step to regard it as a characteristic product. Apologists for the war, including advisers like McGeorge Bundy and W. W. Rostow, both of them former academics, saw it as a struggle for freedom against totalitarianism. Yet what was visible to dissenters in the academy and elsewhere was the attempt by a great power to extinguish the rebellion of a tiny former colony—an attempt that employed vastly incommensurate means and that led, as we now know, to nearly sixty thousand deaths on one side and upward of a million on the other. The saying of the bewildered and murderous army officer of that time, "We had to destroy the village in order to save it"—placed alongside the proposals of academic researchers at Harvard and MIT who theorized the "pacification" policy in Vietnam—would pass into the understanding of the academic left as a revelatory maxim. It gave a vivid illustration of the belief that knowledge is power and that the power of enlightened authority is unrestricted.[3] Max Horkheimer and Theodor Adorno's *Dialectic of Enlightenment*, a European prophecy written in America during World War II and reissued in 1969, drew a conclusion for which the soldier's maxim was the sole necessary premise: "The spirit of enlightenment replaced the fire and the rack."[4] This was the antithesis of the view of imaginative intelligence offered by Ernst Cassirer in the *Essay on Man*, the work of another émigré scholar written at the same time as the *Dialectic*: "It is symbolic thought which overcomes the natural inertia of man and endows him with a new ability, the ability constantly to reshape his human universe."[5] Plainly the ideals of enlightenment and of free inquiry have to be looked at more nearly in Cassirer's spirit to allow any scope for the clash of opinions on which democratic education depends. But the legitimacy of liberal tolerance suffered a loss, in the years 1965–1975, the depth of which is impossible to fathom, and of which we have yet to hear the last reverberations. A significant part of a long generation of educated citizens, many of them hopeful of social improvement, some of them interested in doing something to achieve it, had been severed from the faith that enlightenment enlightens.

Some members of the student left of those years stayed on in academic positions—Angela Davis, for example, who became the intellectual voice of American communism long after the party had ceased to be a force on the political scene. Others like Staughton Lynd went from university teaching to urban organizing. My experience as a political liberal at the younger edge of that generation has been that only recently have those who received their graduate training in the late 1960s or the 1970s been willing in any numbers to consider themselves as liberals. Since universities embody the educated opinion of a nation whose laws and habits are those of constitutional democracy, it might seem that the consequence of the disenchantment of the early 1970s would be an "inner emigration" by reformers skeptical of what was then called *the system*. Almost the reverse occurred. Scholars who believed that scholarship itself is an all-important vehicle for social reform became, starting in the mid-1970s, the most visible body of opinion within universities, in certain subjects above all: American studies; American history; the modern languages and literatures; and the many subfields that were carved out with this understanding of scholarship intimately in view—gender, racial, ethnic, cultural, and postcolonial studies in most of their varieties.

That a group of persons make up the most visible body of opinion does not mean that theirs are the only articulate views, or that they constitute a majority, or that their efforts to merge curricular and communitarian aims will be often or everywhere decisive. Yet organized opinion is at an advantage, in relation to unorganized opinion. Though the comments from political conservatives on the politicization of learning have not been reliable about the degree, intent, or placement of coercive tactics from this wing of committed scholarship, and the reactions are driven clearly enough by interest and fancy when they project the dangers of the academic left to American culture generally, they nevertheless proceed from an adequate sense of the utility of organized opinion:[6] a fact of which the technocrats in charge of higher education are apt to have a far less certain grasp.

I am concerned with the genealogy and the motives of a new academic understanding of scholarship as social action. Its likely future has to be inferred from the direction and the success of its existing projects. Financial constraint will be an element, more pressing than it has been for some time, in shaping the scholarly conduct of the next generation. However that in turn affects the ideology of social commitment—whether it is allowed to retard or advance a radical communitarian curriculum—the local choices of schools and even departments are beginning to be exposed to a kind of scrutiny that is unfamiliar on every side. College alumni now profess an absorbing interest in how their money is spent, and a national watchdog association has been formed on the right to organize the suspicions of donors against those inside the universities who may not have their interests at heart. Meanwhile, the common front that the academic left had appeared to present throughout the 1980s is growing both generalized and diffuse. Most scholars-in-training inherit a quantum of the relevant views, and the proportion who would want to say their work is eminently directed at social reform may have climbed from 10 to 20 percent, but what they mean by reform has grown elusive and is apt to find its boundary within the profession. I consider all of these developments unfortunate—the expansion and diversification of a communitarian curriculum without sufficient time for reflection; the intensified scrutiny to which all subsidy for education has consequently been exposed; and the complacent narrowing of the activist constituency from fellow citizens to fellow professionals.[7] But this essay is mostly an effort of description. It aims to sketch the internal dynamic of an idea of scholarship that made such developments probable.

———

The commanding visions of society have often had their source in a sense of social loss or paths not taken. E. P. Thompson's *Making of the English Working Class*, the one classic of scholarship to emerge from the New Left, was gripped by a fear: that the rationalization of life that came with industrial modernity had crushed a kind of community basic to human decency. It was likewise animated by a hope: that the exploration of a lost culture, which historical recovery could prove to have been substantial, would give fresh stimulus to the emancipation of persons and communities. Thompson was faithful to two traditions, the romanticism of Blake and the young Wordsworth, who were subsidiary heroes of his story, and the resistance to capitalism by working-class radicals from the 1790s to the Chartist protests. "In the failure," wrote Thompson, "of the two traditions to come to a point of junction, something was lost. How much we cannot be sure, for we are among the losers."[8] The enemy in this account was not just the Whig order and its master, capitalism. It was also Whig history—history that teleologically favors the interests of the present. There is a question how far any history, conceived as a record of the past that shows some forward motion, can avoid being read as a version of Whig history. In this sense Thompson was as present-minded as Macaulay or Lecky. But in his story, the progressive moral was turned upside down. We are no longer to avow a primary interest in the survivals of the past that run closest to the way of life we know today. Rather, we are to take counsel from the heroic defeats of the past, against the bankruptcy of our own success.

The tendency of such history seemed to be antimodern to some extent, and to a larger extent anti-unitary. The professional antagonist of the radical historian of the 1960s was "consensus history"; and the move away from consensus touched those who would least have cared to abet it. The history department of Yale University, ranked number one in the nation in 1995, is not remarkably colored by political radicalism or professional susceptibility. Yet it was once a department renowned for its strength in American political history. At present, a student who wanted to study the ideas of the Founding Fathers, or the career of Lincoln, or the politics of the New Deal, would find no senior professor who made a practice of teaching those subjects. Nor is this an anomaly. The department at the University of California at Berkeley, also among the top in the nation, some years ago closed out its only existing position in British history. These developments are the result of a coincidence. The anti-Whig prejudice emerged at just the right moment to assist the planned obsolescence that history, like all other fields, is obliged to impose on any research program that has dominated the scholarly literature for long enough, and the research program in question here was the political history of Europe and America. The demands of advocacy and the needs of professionalism therefore marched together. The "European roots of American culture," of which so much was heard in the 1950s, were already on their way to removal by the 1970s.

For reasons that remain partly obscure, history, without producing a book as widely read in universities as Thompson's in the three decades since, has in that time become the most influential of the liberal arts, the one whose name and presence make scholars in rival fields most pious and emulative. Historicism—the belief that thought and action in the past can be wholly understood as effects of environment, with the style of interpretation that follows from this belief—derives some measure of its prestige from its convergence with postmodernism: a redundant term that suggests a lack of conviction and has come to mean in practice an eclectic pliability to the most various convictions. Postmodernism and historicism in its recent forms are doubtless also products of a long deferral of hope, the sensation of being trapped between two gigantic obstacles that the Cold War did at last produce in most of those who experienced it. The renewal of emphasis, in the early 1990s, on "personal agency" might suggest a lightening of this burden and of the pessimistic superstition that accompanied it—that we are all now, just as our ancestors were, the determined creatures of environment and our words the creations of nothing but social context. The belief in agency *seems* to offer a way out, but, when one looks at the current uses of the idea, its picture of human action tends to be circumstantial and contingent, the more modest and lowercase the better. The grand narratives are gone, we have been told, just as we are also told that all knowledge depends on narrative;[9] well then, if we must have a story to understand ourselves, let us make it as unpresuming as we can: we will not be held captive within any frame, even if that means painting ourselves out of the story.

The acts of charitable reconstruction that Whig history, once inverted, properly favors can produce an estranged response from those who encounter the new history without a theoretical code, or in the absence of rhetorical effects of an impassioned advocacy. "History," wrote Auden, "to the defeated / may say alas but cannot help or pardon." But Marxism too was a variant of Whig history. Anti-Whig etiquette has made it a requirement of manners and of professional dogma to pardon the defeated conspicuously and withhold all pardon from the victors. Here the consequences of professional change have only gradually come into view outside the profession. The Smithsonian Institution was set in 1994 to mount an exhibit that would mark the fiftieth anniversary of the end of World War II. Part of the effort was going to be a reconstruction of the Enola Gay, the plane that dropped the atomic bomb on Hiroshima. By early 1995 a fury of contention over the catalogue text finally caused the exhibit to be scrapped; in the end, not one American received the history lesson the Smithsonian had paid for and that many must have been hoping to see. How did this happen? Scholars trained in a new research program may at first turn almost exclusively to university teaching, but later, as the program succeeds, they make their way into positions as textbook writers and curators.

Consultants on the Smithsonian text were in possession of facts about the dropping of the bombs in August 1945 that ought to be known by a wider public, facts that could have been made known without the assault on national feelings that closed the show. Some of those facts are the following: that the Truman administration was intent on keeping Stalin out of eastern Asia, and by July Russia's entry into the war against Japan was imminent; that the bombs were dropped in obedience to a select portion of the expert advice the administration canvassed—Stimson had pressed for the decision but Eisenhower opposed it; that the idea of inviting the Japanese to witness the exploding of a "demonstration" bomb was never deliberately considered; that the official estimate produced at the time of lives that would be lost in a full invasion of Japan was not in the range of the millions later quoted by Churchill and others, but 46,000.[10] The dissemination of these data in a national exhibit would have caused irritation; but the effect was compounded to a catastrophic degree by the total shape of the text. An exhibit was proposed that brought into relief the racist motives for prosecuting the war against Japan and recalled the unique and admirable qualities of Japanese culture. Little was said about American culture. In short, the text appeared to speak with a sorrowing advocacy and with an extracurricular solicitude on behalf of the vanquished.

It was this selective sympathy that assured the virulence of the public reaction. Newspapers that in calmer times would hardly report on such an event delivered ferocious editorials. The *Cincinnati Enquirer* may stand for many other papers in its comment that "a venerable institution has turned what could have been a poignant tribute to the 50th anniversary of World War II's conclusion into a dud that damaged its reputation and left veterans bitter and betrayed," and in the incredulity with which it recounted the facts: "The exhibit asked 'Would the bomb have been dropped on the Germans?' Then it answered: 'Some have argued that the United States would never have dropped the bomb on Germans because Americans were more reluctant to bomb "white people" than Asians.'"[11] Eventually, the exhibit was mounted, in a much diminished form, but not before the Reserve Officers Association had called for its cancellation and the president of the Air Force Association, R. E. Smith, had testified in the Senate Rules Subcommittee on Smithsonian Oversight that he had counted 49 photographs of Japanese casualties and 3 of Americans, and that less than 1 page out of 295 dealt with Japanese military activity prior to 1945.[12] A note of late-found diplomacy was struck by I. Michael Heyman, the director of the Smithsonian: "In this important anniversary year, veterans and their families were expecting, and rightly so, that the nation would honor and commemorate their valor and sacrifice. They were not looking for analysis and, frankly, we did not give enough thought to the intense feelings such analysis would evoke."[13] But this answer by a curator, for his censored and therefore twice-compromised scholars, was condescending and unworthy. It also betrayed a chronic misreading of the nature of the problem.

From none of the reactions to the exhibit was it clear that analysis was sure to be resented. The statement about white Americans not wanting to bomb white Europeans was dubious *as history*, and those with memories long enough, or a modicum of acquaintance with the available documentary footage, would know how the bombing of Dresden, Berlin, and other German cities refuted the inference to be drawn from the text. This was not analysis but speculation, and of a kind that implied a hostile disposition in the speculator. In the same way the statements about American racism, and the subdued interest in the atrocities committed by the Japanese, were resented not because they were analysis but because they suggested a patent antipathy to the nation that had subsidized the exhibit. It is because analysis, and the education that comes with it, are jobs worth doing well that the failure of the Smithsonian in 1995 represented so acute a loss. And a loss on a very large scale: this has become the classic specimen that a lawmaker now may cite in giving the knockdown, half-baked argument for withdrawing support for such cultural entities as National Public Radio or the National Endowment for the Humanities (NEH). Unhappily, a similar example had come into view several months earlier, with the publication in 1994 of the *National Standards* for teaching American history in grades 5–11.

These standards—a handsome paperback with explanatory charts and photographs and eleven pages at the back listing the persons, organizations, and focus groups that created it—were delivered by the National Center for History in the Schools at the University of California at Los Angeles. They drew upon a generous grant from the NEH. As soon as the standards emerged, they were pilloried by journalists of the political right as a reflex result of politically correct thinking. That description was false. The standards shown at the time were a disaster, but a far more incoherent one than political correctness would have produced. They were rather a typical committee production, the outcome of professional timidity, acquiescence, and a muddled eclecticism. The heroes of the story are not radicals; they are not persons; they are social causes and effects—conditions in which this or that migration took place, this or that opinion became possible—and preconditions of those conditions. The *National Standards* of 1994 disclose what it would be like to try to teach Americans, from the age of ten to seventeen, the look and feel of American history *as the recent development of the field has made it over.* It may be replied that the cultural, social, military, and economic histories written in our time lean upon, and suppose a prior knowledge of, the kind of political and intellectual history that was consolidated by the generation of Perry Miller and Richard Hofstadter and David Potter. Perhaps; but that is more than seems to have been known to the dozens of grade-school and high-school teachers who sat in the focus groups and reproduced from their college mentors the atomization of context that is the prevailing version of consensus.

The history of the heroic and defeated was here bureaucratized as the history of the hard to represent and the hard to see. That, as the *Standards* proved, can include most people at most times. But it cuts down the Americans on whose appearances in the national story many have long relied for edification. There was very little in the *Standards* of a character-istic or even a consistently political sort, on Washington or Jefferson or Lincoln or FDR. Almost every mention of Martin Luther King was accom-panied by a matching and equal mention of Malcolm X. It is understand-able that the inclusive impersonality of this approach would be mistaken for a radical exclusionism by the slightly informed and slightly curious. In fact it had a tamer source, and the resultant tedium exhibited the revenge of success against the ambition to rescue every group, every culture, every milieu from what Thompson called "the enormous condescension of pos-terity." It has now become the distinguished of any class who have to be rescued from a posterity that levels all as a compliment to its own impartiality. How conscious was the process that produced such effects? Hardly conscious, or so I suspect from some experience of committees. The inhibitions required to make this sort of story had been internalized in advance.

Much of the content of the *Standards* was familiar. Their uncertainty regarding their audience was novel. Here, for example, are two specimens from the revolutionary period—questions a student in grades 9–12 was expected to answer as a proof of mastery:

> Drawing upon ideas of religious groups such as Virginia Baptists, mid-Atlantic Presbyterians, and millennialists, assess how religion became a factor in the American Revolution.

And again:

> Marshall evidence to explain how a Loyalist and a Patriot would view each of the following: The Tea Act of 1773, the Boston Tea Party, the "Intolerable" Acts, the cause of the skirmish at Lexington Green. *How might a Loyalist have rewritten the natural rights theory of the Declaration of Independence? How might a Loyalist have answered the charges in the Declaration of Independence?*[14]

The apt answerer of these questions would exhibit mastery indeed—a mastery appropriate to a Ph.D. candidate on a general oral examination. The questions were extraordinarily intricate, sharp, and deep and bore almost no relation to the attractable interests of a fifteen-year-old, who might be drawn to the characters of John Adams, Benjamin Franklin, and others whom the standards hardly addressed. It can be seen from these questions how far the result commonly lies from any radical concern for the oppressed. Almost all that remains of it is the wish to think with anyone but the victor, anyone but the Whig—even if that means, as it does here, the mind of a rational Tory fully stocked with reasons-of-state against the rights of man.

A principle of broad empathy was implied throughout the 1994 *Standards* by an ameliorative language of agency; the teacher was urged to "challenge prevailing attitudes of historical inevitability by examining how alternative choices could produce different consequences."[15] In this view of "alternative choices" exported from the present to the past, even the worst sufferings can be seen to have worked toward the creation of a culture whose value is still to be ascertained. Thus, "while coming to grips with [slavery and expropriation from lands], students should also recognize that Africans and Native Americans were not simply victims, but were intricately involved in the creation of a colonial society and a new, hybrid American culture."[16] The compromise with determinism, hammered out on the bodies of words like "agency" and "hybrid," is not easily to be resisted, all hope being preferable to despair. But some kinds of suffering need to be called suffering, and slavery is one of these. The 1994 *National Standards* added up to a mosaic of unamalgamating good intentions, founded on the venerable but now indistinct memory of the worth of a usable past. The aim had become to produce user-friendly pasts at the sacrifice of dramatic interest and memorableness. The grade-school or high-school teacher who might actually look to the *Standards* for assistance was nowhere guided to a better authority than itself on any period or person whatever. There was no mention of works of vivid authority on key subjects, such as Don Fehrenbacher's *Dred Scott Case*, or inventive works on contested subjects, such as Tsvetan Todorov's *Conquest of America*. In fact, above grades 5 and 6, there was no mention of a book.

Between the writing and editing of the present essay, the National Center for History in the Schools released a thoroughly revised version of the *Standards* for history. This "basic edition" of 1996 offers an extractable narrative and a digest of nonoptional facts, and it exhibits the virtues many had looked for earlier: pedagogic aptness and focus and a practical concern with a common history to be mastered by the generality of students. The 1996 *Standards* thus embody not only a prudent condensation of the 1994 version but also a redefinition of purpose. Yet nowhere does the text make mention of the controversy that rendered the new edition almost a diplomatic necessity. The previous text had not been presented originally as a draft but as the final product, and no one aware of the impact of the sustained and hostile response can suppose these changes would have seen the light but for the exigent resistance. If the result suggests that a licensed curricular project may, in the current climate, eventually produce an appropriate curriculum for public schools, it also leaves in doubt to what extent such pragmatic effects are probable without intervention from an articulate public.

The direction of teaching in which politically minded scholarship has most often ventured in recent years comes under the heading of cultural identity. Diversity need not be a code word for people who look different and think alike. It is, however, the preferred American euphemism for the collective labor of cheering and elevating the self-esteem of a group. The process requires a euphemism because it is widely understood, though seldom said aloud, that the interests of such a group may overlap but cannot coincide with those of the society as a whole. Edmund Burke said in a speech on the relief of Protestant dissenters in 1773, "Do not promote diversity; when you have it, bear it."[17] American educators, in the past decade, on an impetus from the academic left and later with a momentum of their own, have taken up the work of promoting diversity. Why do they subsidize it? For the policy has its workaday innovations seldom far from view—holding curricular and extracurricular seminars on "difference," proposing segregated housing and eating as an amenity of education. Demographics offer one explanation, and one that is credited with profound effects by Lynn Hunt in her contribution to this volume. It seems to me neither a theoretically sufficient nor a uniquely efficient cause. Educational policy is not a projectable outcome of demographics, any more than human action is a projectable outcome of genetics. The entry into universities of persons ever more various in their backgrounds might just as plausibly have prompted a stress on the value of scholastic rituals promoting unity and harmony. Another source of the change went hand in hand with demographics: a moral supplement to the process of identification with a lost culture, which the success of social history had legitimated by the 1970s. I will call the supplement, borrowing a term from ego psychology, *dis*identification. The meaning of the term can best be clarified by an anecdote.

At a seminar some years ago, I listened to a presentation by a young cultural historian on suttee, the custom by which a Hindu widow was burned on the funeral pyre of her husband. The British in India, after discountenancing the custom for many years, eventually prohibited it in

1829. The scholar had done a good deal of work on the ideology of the abolitionists, including the civil service memoranda that passed at India House, and he took a jaundiced view of the motives of these imperial reformers. They were administering their own form of "enlightened" knowledge in the interest of domination; the crushing of an ancient superstition was part of the work of social control. All this sounded almost routine, in its academic setting, except that not a word of comment appeared, for all the irony at the expense of the British, regarding the morality of the ritual sacrifice of Indian women. In the question period, the scholar was asked about this. He replied that he was Western and judged the British without hesitation as precursors of his own culture. In principle, he refrained from judging the customs of another culture. Including slavery and human sacrifice? Including them. The moment was the more startling in that the presenter was intelligent, not, it seemed, a misogynist, not particularly an ideologue, and not particularly anti-West. The suspension of judgment here seemed to touch a limit.

Disidentification entered the curriculum of the Western intellectual in the postwar years from many tributaries—most potently from Sartre's preface to Fanon's *Wretched of the Earth,* an essay almost as eloquent and far more reckless and aggressive than the text of that book. Sartre there referred to what he called, in the colonial context, "the strip-tease of our humanism," and challenged his readers:

> There you can see it, quite naked, and it's not a pretty sight. It was nothing but an ideology of lies, a perfect justification for pillage; its honeyed words, its affectation of sensibility were only alibis for our aggressions. . . . "We aren't angels, but we, at least, feel some remorse." What a confession! Formerly our continent was buoyed up by other means: the Parthenon, Chartres, the Rights of Man, or the swastika. Now we know what these are worth; and the only chance of our being saved from shipwreck is the very Christian sentiment of guilt. You can see it's the end; Europe is springing leaks everywhere. What then has happened? It simply is that in the past we made history and now it is being made of us.[18]

Several details are remarkable here: the assumption that it could be legitimate for a social critic like Sartre to weigh the culture of Europe in the balance with its crimes; the tabloid association of culture-as-such with a few high-visibility monuments that have nothing in common except their renown; the casual insertion of the Nazi emblem into Europe's hit parade, followed by the canceling of its worth along with the rest, as if it bore a family resemblance to them. But the mood of such writing defies analysis; Sartre was offering a spurious façade of an argument. It nevertheless carried enormous weight in our time with young scholars more assured of their sensibility than of their political bearings.

Sartre's preface was quoted prominently in "Repressive Tolerance," the essay of 1965 by Herbert Marcuse that did more than any other work to justify the authoritarian conduct of the academic left. Marcuse asserted that liberal democratic tolerance was a sham. Tolerance is authentic only when (1) every person who might possibly be heard from has the chance to speak; (2) preachers of hateful intolerance are not among the voices that are heard; and (3) the speakers are being genuinely attended to, and not just counted as place-fillers to make out a "spectrum" of opinion. That the last of these demands is metaphysical—beyond testing—is as obvious as that the first two exclude each other. But so broad a rehearsal of the argument gives no sense of the satisfying finality with which Marcuse's practical deductions are broached. His central contrast is between the apparent tolerance (actually repression) that the establishment maintains and the revolutionary intolerance (preparing the way for authentic toler- ance) that must be practiced by the militant avant-garde of human emancipation. Tolerance that is more than a sham will only come from a revolution triumphant: "The small and powerless minorities which strug- gle against the false consciousness and its beneficiaries must be helped: their continued existence is more important than the preservation of abused rights and liberties which grant constitutional powers to those who oppress these minorities. . . . When tolerance mainly serves the protection and preservation of a repressive society, when it serves to neutralize opposition and to render men immune against other and better forms of life, then tolerance has been perverted." When, that is, the minds of the majority have been stunned and tranquilized and their human faculties poisoned at the source by the "words and images which feed this [false] consciousness," we must conduct a program of reverse propaganda on behalf of humanity. And we must do it by prohibiting, through either legal sanction or extralegal force, the works of fiction and acts of persuasion that we find morally intolerable. As Marcuse remarks in his 1968 "Post- script" to the essay, "there are issues where there is no 'other side' in any more than a formalistic sense."[19] Here then was the germ of the academic speech codes of the 1980s and 1990s—at the University of Wisconsin, at Stanford, and elsewhere.[20] Court by court they are being found unconsti- tutional, as Marcuse warned they would have to be. But new experiments of the kind spring up as quickly as the old are invalidated: a code was ratified in 1995 at the University of Massachusetts at Amherst that is as stringent and categorical as any yet ventured.

Self-repression has long been the counterpart of the banishment of "regressive" voices. And the analogy by which the scholar stands to the subject as the colonizer to the colonized has made the wary still warier, even as it has become the basis of a new style of uncritical support for non-European cultures. Alain Finkielkraut in *The Undoing of Thought* summarizes the postcolonial ideology of UNESCO in a way that renders unambiguous its connection with a usual stress of postcolonial studies:

> It is claimed in the present day resolutions of the Organization that human beings draw all their substance from the community to which they belong; that the personal identity of individuals is the same as their collective identity; that everything about them—beliefs, values, intelligence and feelings—proceeds from that combination of climate, life-style and language which used to be called *Volksgeist*, but which is now known as culture. In this perspective the end of education is seen to be, not to give each person the wherewithal to sort out his own ideas from the enormous mass of beliefs, opinions, customs, and outlooks which comprise his heritage; but on the contrary to have him immersed willy-nilly in that flood of experience.[21]

This analysis brings out how thoroughly an anthropological definition of culture—presupposed, of course, in the assurance a historian could feel about "working-class culture"—has smoothed a path for populist surveys and interpretations of the culture of everyday life.[22]

Such a strenuous embrace of a plurality of cultures may seem to embody a freedom from moralism and the jealous spirit of licensing. But there has always been a strong moral undertone in the conviction with which anthropologists speak of the "subtle violence" of uprooting native Americans or Hispanic immigrants from their cultural setting by the requirement of learning English or studying European history. This is where the remedy of multiculturalism comes in to offer plausible relief. It codifies, in the most intricate imaginable degree, the abstinence, the tentative recusal or disavowal of judgment, that might otherwise embarrass the Western scholar as a too hastily improvised contradiction. The contradiction is manifest, as Finkielkraut points out, but it can be expressed more genteelly in the form of irony: "They have been brutally uprooted, and to soften this somewhat, we bind them hand and foot and pass them over to their communities. We think we are enlarging the arena of human rights, to the extent of allowing everyone to live within his own culture. In practice we limit access to that arena to Westerners."[23] The Western scholar who agrees to live on terms with this irony is safely nested in a culture that is literally untenable. How can a practice of education derived from the Enlightenment, a practice that is in a large measure individualist, claim the binding privilege that belongs to culture anthropologically defined? To effect this transition an innovation of great ingenuity was required. The privilege had to be turned into an impoverishment. Here the important work was done by the group therapists and diversity managers who went to work in the 1970s in corporate T-groups and in the 1980s in colleges—to devise, for example, the innovation of an ethnically divided orientation week.[24] The protocol they teach regarding the "subject position" has since made its way into the classroom and the curriculum.

The subject position is the web of social and material traits that are taken to reveal "where I'm coming from"—environmental facts that I admit as conditioning everything I say and do, in ways that are bound to be partly invisible to me. Richard Ohmann began his polemical survey *English in America: A Radical View of the Profession*, in 1976, with an early version of the self-humbling formula: "My argument is the argument of someone who is American, male, white, 44, and privileged; who has been marked by Shaker Heights, Ohio, by the Harvard Society of Fellows, by Wesleyan University, by professional successes and failures, by students and colleagues, by the Vietnam war, by the crises in American society these past fifteen years."[25] One notices the characteristic trend from the modest to the aggrandizing. The ego-purge enacted in public is fated to be read as egotistical, and Ohmann's experiences in Shaker Heights and Middletown gather an importance that finally makes them identical with the crises of American society. *English in America* was described in a review by Steven Marcus in the *Times Literary Supplement* as the professional autobiography not of the twice-born but the just-born. In this stance, the book foreshadowed the confessional turn in literary studies in the 1990s.

Ohmann described vicariously and in a tone of raw grievance "the voraciousness, the callousness, of America's assault on land and people," and the "tradition of voraciousness and callousness that goes back to our first arrivals, when freedom-loving settlers made the perfectly casual assumption that they could use the land however they liked, expelling and murdering and cheating."[26] Pronouncements on the origins and nature of the American mind alternate, in *English in America* as in later books of its genre, with the rock-bottom trivia of microprofessional critique.[27] But in the course of his survey Ohmann paused to acknowledge one opponent of some substance. Quoting Sidney Hook to the effect that the duties of the scholar and the duties of the citizen are different, that not every choice is a political choice, and that an institution's refusal to take a position on a political question is not thereby a political decision, any more than its refusal to take a position on a religious question is a religious decision, Ohmann replies uncontentiously that Hook's view differs "sharply from any view of politics that I would find illuminating." Politics he defines as "the attempt to exercise power and serve interests"[28]—any exercise of power, any serving of interests, is political. But as the growth of confessional criticism shows, the talk of scholars about politics and their talk about "complicity" has become, to a remarkable degree, uninhibited talk about themselves.

That they see this themselves, and consciously "foreground" the fact, gives much of the current discourse an eerie atmosphere of postmortem effects. How did the ethic of social engagement pass into the self-regard of confessional therapy without renouncing the name of its parent faith? An answer more cogent than any other I have found is suggested by Julie Ellison's essay "A Short History of Liberal Guilt"; Ellison's conclusion is that "guilt spawns theory."[29] A field of renewed interest for literary studies, in which Ellison has published several essays, is the late eighteenth century—the age of sentiment, of the debate over chivalry and natural rights, and the first wave of intense concern with the aspect of sexual difference we now would call gender. Not only the 1780s and 1790s but, as she rightly observes, "the entire eighteenth century is being transformed from the rational Enlightenment into the heyday of sensibility under the pressure of our need to understand the viability of social emotion in the U.S. today."[30] This perceptive judgment misses one piece of the combination that has made the analogy pertinent. The actors in the typical exchange of sensibility, the scene of shared feelings in the 1790s or the 1990s, have been aristocrats of some kind and the flatterers of aristocrats. Writers like Sterne and Mackenzie came to be cherished by an audience that looked on the cultivation of sentiments as the final proof of consummated luxury. The same is true of the audience of such scholar-therapists as Homi Bhabha (in the field of postcolonial studies) and Patricia Williams (in the field of law and rhetoric).

By creating a perpetual residence for the controlled performances of sentiment, affirmative action fostered a climate entirely at odds with the dry egalitarianism that drove the program in principle. Anyone who has witnessed the demeanor of one of the new therapists as he or she addresses the guilty audience will have remarked that the performers are, in their daily lives and conduct, aristocratic. The privilege of manners they routinely command would seem exorbitant in the eyes of a common citizen of a democracy; the matter is clarified when one recalls the eighteenth-century gentleman's ideal of presumptive virtue: "that proud submission, that dignified obedience, that subordination of the heart" which can never be earned but with which one is received as a consequence of merely being what one is. The spell that holds performer and audience captive is sustained by a knowledge both parties agree to keep unspoken. For the performer has been brought in to represent symbolically a class of the miserable on whom the audience wants to confer an unquestioning pity. As Ellison shows, the performer is thereby given to speak a language that would draw the reproach of coercion on any scholar not so licensed: "We must force [Rorty] to dialogue in order to teach him the social theory of pain and suffering."[31] In an imperative utterance such as this, the meaning of *to dialogue* (used as an intransitive verb) is that of the B-movie standby: "We have ways of making you talk."

Thus Nietzsche's analysis of pity is confirmed from an unexpected angle. It is a game in which one wins and both lose.[32] The number of players has been small, so far, but the few have realized ponderable effects from the embrace of publishers and the funding of special programs in departments with money to spare. And there have been some remarkable extensions of tactical ingenuity. Gayatri Spivak, when her white male students docilely assume their subject positions in the prescribed manner, now tells them to stop feeling guilty and get to work: their abjection is proof of the oppression they share with other peoples. It is a generous conclusion, "unexpectedly protestant" as Ellison says. But something must follow from an injunction like this, in scholarship or political practice. It is not yet clear what that can be. Meanwhile, an essay in the same issue of the journal in which Ellison's appears would seem to offer testimony of the staying power of the sentimental exchange. A gender theorist responds to a criticism of her theory by two counter-theorists. Heterosexuals, they are called to the carpet for having formulated a "severely normative critique": "nowhere . . . do the authors name their own speaking position" and the "omission is not, of course, mere oversight; the use of an objective, moralizing, and universal voice is one of the standard tropes of homophobic discourse." Further debate is impossible since "by conducting their critique from this unmarked position . . . they foreclose all scrutiny of the political determinations and the ideological investments of their 'return look.'"[33]

The name of Richard Rorty came up briefly in the preceding section, on the wrong end of a shaming aside by a postcolonial authority: "We must force [Rorty] to dialogue." This reversion to force comes from a belief that education must be public in a sense opposed to every personal "dialogue of the mind with itself," and Rorty is its natural target because he holds a singular position among scholars interested in reform outside the university. He is one of the few living American philosophers who have had a broad impact in other fields of the humanities, and of those few he is the only one whose idea of liberalism springs from deeper sources than those supplied by the current Anglo-American philosophical idiom. Rorty has derived from John Stuart Mill and Walt Whitman an insistence that a distinction between private and public experience is an inseparable good of modern democracy. The distinction, as Mill and Whitman explored it,[34] aims at getting an educated citizenry beyond the charm of just such games as the conjunction of *force* and *dialogue* suggests. The talk therapy in the mass culture today, which the academic culture has begun to follow, offers public catharsis for private griefs, and in doing so implies that all questions of personal practice and general morality are equally open to relief by a process of forced dialogue, shared sentiments, commiseration, and, if possible, absolution. The result is to aestheticize suffering by absorbing every concern into the reciprocal gaze of speaker and spectator. That gaze and its objects are for private contemplation, Rorty argues, whereas suffering and its subjects are for public engagement and assistance. A fair criticism of the distinction as he presents it[35]—between free play and moral action, aesthetic solitude and social solidarity—is that public and private have never in practice been quite so distinct. Not even Mill in *On Liberty* seems to have imagined that they were.

But his argument here, so unusual on the academic left, is perhaps best read as a corrective. Anyone looking at the morale of the educated classes today will be struck by a disturbing symmetry between two axioms: that everything about my conduct is the product of environment, conditioning, "determinations"; and that what *appears* unique or arbitrary or salient about me is not really mine. The latter belief owes much of its currency to a rival description of public and private by John Rawls, who in *A Theory of Justice* treated individual gifts, endowments, and character as not belonging to the person they inhabit. Among the conditions of Rawls's argument for social fairness is "an agreement to regard the distribution of natural talents as a common asset and to share in the benefits of this distribution whatever it turns out to be. Those who have been favored by nature, whoever they are, may gain from their good fortune only on terms that improve the situation of those who lost out." Rawls's idea of fairness, the broad outlines of which are close to the common sense of the New Deal settlement, feels much less surprising than the premise that personal talents are cooperative assets. Yet he believed the following assertion to be a simple correlative of the agreement he had sketched: "It seems to be one of the fixed points of our considered judgments that no one deserves his place in the distribution of native endowments, any more than one deserves one's initial starting place in society. The assertion that a man deserves the superior character that enables him to make the effort to cultivate his abilities is equally problematic; for his character depends in large part upon fortunate family and social circumstances for which he can claim no credit."[36] The real source of such a prescription for merging personal gifts and qualities (including character) with the cooperative holdings of society can hardly be that the intuition about our not deserving them is "one of the fixed points of our considered judgments." It is far from being such a fixed point and only a sort of pun on deserving could make it seem so.

To say of my starting point in life that "I deserved it" certainly makes no sense. "I was lucky" or "I was unlucky" seems true to the sense of most people. But to say of my ear for music or the arm that made me a fast server in tennis "I do not deserve it" seems as odd as it would be to say "I do deserve it." It comes with me. It is an accident. It may be important or

it may not be, but nothing can or should be done to remedy it.[37] But here
again is the symmetry: on the one hand, determination of the person by
race, moment, milieu, culture; on the other hand, transfer of the person to
the collectivity that deserves his or her qualities. Rawls appears to have
reasoned back from the desirability of cooperative protection to the sup-
position that the things protected are assets, and further back to the "fixed
point of our considered judgment" that talent or endowment or genius or
gift or character may truly be understood as an asset, a kind of property.

The definition of character as an asset suggests no interesting reflection
on the relations of private to public experience. Still, a verbal usage of this
tenor supports the contemporary tendency to rate every personal undertaking on the index of collective need. When it is said that one's gifts do
not belong to oneself, the thought may as well be extended. What of a
passion felt with peculiar strength? What of an artistic or professional
calling? One is brought back to a persuasion that seems to be shared by
the cooperative therapist and the patient of advocacy theory. They do not
see how their work can belong to them. This mood of self-divestment is
prompted by a doubt that is none the less corrosive for being half-formed.
America is moving from an industrial society controlled, as J. G. A. Pocock
observes, by an "appropriative animal" who employed labor "to process
his environment in production" to a postindustrial society in which the
relation between self, property, and the available materials for appropriation appears more dubious than ever before. "It is not surprising," Pocock
goes on, "that postindustrial societies should display movement toward
postappropriative philosophies of individuality and society, and even toward postindividualist philosophies of humanity itself; though whether
you can sacrifice individualism and retain individuality, or individuality
and retain humanity, continues to be a question."[38] This speculation opens
a longer perspective than is strictly relevant to a discussion of American
education. The warning has anyway the merit of suggesting how little
Cassirer's sentiment of man's "ability constantly to reshape his human
universe" can now be taken for granted in education. It has become the
name of a hope and not a certainty.

I close with a remark of traditional resonance that need not imply
excessive hope. The American sense of intellectual experience and the
world has never been much like the European sense. In Europe there is a
thing called learning—a monument that is a property and that can be
appropriated. Here there are words and imaginings, moments of lives that
one encounters in books, and that join one's sense of life. The wisdom of
books is never planted. If I find it, it was made for me. There is a question
whether an American scholar, in keeping with the "sad self-knowledge" of
our tradition, can ever instruct against this view that books are made for
us, that they are only significant as rebuilt by ourselves. The first known

use of the phrase "creative writing"—a phrase with a history, and with much to atone for—occurs in the same essay on the vocation of scholars in which Emerson speaks of "creative reading." We are still living with the tension he recognized between the old-world monumental culture—which bears with it a kind of authority necessary in education—and the deference to personal experience that has priority for us but that can scarcely reconstitute itself as pedagogic method. After World War II, American universities discovered in their midst a host of scholars who were among the last and most admirable descendants of the European Enlightenment: Erwin Panofsky, Hannah Arendt, Erich Auerbach, Franz Neumann, and many others. Their presence, the genuineness of their authority, helped to defer for a long generation the encounter American scholars have always evaded between authority and imagination.

Teaching has its undemocratic side; it is hard for us to say so. And an individualist culture of education seems a contradiction in terms, something no institution should be asked to promote. The teacher will say what he or she thinks and will be taken as an authority. Yet a piece of us knows that to act like this is cheating, or conniving with the neglect of a truth about experience. Our awareness implies a premise of learning that can be missed in the company of those who put up a flawless front of pieties about equality, as it can be missed among those, more common in education than in the other professions, who are democrats on sufferance and have made their peace with appearances. The student who lives to read still knows what these have forgotten: that authority is necessary and that in education it is only ideal, never finite or local. It was Dewey's faithfulness to this idealism that lengthened his early interest in education and made him speak of inquiry and knowledge, imagination and experience, as if all were almost synonymous. "Ends are, in fact, literally endless,"[39] and the curriculum that does not premeditate social aims can be fertile for reform in ways untested by the programmed schools of commitment. This view of thought and action has had many lives in more unpromising settings than ours. It may become familiar once more. To want to bring life into the classroom will then seem as much a solecism as the idea that you could ever take life out of it.

Notes

1. See Michael Oakeshott, *The Voice of Liberal Learning*, ed. Timothy Fuller (New Haven, 1989), 105–35.

2. Max Weber, "Science as a Vocation," in *From Max Weber*, ed. H. H. Gerth and C. Wright Mills (New York, 1946), 147. By science Weber meant the dis-

ciplines of learning; what he supposed it to exclude is made plain in the companion essay, "Politics as a Vocation."

3. Noam Chomsky's *American Power and the New Mandarins* (New York, 1969) was a book of enormous impact at the time, particularly for the full-scale iconoclasm of its essay "Objectivity and Liberal Scholarship." Chomsky's intentions and rhetoric belonged to the rational Enlightenment, for which he aimed to speak as an authentic representative by exposing the swindle of pretenders. In this, he differed markedly from exponents of emancipatory violence of the school of Frantz Fanon.

4. Max Horkheimer and Theodor W. Adorno, *Dialectic of Enlightenment* (New York, 1982), 31. The *Dialectic* entered the consciousness of American intellectuals through the medium of Herbert Marcuse's *One-Dimensional Man* (1964). That resonant work of pamphleteering brought the Horkheimer-Adorno thesis—that technology and the mind in its service only know an object in order to conquer it—into a consideration of the self-imposed limits of academic culture and the confined spectrum of the available opinions in the mass culture. Marcuse acknowledged a debt to social critics like Vance Packard and C. Wright Mills, who had pointed out instrumentalities of tacit as well as overt repressiveness in the social order of the Cold War. His conclusions went beyond theirs to yield a picture of American democracy as virtually totalitarian.

The reputation of *One-Dimensional Man* faded with a thoroughness in the late 1970s that it would be wrong to take at face value. The book had prepared the way for the American assimilation of the writings of Michel Foucault. Indeed, until the translation of the *History of Sexuality* in the late 1980s, Foucault was read by his most prominent American expounders much as if he were Marcuse, with the social-critical element (often associated with the Frankfurt School) emphasized and the sadistic-individualist element (explicitly derived from Nietzsche) suppressed.

5. Ernst Cassirer, *An Essay on Man* (New Haven, 1944), 62.

6. See, e.g., Lynne V. Cheney, *Telling the Truth*, an official publication of the National Endowment for the Humanities (Washington, D.C., 1992), lately expanded into a book of the same title (New York, 1995).

7. I give reasons for this stance in *Politics by Other Means* (New Haven, 1992), 98–164.

8. E. P. Thompson, *The Making of the English Working Class* (New York, 1963), 832. An anthology of work by various hands, *Towards a New Past*, ed. Barton Bernstein (New York, 1968), registered early the depth of Thompson's influence among younger American historians. It appeared then in the shape of a broad resolution to write history "from the bottom up"; distinguished full-scale examples of this kind of history, e.g., Sean Wilentz, *Chants Democratic* (New York, 1984), were delayed almost a generation.

9. An argument advanced most influentially by Alasdair MacIntyre in *After Virtue* (Notre Dame, Ind., 1981).

10. See Gar Alperovitz, *The Decision to Use the Atomic Bomb* (New York, 1995), 633.

11. Unsigned editorial, *Cincinnati Enquirer*, February 6, 1995.

12. Testimony of R. E. Smith, May 11, 1995, courtesy of the Federal Document Clearing House.

13. I. Michael Heyman, quoted in unsigned editorial, *Washington Post*, February 7, 1995.

14. *National Standards for United States: Exploring the American Experience* (Los Angeles, 1994), 11.

15. A useful moralizing aim, though some events are less resistible than others, and the student should be encouraged to see this too. The risk of importing our sense of "possibility" into the past is that we lose sight of the partiality or blindness of its inhabitants, human frailties that enter into what they think they know of impossibility. The upshot can be a complacent (oddly Whiggish) sense of the court of history as residing in ourselves. On the dangers of such "backshadowing," see Michael André Bernstein, *Foregone Conclusions* (Berkeley and Los Angeles, 1995).

16. This complex view of the "hybridity" of Americans appears to be derived from Albert Murray's book of essays *The Omni-Americans* and Ralph Ellison's *Going to the Territory*, among other books; and it would not hurt to name the books. On the systematic reticence of the 1994 *Standards* regarding secondary literature of high quality, see below.

17. Edmund Burke, *Works*, 12 vols. (New York, 1869), 7:36.

18. Jean-Paul Sartre, preface to Frantz Fanon, *The Wretched of the Earth*, tr. Constance Farrington (New York, 1968), 27.

19. Herbert Marcuse, "Repressive Tolerance," in Robert Paul Wolff et al., *A Critique of Pure Tolerance* (Boston, 1969), 110–11, 116.

20. A history of the rise of the speech codes and a libertarian polemic against them are combined in Nat Hentoff, *Free Speech for Me—But Not for Thee* (New York, 1993).

21. Alain Finkielkraut, *The Undoing of Thought*, tr. Dennis O'Keefe (London, 1988), 79.

22. Many of them influenced by Pierre Bourdieu, *Distinction*, tr. Richard Nice (Cambridge, Mass., 1984). Bourdieu's "Postscript: Towards a 'Vulgar' Critique of 'Pure' Critiques," suggests that his theoretical position emerged in reaction against Kant's *Critique of Judgment*, which he curiously misreads as a defense of good taste.

23. Finkielkraut, *The Undoing of Thought*, 105.

24. This is one of several current forms of codification that draw theoretical sustenance from the culturalist program in law and the social sciences; see "Culturalism, the Euthanasia of Liberalism" (*Dissent* [Winter 1995]: 89–102), where I define culturalism as the thesis "that there is a universal human need to belong to a culture—to belong, that is, to a self-conscious group with a known history, a group that by preserving and transmitting its customs, memories, and common practices confers the primary pigment of individual identity on the persons it comprehends. This need, culturalism says, is on a par with the need to be loved by a father and a mother" (p. 89). Culturalism in this sense—the diversified reenforcement of prejudice—is a recent investment of educational policy. Though some liberal theorists are among its apologists, its deeper affinities are with nationalism and nineteenth-century race thinking.

Academic-culturalist doctrine exists in symbiosis with the political push for cultural self-definition as a human right. Charles Taylor, in *Multiculturalism and the Politics of Recognition* (Princeton, N.J., 1992), has argued for cultural recognition as a political right—recognition being defined as some mixture of set-aside public space, measurable approval or applause, and sanctions against "misrecognition" (a difficult concept). The charm of this quasi-legal suggestion has prompted a curious shuffle of alliances in Europe and America. Thus Taylor, a social democrat and advocate of Quebecois nationalism, owes much of his reputation in France to the admiring attention of Alain de Benoist, the philosopher of the French New Right. Benoist's doctrines have in turn been appreciatively expounded in a special issue of the American Marxist journal *Telos* (Summer 1994). For a record of these affiliations and some pertinent questions, see Pierre Birnbaum, "From Multiculturalism to Nationalism," *Political Theory* 24, no. 1 (1996): 33–45.

25. Richard Ohmann, *English in America: A Radical View of the Profession* (New York, 1976), 4.

26. Ibid., 63.

27. See, e.g., D. J. Gless and B. H. Smith, ed., *The Politics of Liberal Education* (Durham, N.C., 1992); for a skeptical estimate of the academic literature now backing the thesis that "academic politics is politics," see Russell Jacoby, *Dogmatic Wisdom* (New York, 1994), 160–91.

28. Ohmann, *English in America*, 44.

29. Julie Ellison, "A Short History of Liberal Guilt," *Critical Inquiry* 22, no. 2 (1996): 370. I am much indebted to this survey both for quotations and for speculative hints. Ellison's research has been extensive; her irony is underplayed.

30. Ibid., 358.

31. Ibid., 355, quoting Homi Bhabha.

32. Friedrich Nietzsche, *On the Genealogy of Morals*, tr. Walter Kauffman (New York, 1967). One of the few frank discussions of the ideology and effects of institutionalized pity is Shelby Steele, *The Content of Our Character* (New York, 1990), especially 77–148.

33. Diana Fuss, "Critical Response," *Critical Inquiry* 22, no. 2 (1996): 383–84. The refusal to engage in debate with a rival constituency—often a constituency posited for convenience by the refuser—is a symptom of the unworldliness of theory, in the sense of the word explored by Edward Said, "The Politics of Knowledge," *Raritan* 11, no. 1 (1991): 17–31. Said believes that a habit of deference to the subject position ignores certain self-evident truths about human work: "that, given the very nature of human work in the construction of human society and history, it is impossible to say of it that its products are so rarefied, so limited, so beyond comprehension as to exclude most other people, experiences, and histories. . . . This kind of human work, which is intellectual work, is worldly. . . . It is not about things that are so rigidly constricted and so forbiddingly arcane as to exclude all but an audience of like-minded, already convinced persons" (p. 20).

34. On Whitman's importance as a theorist of democracy, see George Kateb, *The Inner Ocean* (Ithaca, N.Y., 1992), 152–71 and 240–66. Whitman better than any other writer evokes the untranslatable character of democratic identity and the

"tally" of a self with its evidences of its own being. He trusts "the almost transub-stantiating power of the equal franchise to achieve its effects"—effects visible in the way "the democratic individual is always encouraged to recognize others as being as real as oneself" (pp. 160 and 163).

35. See Richard Rorty, *Contingency, Irony, and Solidarity* (Cambridge, 1989).

36. John Rawls, *A Theory of Justice* (Cambridge, Mass., 1971), 101 and 104.

37. A strong critique of this element of Rawls's thinking is in Robert Nozick, *Anarchy, State, and Utopia* (New York, 1974). Rawls, as Nozick observes, presses "*very* hard the distinction between men and their talents, assets, abilities, and special traits. Whether any coherent conception of a person remains when the distinction is so pressed is an open question" (p. 228).

38. J. G. A. Pocock, "Edward Gibbon in History," in *The Tanner Lectures on Human Value*, vol. 11, ed. Grethe B. Peterson (Salt Lake City, Utah, 1990), 362.

39. John Dewey, *Human Nature and Conduct*, Modern Library edition (New York, 1930), 232.

Appendix

TABLES AND FIGURES ON B.A.s AND PH.D.s IN THE
HUMANITIES, 1966–1993

THE FOLLOWING set of tables and graphs was prepared at The Andrew W. Mellon Foundation, chiefly by Joan Gilbert and Fred Vars, whose help in this regard is gratefully acknowledged. This material is intended to serve as a freestanding graphic essay on the condition of the humanities.

The data used for the years 1966–1993 come from the *IPEDS Completions Survey/Degrees Conferred in Institutions of Higher Education*, compiled by the National Center for Education Statistics. These data are part of the data library supported by the Computer-Aided Science Policy Analysis and Research data base system. Slightly more than 1,400 B.A. degree–granting institutions are included in this data base. The Carnegie Classification of 1987 has been used to define the institutional types on the basis of the level of degree offered—ranging from prebaccalaureate to the doctorate—and the comprehensiveness of their missions. All categories are included in the figures that refer to "all institutions," but several categories have been singled out for separate treatment because they show significant variations in the number of humanities degrees granted. The categories are defined as follows:

Research I universities. These institutions offer a full range of baccalaureate programs, are committed to graduate education through the doctoral degree, and give high priority to research.

Research II universities. These institutions offer a full range of degrees but receive lesser amounts of federal support for research.

Doctorate-Granting I universities. These institutions offer a full range of degrees and provide at least forty Ph.D. degrees annually in five or more academic disciplines.

Doctorate-Granting II universities. These institutions annually award twenty or more Ph.D. degrees in at least one discipline or ten or more Ph.D. degrees in three or more disciplines.

Liberal Arts I colleges. These highly selective institutions are primarily undergraduate colleges that award more than half of their baccalaureate degrees in arts and sciences fields.

Liberal Arts II colleges. These institutions are primarily undergraduate colleges that are less selective and that award more than half of their degrees in liberal arts fields.

Observations

Tables 1 and 2. Although the absolute number of bachelor's and doctoral degrees in the humanities increased slightly between 1966 and 1993, a time when the number of degrees in both categories overall was more than doubling (see Figure 3), the humanities percentage of the total number of degrees has decreased, as has the percentage of science degrees. The degrees in social science have held their percentage place in the total.

Figure 1. The figure shows the long-range change in the percentage of undergraduate majors in the liberal arts from 1890 to 1992. The figures from 1890 to 1961 are from Douglas L. Adkins, *The Great American Degree Machine: An Economic Analysis of the Human Resource Output of Higher Education* (Berkeley, Calif.: Carnegie Commission on Higher Education, 1975). Adkins has made an effort to disaggregate the figures in such a way as to give the same meaning throughout to the following subjects: foreign languages and literature, English, philosophy, art, and music.

Figure 2. B.A. production and Ph.D. production in the humanities in all institutions move fairly closely in tandem. The more B.A.s, apparently, the more Ph.D.s. If allowance is made for the fact that in the past the average time to earn humanities Ph.D.s has been seven years and that for B.A.s four years, the lines are almost identical. Probably both Ph.D. production and B.A. production respond nearly simultaneously to forces such as the strength of the job market and levels of interest in professional training (e.g., law, medicine, and business).

Figures 3 and 4. All liberal arts subjects (humanities, natural sciences, social sciences), while remaining relatively flat in absolute numbers, are dropping as a percentage of the total number of B.A.s granted in all institutions. Combined, they dropped (Table 1) from 48 to 35 percent of the total from 1966 to 1993, while the humanities alone were dropping from 21 to 13 percent.

Figures 5 and 6. During this same period there were increases of arts and sciences Ph.D.s in absolute numbers, particularly in the natural sciences, but as a percentage of the total number of doctorates granted in all institutions, sciences and humanities Ph.D.s dropped sharply, while those in social sciences increased slightly. Doctoral degrees in the humanities, social sciences, and natural sciences combined went from 61 to

50 percent of the total doctoral degrees granted, as shown in Table 2. In the humanities alone the drop was from 14 to 9 percent of the total.

Figures 7–9. In the Liberal Arts (LA) I and II colleges and Research I universities, the traditional bastions of the humanities in American education, the number of B.A. degrees in the humanities has also been dropping steadily as a percentage of the overall number of B.A.s granted, but at different rates in different types of institutions. Whereas in LA I colleges (Figure 7) the number of B.A. degrees in each humanities subject has shown some decrease—and the overall percentage of total humanities degrees dropped by about 10 percent of the total—in LA II colleges (Figure 8) there has been a drop from 26 to 10 percent of the total in the absolute number of humanities B.A.s, and a corresponding decrease in each of the major humanities disciplines. In Research I universities (Figure 9), most of which contain distinguished liberal arts colleges, though there has been some recovery in recent years, the number of humanities B.A.s has dropped in the total by about one-fourth from what it was in 1966.

Figure 10. The decrease in the number of humanities Ph.D.s in Research I universities roughly corresponds, as Figure 2 suggests it would, to the drop in humanities B.A.s. From 1966 to 1993 total humanities doctoral degrees dropped from about 15 to 11 percent of the total doctoral degrees conferred.

Figure 11. The figure shows a drop in all humanities Ph.D.s in second-level doctoral degree–granting institutions of about 20 percent, from about 10 percent to less than 8 percent of the total Ph.D. degrees granted. Obviously, the humanities did not fare so well at the doctoral level in these institutions as they did in the more prestigious Research I universities.

Figure 12. There was approximately a threefold increase in the number of women receiving Ph.D.s in all disciplines, in all universities, over the period 1966–1993. In all humanities the increase of women has been equally striking, from just below 20 percent to just below 50 percent of the total. English and foreign languages now award about 60 percent of their Ph.D.s to women, while history and philosophy remain below 40 percent.

Figures 13 and 14. The increase of women taking Ph.D.s in the humanities has not been matched by a similar increase in the number of women taking B.A.s in these fields at LA I colleges and Research I universities. In those schools, where there has traditionally been heavy enrollment by women in the humanities, the level of majors has remained about the same.

Figures 15 and 16. The humanities have not been popular with the various minority groups entering the academic world since 1977. After a sharp drop in the mid-1980s, the percentage of B.A.s has recently improved somewhat, but B.A.s and Ph.D.s have both dropped off over time. Interestingly, Hispanic interest in Humanities Ph.D.s has been stronger than that of any other ethnic group.

TABLE 1
Bachelor's Degrees Conferred in All Institutions (thousands), 1966–1993

Year	All disciplines	Social sciences		Humanities		Natural sciences	
		Number	Percent	Number	Percent	Number	Percent
1966	524	81	15.5	108	20.7	61	11.6
1967	562	92	16.3	119	21.2	65	11.5
1968	637	109	17.2	136	21.3	72	11.3
1969	734	130	17.6	157	21.4	81	11.1
1970	798	144	18.1	165	20.7	83	10.4
1971	846	155	18.3	166	19.7	82	9.7
1972	894	164	18.4	168	18.8	82	9.2
1973	930	171	18.4	164	17.7	87	9.3
1974	954	173	18.2	158	16.5	92	9.6
1975	932	163	17.5	145	15.5	91	9.8
1976	934	157	16.8	135	14.4	93	9.9
1977	928	149	16.0	125	13.5	91	9.8
1978	930	144	15.2	117	12.6	88	9.5
1979	931	139	14.9	112	12.1	85	9.1
1980	940	136	14.4	109	11.5	82	8.7
1981	947	133	14.0	106	11.2	79	8.4
1982	964	134	13.9	105	10.9	78	8.1
1983	981	129	13.1	102	10.4	77	7.9
1984	986	126	12.8	103	10.5	77	7.8
1985	991	125	12.6	101	10.2	79	7.9
1986	1,000	128	12.8	102	10.2	78	7.8
1987	1,004	132	13.1	104	10.3	76	7.5
1988	1,006	137	13.6	108	10.7	71	7.1
1989	1,030	147	14.2	116	11.2	70	6.8
1990	1,062	159	15.0	125	11.8	69	6.5
1991	1,108	170	15.4	136	12.2	72	6.5
1992	1,150	182	15.8	146	12.7	76	6.6
1993	1,179	187	15.8	150	12.7	81	6.8

TABLE 2
Doctoral Degrees Conferred in All Institutions (thousands), 1966–1993

Year	All disciplines	Social sciences		Humanities		Natural sciences	
		Number	Percent	Number	Percent	Number	Percent
1966	18.2	2.7	14.6	2.5	13.8	5.9	32.3
1967	20.6	3.1	15.1	2.9	14.0	6.5	31.5
1968	23.1	3.5	15.0	3.3	14.3	7.3	31.6
1969	26.2	3.9	15.1	3.7	14.3	8.0	30.4
1970	29.9	4.5	15.1	4.3	14.3	8.8	29.5
1971	32.1	5.0	15.6	4.5	14.0	9.2	28.7
1972	33.4	5.4	16.1	4.8	14.4	8.9	26.6
1973	34.8	5.8	16.7	5.2	14.8	8.7	25.0
1974	33.8	5.9	17.5	5.0	14.7	8.1	23.9
1975	34.1	6.1	18.0	4.8	14.0	8.0	23.4
1976	34.1	6.3	18.6	4.6	13.6	7.7	22.5
1977	33.2	6.2	18.8	4.2	12.7	7.5	22.7
1978	32.2	6.0	18.7	3.9	12.2	7.2	22.5
1979	32.8	5.9	17.9	3.7	11.4	7.4	22.5
1980	32.6	5.9	18.1	3.5	10.8	7.4	22.8
1981	33.0	6.1	18.4	3.4	10.3	7.6	23.0
1982	32.7	5.8	17.7	3.3	9.9	7.7	23.5
1983	32.8	6.1	18.5	3.0	9.3	7.3	22.3
1984	33.3	6.0	17.9	3.1	9.2	7.4	22.3
1985	33.0	5.9	18.0	2.9	8.9	7.5	22.8
1986	33.7	6.2	18.4	3.0	8.8	7.7	22.7
1987	34.2	6.2	18.2	3.0	8.8	7.8	22.8
1988	34.9	5.9	17.0	2.9	8.4	8.2	23.4
1989	35.8	6.3	17.7	3.0	8.4	8.3	23.1
1990	38.3	6.5	16.9	3.3	8.6	8.9	23.3
1991	39.4	6.6	16.7	3.5	8.8	9.4	23.8
1992	40.7	6.6	16.2	3.8	9.2	9.7	23.8
1993	42.2	7.1	16.8	3.8	9.1	10.0	23.7

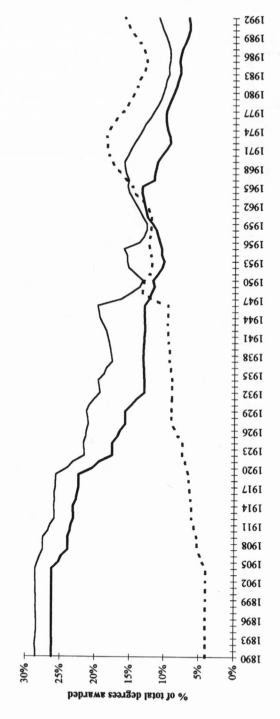

FIGURE 1. Redistribution of majors, 1890–1992. *Key:* - - -, social sciences; ——, natural sciences; ——, humanities.

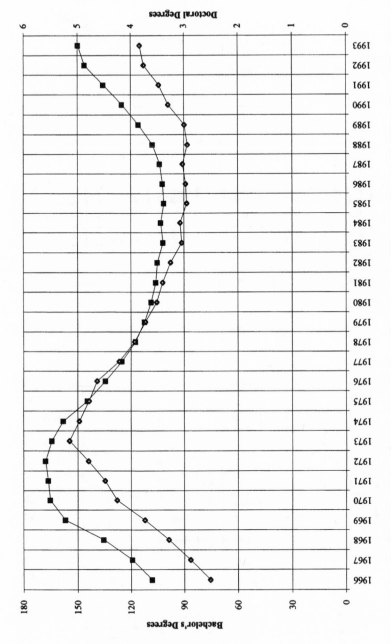

FIGURE 2. Degrees conferred in humanities subjects in all institutions (thousands), 1966–1993. *Key:* —■—, bachelor's degrees; —◇—, doctoral degrees.

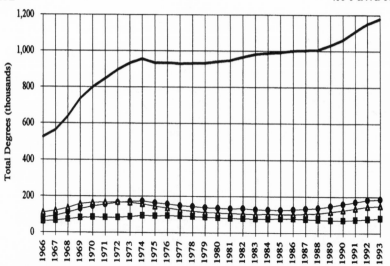

FIGURE 3. B.A. degrees conferred in all institutions, 1966–1993. *Key:* ——, all disciplines; –■–, natural sciences; –●–, social sciences; –Δ–, humanities.

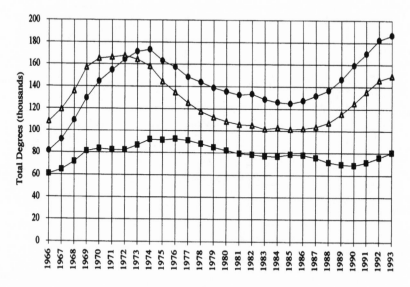

FIGURE 4. B.A. degrees conferred by subject in all institutions, 1966–1993. Symbols as in Figure 3.

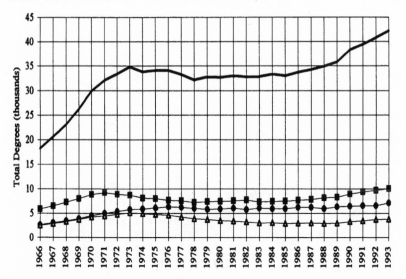

FIGURE 5. Doctoral degrees conferred in all institutions, 1966–1993. Symbols as in Figure 3.

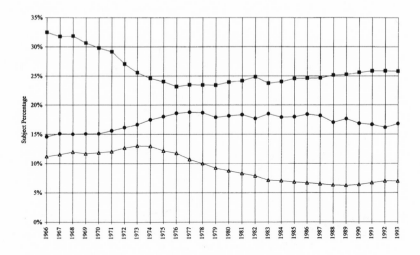

FIGURE 6. Subject percentages of doctoral degrees conferred in all institutions, 1966–1993. Symbols as in Figure 3.

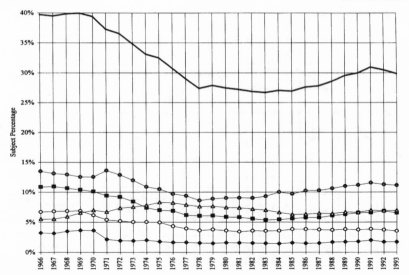

FIGURE 7. Percentage of B.A. degrees conferred in humanities subjects in Liberal Arts I colleges, 1966–1993. *Key:* ——, total humanities; –■–, history; –❸–, English and literature; –○–, foreign languages; –◆–, philosophy and religion; –△–, arts and music.

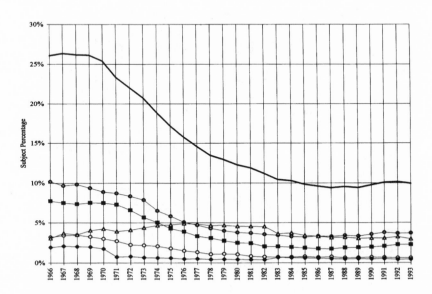

FIGURE 8. Percentage of B.A. degrees conferred in humanities subjects in Liberal Arts II colleges, 1966–1993. Symbols as in Figure 7.

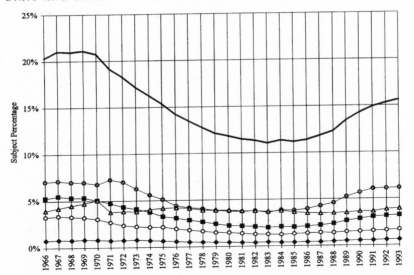

FIGURE 9. Percentage of B.A. degrees conferred in humanities subjects in Research I universities, 1966–1993. Symbols as in Figure 7.

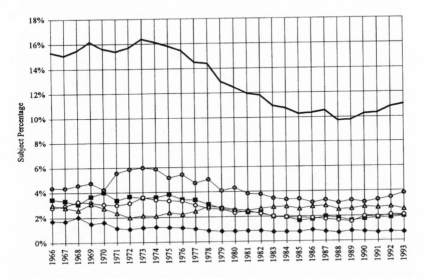

FIGURE 10. Percentage of doctoral degrees conferred in humanities subjects in Research I Universities, 1966–1993. Symbols as in Figure 7.

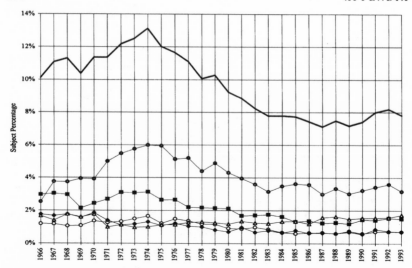

FIGURE 11. Percentage of doctoral degrees conferred in humanities subjects in Research II and Doctorate-Granting I and II universities, 1966–1993. Symbols as in Figure 7.

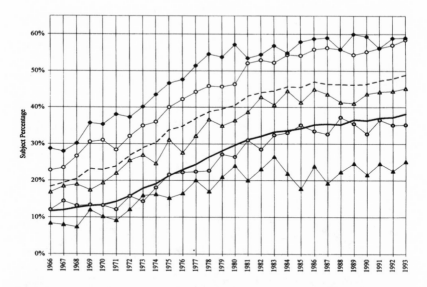

FIGURE 12. Percentage of doctoral degrees conferred on women by academic discipline in all institutions, 1966–1993. *Key:* ——, all disciplines; - - -, all humanities; –⊕–, history; –O–, English and literature; –◆–, foreign languages; –▲–, philosophy and religion; –Δ–, arts and music.

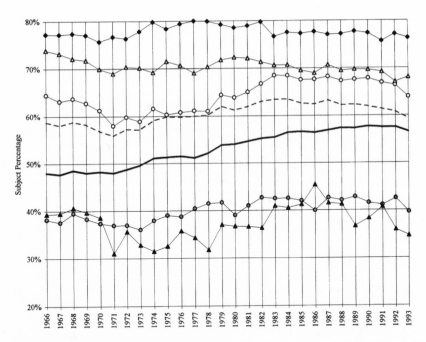

FIGURE 13. Percentage of B.A. degrees conferred on women in Liberal Arts I colleges, 1966–1993. Symbols as in Figure 12.

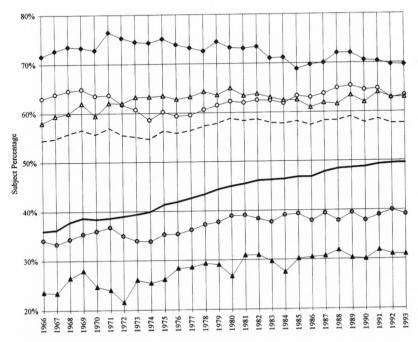

FIGURE 14. Percentage of B.A. degrees conferred on women in Research I universities, 1966–1993. Symbols as in Figure 12.

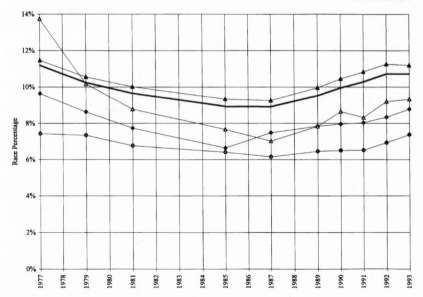

FIGURE 15. Percentage of B.A. degrees conferred in humanities subjects in all institutions by race and ethnicity, 1977–1993, selected years. *Key:* ——, all races; –⦿–, black; –◆–, asian; –Δ–, hispanic; –▲–, white.

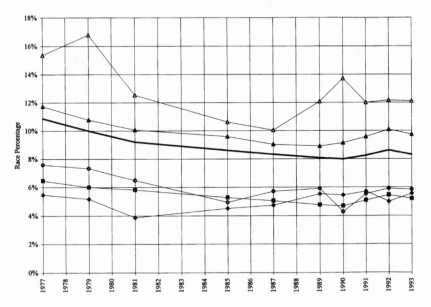

FIGURE 16. Percentage of doctoral degrees conferred in humanities subjects in all institutions by race and ethnicity, 1977–1993, selected years. Symbols as in Figure 15.

About the Contributors _____

David Bromwich is the author of *Hazlitt: The Mind of a Critic*, *A Choice of Inheritance*, and *Politics by Other Means*. He is Honsum Professor of English at Yale University.

John H. D'Arms, classicist, ancient historian, and G. F. Else Professor of the Humanities at the University of Michigan, recently completed ten years as dean of the Horace H. Rackham School of Graduate Studies and five years as vice-provost for academic affairs. He is a member of the National Council on the Humanities, a trustee of the National Humanities Center, and a former member of the board of directors of the American Council of Learned Societies. The author of *Romans on the Bay of Naples* (1970) and *Commerce and Social Standing in Ancient Rome* (1981), he is currently writing about food and status in the Roman world. D'Arms was director of the American Academy in Rome from 1977 to 1980.

Denis Donoghue is University Professor and holds the Henry James Chair of English and American Letters at New York University. His most recent book is *Walter Pater: Lover of Strange Souls* (1995).

Carla Hesse is professor of history at the University of California, Berkeley. She is the author of *Publishing and Cultural Politics in Revolutionary Paris, 1789–1810* (1991) and coeditor, with R. Howard Bloch, of *Future Libraries* (1995). She is also the co-chair of the editorial board of *Representations*, a journal of cultural studies.

Gertrude Himmelfarb is professor emeritus of history at the Graduate Center of the City University of New York. Her most recent book is *The De-Moralization of Society: From Victorian Virtues to Modern Values* (1995).

Lynn Hunt is Annenberg Professor of History at the University of Pennsylvania. She is the author of three books on the French Revolution and has edited four books on various questions of historical method, including most recently, with Jacques Revel, *Histories: French Constructions of the Past* (1996). She is the coauthor with Joyce Appleby and Margaret Jacob of *Telling the Truth about History* (1994).

Frank Kermode was King Edward VII Professor of English Literature at Cambridge University and is an honorary fellow of King's College. His latest book is a memoir, *Not Entitled* (1995).

Alvin Kernan is Avalon Professor of Humanities, Emeritus at Princeton University, and presently senior adviser in the humanities at The Andrew W. Mellon Foundation. His most recent book is *Crossing the Line: A Bluejacket's World War II Odyssey* (1994).

Louis Menand is professor of English at the Graduate Center of the City University of New York. He is the editor of *The Future of Academic Freedom* (1996).

Francis Oakley, president emeritus of Williams College, is currently Edward Dorr Griffin Professor of the History of Ideas at the college. His most recent books are *Omnipotence, Covenant, and Order: An Excursion in the History of Ideas from Abelard to Leibniz* and *Community of Learning: The American College and the Liberal Arts Tradition.* He has served since 1993 as chairman of the American Council of Learned Societies.

Christopher Ricks teaches at Boston University. *Essays in Appreciation,* a new collection, was published in 1996, as was his edition, *Inventions of the March Hare: Poems 1909–1917 by T. S. Eliot.*

Margery Sabin is Lorraine Chiu Wang Professor of English at Wellesley College. She is the author of *English Romanticism and the French Tradition* (1976) and *Dialect of the Tribe: Speech and Community in Modern Fiction* (1987). Her current work on literary approaches to colonial and postcolonial narrative has appeared in the form of essays and reviews in *Raritan Quarterly, Essays in Criticism, College English,* and *Victorian Studies.*

Index

Academic Revolution, The (Jencks/ Riesman), 212–13
Acquisitive Society, The (Tawney), 203
Adelman, Janet, 129, 131
Adkins, Douglas L., 246
Adorno, Theodor W., 222, 240n4
Aeschylus, 169
Aesthetic Dimension, The (Marcuse), 137
Aesthetics and Ideology (Levine), 138
Affirmative action, 5, 27, 29, 235
After Theory (Docherty), 171
Against Interpretation (Sontag), 211
Altman, Robert, 183
American Antiquarian Society, 43
American Association for the Advancement of Science, 202
American Association of University Professors, 201, 204
American Council of Learned Societies (ACLS), 7, 32, 35, 38–39, 40, 41, 44, 45, 46, 66, 118
American Historical Association, 24, 72, 145–46, 156, 202
American Mathematical Society, 202
American Medical Association, 204
American Physical Society, 202
American Political Science Association, 202
American Power and the New Mandarins (Chomsky), 240n3
American Renaissance, The (Matthiessen), 220
American Social Science Association, 202
American Sociological Society, 202
Amherst College, 8, 9, 86–91, 96, 100
Anatomy of Criticism (Frye), 210
Andrew W. Mellon Foundation, 38, 43, 45, 46, 50
Anni Mirabiles (Blackmur), 123
Anticommunism, 221–22
Arendt, Hannah, 239
Aristotle, 137
Armstrong, Nancy, 97
Arnold, Matthew, 74
Association of American University Presses, 42
Attitudes Toward History (Burke), 221

Auden, W. H., 225
Auerbach, Erich, 239
Austell, Mary, 74
Austen, Jane, 97
Australia, 18, 30n5

Baird, Theodore, 86, 87, 100
Baldwin, James, 74
Ball State University, 66, 80n23
Barraclough, Geoffrey, 76
Barthes, Roland, 153
Bartholomae, David, 98, 99–100
Beard, Charles, 147
Beardsley, Monroe C., 188, 191
Beck, Jonathan, 85, 91
Belsey, Catherine, 129, 132, 176
Benda, Julien, 177
Benjamin, Walter, 112, 133
Bennett, Arnold, 174
Bennett (William) Report, 66
Benoist, Alain de, 242n24
Bentley, Alvin M., 51
Bergen Community College, 80n23, 80n25
Bergonzi, Bernard, 176
Berlin Wall, 53
Bersani, Leo, 97
Bhabba, Homi, 235
Bibliothèque Nationale de France, 110, 113
Biggins, Dennis, 129
Black, Max, 191
Blackmur, R. P., 123, 138
Blake, William, 133, 224
Bloch, Howard, 112–13
Boorstin, Daniel J., 24
Botticelli, Sandro, 164
Bourdieu, Pierre, 137
Bowen, William, 12, 212
Brint, Stephen, 205
Bromwich, David, 212
Brontë, Charlotte, 74
Brooks, Cleanth, 125, 128, 207–8
Brooks, Peter, 97
Brower, Reuben, 86, 88, 95
Brown, Denise Scott, 211
Brown University, 51
Bundy, McGeorge, 221
Burke, Edmund, 230

Burke, Kenneth, 128, 221
Butler University, 80n24
Butterfield, Herbert, 146

Calinescu, Matei, 132
Cambridge University, 87
Canada, 18, 30n5
Carlyle, Thomas, 74
Carnegie Corporation, 38, 46
Carnegie Foundation for the Advancement
    of Teaching, 33, 65, 68
Casey, John, 177
Cassirer, Ernst, 222, 239
Castleton State College, 80n24
Cather, Willa, 89
Center for Advanced Study in the
    Behavioral Sciences, 35
Center for the Advanced Study of the
    Visual Arts (CASVA), 42–43
Chaucer, Geoffrey, 73, 74, 87
Cheney (Lynn) Report, 66
Chomsky, Noam, 240n3
Churchill, Winston, 226
Clark University, 201
Clerisy, 173–74
Coalition for Networked Information, 118
Cold War, 53, 212, 213, 225
Coleman, David, 188
Coleridge, Samuel Taylor, 173
Collectivity, 95–96
Color Purple, The (Walker), 74
Conquest of America (Todorov), 229
Constant, Benjamin, 115
Corbett, Edward, 136
Cornell University, 66, 79n19, 201
Cornell University Library, 118
Crews, Frederick, 8, 92–93
Crick, Bernard, 183
Croly, Herbert, 203, 204, 205
Culler, Jonathan, 195
Culturalism, 241–42n24
Cultural Literacy (Hirsch), 133
Culture and Imperialism (Said), 138
Culture of Literacy, The (Godzich), 136

Dada, 166, 167
Damrosch, David, 212
Davie, Donald, 180
Davis, Angela, 222
Davis, Natalie Zemon, 150, 156
Dead Certainties (Schama), 150–51

Death of Woman Wang, The (Spence), 150
Deconstruction, 76, 86, 95, 131; in literary
    criticism, 210–11; metaphor and,
    185–86; postmodernism influenced by,
    143, 144, 151, 153
de Man, Paul, 89, 134, 210
Demassification, 110
Democratization, 17–30; decline in status
    and, 20–23; digitalization and, 111;
    intellectual consequences of, 28–30;
    social pressures and, 23–27
Demos, John, 150
Department of Defense, 52
Department of Energy, 52
Derrida, Jacques, 10, 143–44, 152, 153,
    180, 195, 210
Despatialization, 112–114
Dewey, John, 143, 220, 239
Dialectic of Enlightenment
    (Horkheimer/Adorno), 222, 240n4
Dickens, Charles, 73
Dickinson, Emily, 74
Digitalization, 107–19; communication
    and scholarship and, 111–17;
    communication transparency and
    representation and, 118–19; library
    downsizing and, 108–11
Dilthey, Wilhelm, 175
Disidentification, 230–31
Diversity, 230
Division of Social Labor, The (Durkheim),
    203
Docherty, Thomas, 171
Donne, John, 74, 97
Don Quixote (Cervantes), 153
Douglas, Lawrence, 64
Douglass, Frederick, 74
Drama and Society in the Age of Jonson
    (Knights), 128
Dred Scott Case (Fehrenbacher), 229
Duguid, Paul, 110
Dürer, Albrecht, 162–63
Durkheim, Emile, 203
Dylan, Bob, 93

Eagleton, Terry, 9, 95, 129–30, 131–32,
    184–85
*Economic Interpretation of the Constitution
    of the United States, An* (Beard), 147
Education and the University (Leavis),
    125–27

Eisenhower, Dwight D., 226
Elbow, Peter, 99
Eliot, Charles William, 202
Eliot, George, 155
Eliot, T. S., 97, 128, 180, 185, 190, 192, 194, 208
Ellison, Julie, 235, 236
Elton, Geoffrey, 149
Emerson, Ralph Waldo, 74, 173, 239
Empson, William, 9, 86, 127, 128, 136, 137, 180
English in America: A Radical View of the Profession (Ohmann), 234
Enlightenment, 144, 166, 171
Enola Gay exhibit, 12, 225–27
Episteme, 10
Essay on Man (Cassirer), 222
Essentialism, 211
Euphorion, 169
Evans, Malcolm, 129

Facts, Artifacts, and Counterfacts (Bartholomae), 99
Fanon, Franz, 231
Fehrenbacher, Don, 229
Feminism, 5, 29, 70, 76; in history, 151, 152; in philosophy, 154; subjectivism and, 155
Feminization, 20–22, 28
Fiction and the Reading Public (Q. D. Leavis), 128
Figuratively Speaking (Fogelin), 186–87
Finkielkraut, Alain, 232–33
Fogelin, Robert J., 186–87
Folger Shakespeare Library, 43
Ford Foundation, 38, 46, 47
Formalism, 211
Forms of Lyric (Brower), 95
Foucault, Michel, 10, 143, 144, 148, 152, 159n29, 165, 240n4
France, 18, 30n5, 115
Francia, Louis, 164
Freire, Paulo, 100
French, Marilyn, 129
Frieze, Henry S., 50
From Left to Right, 94
Frost, Robert, 86–87
Frye, Northrop, 210
Fuller, Margaret, 74
"Function of Literary Theory at the Present Time, The" (Miller), 135

Future Libraries (Bloch/Hesse), 112–13

Gadamer, Hans-Georg, 100
Gaither Report, 47
Gardner, Helen, 124, 125
Gates, Bill, 117, 119
Geertz, Clifford, 213
Genette, Gérard, 117
Germano, Bill, 170–71
Getty Art History Information Program, 118
Getty Center for the Study of the Arts and Humanities, 43
Ghirlandaio, Domenico, 164
Globalization, 71
Godzich, Wlad, 136
Gohlke, Madelon, 9, 129, 130
Goldberg, Jonathan, 129, 130
Golden Bowl, The (James), 85
Gombrich, E. H., 164–65
Gommes, Les (Robbe-Grillet), 162
Gottschalk, Louis, 146
Graff, Gerald, 214
Grafton, Anthony, 67, 68
Great American Degree Machine, The (Adkins), 246
Greenblatt, Stephen, 153, 173
Guarino Guarini da Verona, 68
John S. Guggenheim Foundation, 32, 35, 38, 39–41, 44, 45, 46–47
Guillory, John, 128–29, 133
Gunn, Giles, 173
Gutenberg, Johannes, 167

Handlin, Oscar, 24
Harding, D. W., 124, 136, 137
Hartman, Geoffrey, 210
Harvard University, 48, 88, 201
Haskell, Thomas, 211
Hausman, Carl, 191, 192–93
Hawkes, Terence, 193
Hawthorne, Nathaniel, 73, 74, 92
Heathcliff and the Great Hunger (Eagleton), 184–85
Heidegger, Martin, 143
Herbert, George, 97
Hercules, 162–63
Hertz, Neil, 89
Hexter, J. H., 24
Heyman, I. Michael, 226–27

Higher Learning in America, The (Veblen), 205
Hill, Geoffrey, 131
"Hinterland of Thought, The" (Harding), 124
Hirsch, E. D., 133
Historicism, 225
History of Literary Criticism and Taste in Europe (Saintsbury), 207
Hoffmann, Stanley, 89
Hofstadter, Richard, 228
Hook, Sidney, 234
Horkheimer, Max, 222, 240n4
Howard University, 80n25
Hughes, Langston, 74
Hugo, Victor, 116
Huizinga, Johan, 166
Humanities and Arts on the Information Highways, 118
Humanities in American Life, 33
Hunt, Lynn, 230
Huntington Library, 43, 51
Hurston, Zora Neale, 89

Illness as Metaphor (Sontag), 184
I Lost It at the Movies (Kael), 211
Institute for Advanced Study, 35, 42
Interdisciplinarity, 28, 88–89, 90, 92, 97–98, 213–14; postmodernism and, 154–55
International Congress of Historical Sciences, 156
Internet, 110

Jackson, Jesse, 66
Jakobson, Roman, 137
James I, King, 129
Jardine, Lisa, 67, 68, 129, 132
Jefferson, Thomas, 116
Jencks, Christopher, 212–13
Jerome, Thomas Spencer, 50
John Carter Brown Library, 51
Johns Hopkins University, 201
Johnson, Lyndon, 221
Johnson, Samuel, 169–70, 180, 188
Joyce, James, 85, 96, 167

Kael, Pauline, 211
Kalstone, David, 89
Katz, Stanley, 214
Keats, John, 192
Kelly, Ned, 174

Kelsey, F. W., 50–51
Kennan, George, 221
Kenner, Hugh, 180
Kernan, Alvin, 170
Kerr, Clark, 5
Kerrigan, William, 172–73
Kimball, Roger, 65, 66, 67
King, Martin Luther, 228
Knight, G. Wilson, 127
Knights, L. C., 127, 128, 132, 137
Kuhn, Thomas, 146, 210

LaForgue, Jules, 180
Lamb, Charles, 183
Langer, Susanne K., 124
Late Histories (Tacitus), 117
Latin America, 72
Learning from Las Vegas (Brown), 211
Leavis, F. R., 9, 86, 125–28, 136, 137, 173–75, 180
Leavis, Q. D., 128, 136
Lecky, William, 224
Lemond, Greg, 188
Leonardo da Vinci, 164
Levine, Arthur, 71–72
Levine, Donald, 213
Levine, George, 138
Lewis, Wyndham, 167
Library of Congress, 111
Lichtenberg, Georg, 192
Literary Criticism: A Short History (Brooks and Wimsatt), 207–8
Literature and Society (ed. Said), 94–95
Lynd, Helen, 220
Lynd, Robert, 220
Lynd, Staughton, 222
Lyotard, Jean-François, 85

John D. and Catherine T. MacArthur Foundation, 38, 45
Macaulay, Thomas Babington, 224
Macbeth (Shakespeare), 9, 122, 124–32, 134, 135, 137
McCarthy period, 221
McDonald, Forrest, 147
Macfarlane, Alan, 129
Macintosh, Fiona, 184
Mackenzie, Henry, 235
McLuhan, Marshall, 190
Making of the English Working Class (Thompson), 223–24

Malcolm X, 228

Mallarmé, Stéphane, 167

Marcus, Leah, 172

Marcus, Steven, 234

Marcuse, Herbert, 137, 231–32, 240n4

Marius, Richard, 172

Martin, Wallace, 207

Marx, Karl, 165

Marxism, 137, 155, 225

Masters, The (Snow), 174

Mather, Cotton, 74

Matthiessen, F. O., 220

Mayer, Arno, 148

Medieval English Dictionary, 50

Melville, Herman, 74

Metaphor (Hawkes), 193

Metaphor and Art (Hausman), 192–93

Metaphor and Thought (ed. Ortony), 191

Methodology, 143, 146–48, 152

Metzger, Walter, 202

Michigan Historical Collections, 51

Microsoft Corporation, 119

Middletown (the Lynds), 220

Mill, John Stuart, 236, 237

Miller, D. A., 97

Miller, George A., 191

Miller, J. Hillis, 135, 138, 155, 156, 210

Miller, Perry, 228

Milton, John, 73, 74, 172–73

Modernism, 9–10, 165, 167, 211; in history, 144–45, 147–48, 151, 152; in poetry, 208

Modern Language Association (MLA), 67, 72, 75, 86, 91–95, 172; Crews and, 8, 92–93; founding of, 202; New Criticism and, 207; postmodernism and, 156; Smith and, 92–94

Moment of "Scrutiny," The (Mulhern), 175

Moore, Marianne, 138

Morgenthau, Hans, 221

Morrison, Toni, 74

Mulhern, Francis, 175

Multiculturalism, 7, 28, 29, 67, 71–75; in history, 148–49, 151, 152; in literature and English, 72–75, 89–90

Multiculturalism and the Politics of Recognition (Taylor), 242n24

National Association of Scholars, 72

National Center for Educational Statistics, 4

National Center for History in the Schools, 227

National Endowment for the Humanities (NEH), 7, 32, 33–35, 38, 41, 44, 49, 50, 227; budget reductions in, 46; disbursements by category, 36–37t; university and college share of budget, 55–56n4

National Gallery of Art, 42

National Humanities Center (NHC), 7, 32, 35, 38–39, 40, 41, 42, 45; budget reductions in, 46; shift in status of, 43–44

National Institutes of Health, 52

National Public Radio, 227

National Science Foundation, 52

National Standards, 227–30

Negative Capability, 192

Ness, Frederick, 75–76

Neumann, Franz, 239

Newberry Library, 43

New Criticism, 75, 76, 86, 92, 128–29, 137, 171–72, 207, 209–10, 215

New Deal, 221, 237

New Left, 223–24

New Thematics, 129, 131, 132

Newton, Sir Isaac, 154

Nietzsche, Friedrich Wilhelm, 143, 235

Nolan, Sydney, 174

Northwestern University, 48

Notes on Virginia (Jefferson), 116

"Notes towards a Supreme Fiction: It Must Change" (Stevens), 194

Notre Dame de Paris (Hugo), 116

Novick, Peter, 24

Oedipus Rex (Sophocles), 184

Ohmann, Richard, 234

One-Dimensional Man (Marcuse), 240n4

On Liberty (Mill), 237

Ortony, Andrew, 191

Paivio, Allan, 191

Panofsky, Erwin, 164, 239

Paradise Lost (Milton), 172

Pater, Walter, 133

Permanence and Change (Burke), 128, 221

Perugino, Pietro Vannucchi, 164

Petrosky, Anthony, 98, 99

Pew Charitable Trusts, 38

Philosophy in a New Key (Langer), 124

Philosophy of Literary Form, The (Burke), 128

Philosophy of Rhetoric, The (Richards), 189–91

Pierpont Morgan Library, 43

Plath, Sylvia, 74

Pocock, J. G. A., 238

Poirier, Richard, 89

Pope, Alexander, 74

Postmodernism, 7, 9–10, 28, 143–57, 165, 167, 171, 225; in history, 144–53, 156; in literature, 144, 152–53; major contributors to, 143–44; methodology compared with, 143, 146–48, 152; on Milton, 172–73; in philosophy, 144, 153–54

Postmodern pragmatism, 84–85

Poststructuralism, 75, 76, 143, 170

Potter, David, 228

Pound, Ezra, 167

Power Center for the Performing Arts, 52

Practical Criticism (Richards), 87

Prêt-à-Porter (film), 183

Princeton University, 48

Principia (Newton), 154

Professional Ethics and Civic Morals (Durkheim), 203

Professionalization, 202–6, 211–12

Promise of American Life, The (Croly), 203

Proust, Marcel, 115

Public and its Problems, The (Dewey), 220

Rabkin, Norman, 95

Rackham, Horace, 51

Rackham, Mary, 51

Rajan, B., 172

Ranke, Leopold von, 145

Ransom, John Crowe, 127–28

Rawls, John, 237–38

Readings, Bill, 84–85

Redrawing the Boundaries (ed. Greenblatt), 172

Reinterpretations of Elizabethan Drama (Rabkin), 95

Religion and the Decline of Magic (Thomas), 129

Renaissance, 163–66, 169, 172

Renascences, 164

"Repressive Tolerance" (Marcuse), 231–32

Rereading (Calinescu), 132

Return of Martin Guerre, The (Davis), 150

Reynolds, Sir Joshua, 133

Rhetoric of Revolution, The, 94

Richards, I. A., 86, 87, 100, 122–23, 128, 137, 187, 189–91

Ricoeur, Paul, 154, 195

Riesman, David, 212–13

Road Ahead, The (Gates), 117, 119

Robbe-Grillet, Alain, 162

Rockefeller Foundation, 38, 45, 46

Rorty, Richard, 143, 153–54, 156, 180, 210, 235, 236–37

Rosenberg, Isaac, 124–25

Routledge & Kegan Paul, 170–71

Rowtow, W. W., 221

Rudenstine, Neil, 212

Sacred Wood, The (Eliot), 128

Said, Edward, 8, 95, 138, 242n33

Saintsbury, George, 207

Sapir, J. D., 191

Sartre, Jean-Paul, 231

Schama, Simon, 150–51

Schorer, Mark, 137

Scott, Joan, 152

Scott, Walter, 150

Searle, John, 180, 185–86

"Semiology and Rhetoric" (de Man), 210

Serres, Michel, 133

Seznec, Jean, 163

Shakespeare, William, 9, 73, 74, 97, 124, 125, 126–28, 129, 130, 131, 133, 134, 137, 185

Shelley, Mary, 74

Shelley, Percy Bysshe, 182

"Short History of Liberal Guilt, A" (Ellison), 235

Smith, Adam, 70, 203, 204

Smith, Henry Nash, 8, 92–94

Smith, R. E., 226

Smithsonian Institution, 12, 225–27

Snow, C. P., 173–75

Social Construction of Reality, The (Berger/Luckmann), 133

Socrates, 4

Some Versions of Pastoral (Empson), 128

Sontag, Susan, 184, 211

Sophocles, 169, 184

Soviet Union (USSR), 18, 29, 30n5

Specialization, 204–6, 208

Spence, Jonathan, 150

Spenser, Edmund, 73

Spivak, Gayatri, 236
Sprat, Bishop, 183
Stalin, Joseph, 226
Stallybrass, Peter, 129
Stanford University, 48, 65–66, 232
Stein, Gertrude, 89
Sterne, Laurence, 235
Stevens, Wallace, 193–94
Stimson, Henry Lewis, 226
Stowe, Harriet Beecher, 74
Strangers and Brothers (Snow), 174
Structuralism, 210–11
"Structure, Sign, and Play in the Discourse
    of the Human Sciences" (Derrida), 210
Structure of Scientific Revolutions, The
    (Kuhn), 210
Subjectivism, 155
Subject of Tragedy, The (Belsey), 132
Suffocating Mothers (Adelman), 131
Swann's Way (Proust), 115
Swarthmore College, 66, 79n19
Sweden, 18, 30n5

Tacitus, 117
Tawney, R. H., 203
Taylor, Charles, 242n24
Taylor, William R., 89
Tempest, The (Shakespeare), 153
Temporal theory, 115–17
Texas Lutheran College, 80n24
Theory of Justice, A (Rawls), 237
Thomas, Keith, 129
Thomas, R. S., 179
Thompson, E. P., 223–24, 225, 228
Tillyard, E. M. W., 221
Todorov, Tsvetan, 195, 229
"Tradition and the Individual Talent"
    (Eliot), 208
Trahison des clercs, La (Benda), 177
Trilling, Lionel, 168, 180
Truman, Harry, 226
Tversky, Amos, 191
Twain, Mark, 74

Undoing of Thought, The (Finkielkraut),
    232–33
UNESCO, 232–33
United Kingdom, 18, 30n5
University of California at Berkeley, 224
University of California at Los Angeles, 227
University of Chicago, 146

University of Massachusetts at Amherst, 232
University of Michigan, 49–53
University of Michigan Press, 50
University of Oregon, 48
University of Pittsburgh, 8, 98–100
University of Tulsa, 80n25
University of Wisconsin, 232
Unredeemed Captive, The (Demos), 150
Uses of the University, The (Kerr), 5

Vasari, Giorgio, 164
Veblen, Thorstein, 205
Venturi, Robert, 211
Veysey, Laurence, 206
Vietnam War, 53, 221–22
*Virgin Land: The American West as Symbol
    and Myth* (Smith), 92

Walker, Alice, 74
Washington and Lee University, 48
Weber, Max, 11, 221
Webster, John, 133
Well Wrought Urn, The (Brooks), 125, 128,
    137
West Germany, 18, 30n5
Whig fallacy, 146, 148
White, Hayden, 152, 213
Whitman, Walt, 74, 236, 242–43n34
Wilde, Oscar, 74
Wilkes University, 80n23
Williams, Patricia, 235
Williams, William Appleman, 148
Williams College, 8, 96–98
William Shakespeare (Eagleton), 129–30
Wills, Garry, 129
Wimsatt, William K., 207–8
Winters, Yvor, 180
Witchcraft in Tudor and Stuart England
    (Macfarlane), 129
Woolf, Virginia, 174
Wordsworth, William, 74, 224
World Wide Web, 110, 112
Wretched of the Earth (Fanon), 231

Xerox Palo Alto Research Center, 110, 118,
    119

Yale critics, 210
Yale University, 48, 224

Zeldin, Theodore, 149, 158n19